CAMBRIDGE
EXAMINATIONS
PUBLISHING

New for March 2004 exam specifications

OBJECTIVE

PET

THE LEARNING CENTRE
HAMMERSMITH AND WEST
LONDON COLLEGE
GLIDDON ROAD
LONDON W14 9BL

D0183682

WITHDRAWN

Louise Hashemi   Barbara Thomas   Student's Book

Hammersmith and West London College

305746

CAMBRIDGE
UNIVERSITY PRESS

PUBLISHED BY THE PRESS SYNDICATE OF THE UNIVERSITY OF CAMBRIDGE
The Pitt Building, Trumpington Street, Cambridge CB2 1RP, United Kingdom

CAMBRIDGE UNIVERSITY PRESS
The Edinburgh Building, Cambridge CB2 2RU, UK
40 West 20th Street, New York, NY 10011–4211, USA
477 Williamstown Road, Port Melbourne, VIC 3207, Australia
Ruiz de Alarcón 13, 28014 Madrid, Spain
Dock House, The Waterfront, Cape Town 8001, South Africa

http://www.cambridge.org

© Cambridge University Press, 2003

This book is in copyright. Subject to statutory exception
and to the provisions of relevant collective licensing agreements,
no reproduction of any part may take place without
the written permission of Cambridge University Press.

First published 2003
Third printing 2003

Printed in the United Kingdom at the University Press, Cambridge

Text typeface Minion 11/13.5pt *System* QuarkXpress® [GECKO]

A catalogue record for this book is available from the British Library

Library of Congress Cataloguing in Publication data

ISBN 0 521 80578 3 Student's Book
ISBN 0 521 80579 1 Teacher's Book
ISBN 0 521 80580 5 Workbook
ISBN 0 521 01017 9 Workbook with Answers
ISBN 0 521 80581 3 Class Cassette Set

Cover design by Dale Tomlinson/Joanne Barker

Produced by Kamae Design, Oxford.

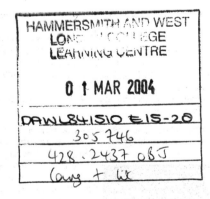

HAMMERSMITH AND WEST
LONDON COLLEGE
LEARNING CENTRE

0 1 MAR 2004

DAWL841510 E15-20
305746
428.2437 OBJ
(ang + lit

305746

Acknowledgements

The authors and publishers would like to thank the teachers and students who trialled and commented on the material:

Argentina: Liliana Luna, Claudia Cecilia Muniz, Marite Stringa, Sylvia Trigub; Australia: Jacque Byrne; Brazil: Angela Cristina Antelo Dupont; Cyprus: Peter Lucantoni; France: Virginie Petit, Robert Wright; Italy: James Douglas, Sarah Ellis, Monica Flood; Malta: Matthew Bonnici; Mexico: Jan Isaksen, Universidad Latino-Americana; Spain: Elizabeth Bridges, Samantha Lewis, Nick Shaw; Switzerland: Nancy Hersche, Julia Muller, Jean Rudiger-Harper, Fiona Schmid; United Arab Emirates: Christine Coombe, Philip Lodge, Anne Scullion; UK: Jenny Cooper, Lynda Edwards, Joe Gillespie, Jane Hann, Roger Scott, Tony Triggs; USA: Gregory Manin.

Picture research by Hilary Fletcher and Val Mulcahy.

The publishers are grateful to Annette Capel and Wendy Sharp for permission to reproduce their original course book concept in *Objective PET* and in all other *Objective* examination course books.

The authors would like to thank Sue Ashcroft and Niki Browne at CUP for their unfailing support and efficiency. They would also like to thank the following people for all kinds of assistance: Rowland, Rhiannon and Rebecca Thomas, Abbas Hashemi, Lorely Britton, Laurie McGeoghegan, Kai and Zoe Tabacek, Grace and Clemmie Newton and Haydn Turoa.

The authors and publishers are grateful to the authors, publishers and others who have given permission for the use of copyright material identified in the text. It has not been possible to identify the sources of all the material used and in such cases the publishers would welcome information from copyright owners. Apologies are expressed for any omissions.

Eikon design illustration on p 79 by Sam Thompson. Recording on p 174 *Somewhere the Sun is Shining* by John Toms, recorded by Topic Records Ltd. All rights of the producer and of the owner of the works reproduced reserved. Unauthorised copying, hiring, lending, public performance and broadcasting of this record prohibited.

Text on p 79 from *The Double Bass Mystery* by Jeremy Harmer, published in 1999 by Cambridge University Press; activity on p 145 (BR) adapted from an idea in *Activity Box* by Jean Greenwood, published in 1997 by Cambridge University Press; text on p 151 from *The Friendship Page* at http://www.friend-ship.com.au/; text on p 162, extracts from Shout Magazine ©DC Thomson & Co. Ltd *What's Your Shopping Style*; text on p 193, extracts from Shout Magazine ©DC Thomson & Co. Ltd *Mind Reader*.

The publishers are grateful to the following for permission to include photographs, logos and other illustrative material:
Action Plus pp 50 (A), 60 (bottom), 61, 98, /©Matthew Clarke p 192 (bottom left, top left); Advertising Archive Ltd p 168 (Persil, Kleenex), 171; Alamy p 50 (H), /©Bill Bachmann p 55 (B right), /©Charlotte p 22 (D), /©Michael Crockett p 86 (H), /©FCL Photography p 35 (taxi), /©Robert Harding Picture Library Ltd p 22 (B), /Stefan Hunziker p 11 (C), /©David Noton p 175 (bottom), /©Jim Pickerell p 175 (top right); Allsport/M. Farr p 100 (centre right), /Mike Powell p 100 (centre left); Alvey & Towers pp 34 (bicycle, plane, tram, coach, lorry, bike), 35 (helicopter, hovercraft, moped, train, car); Aquarius/© Disney p 116 (F); John Birdsall Photo Library pp 73 (left, centre), 183 (left), 193 (left); Britstock-IFA pp 34 (ship), 35 (ferry), /HAGA Hideo Haga p 58 (B bottom), /©Chris Walsh p 53; © Cambridgeshire Collection p 200; Camera Press p 154 (E), /IMAPRESS p 28 (E), /Richard Open p 28 (D); ©Dave Coombs p 76; CORBIS p 93 (A girl) /Francoise Gervais p 183 (centre, right); Greg Evans International/Greg Balfour Evans pp 16 (D), 35 (double-decker bus, ambulance), 148 (D); Mary Evans Picture Library pp 93 (C), 143 (left, right), 154 (F); Eye Ubiquitous/©Peter Blake p 50 (C), /G.Daniels p 174 (top left); Format/©Jacky Chapman p 148 (B), /©Melanie Friend p 192 (top right), /©Pam Isherwood p 22 (G), /©Brenda Prince p 192 (centre right), /Lisa Woollett p 162 (D); Fortean Picture Library pp 142 (B, C, D), /Dezso Stemoczky/SUFOI p 142 (E), /©Frederick C.Taylor p 142 (A); gettyimages/FPG International/ Alistair Berg p 41 (D), /Ken Chemus p 48, /Jacques Copeau p 16 (C), /Brian Erler p 100 (top right), /Sean Justice p 88 (C), /M.Llorden p 28 (C), /Antonio Mo p 40 (bottom right), /Elizabeth Simpson p 58 (C), /Stephen Simpson p 206 (A), /Arthur Tilley p 41 (top centre, E); gettyimages/Hulton Archive p 93 (A boy); gettyimages/ImageBank/Buzz Bailey

p 41 (F), /Barros & Barros p 16 (A), /Peter Cade p 41 (top left), /G&M David de Lossy pp 22 (E), 195, /Alvis Upitis p 28 (B), /White. Packert p 86 (E); getty images/National Geographic/Norbert Rosing p 142 (F); gettyimages/ PhotoDisc/Nick Koudis p 41 (B); gettyimages/Stone/Bruce Ayres p 55 (C left), /Martin Barraud p 50 (D, G), /Christopher Bissell p 30, /Chabruken p 41 (top right), /Nick Dolding p 60 (top), /Terry Doyle p 41 (C), /Erik Dreyer p 73 (right), /Robert Frerck p 205 (top), /Holly Harris p 22 (F), /Johnny Hernandez p 55 (D left), /Zigy Kaluzny p 22 (H), /Joe McBride p 36, /Martine Mouchy p 54, /Euan Myles p 41 (A), /Lori Adamski Peek p 11 (B), /Gregg Segal p 16 (B), /Julie Toy p 16 (F), /Charlie Waite p 55 (D right), /David Young-Wolff p 58 (D top); Ronald Grant Archive pp 28 (F), 116 (all except F, ©1997 Polygram Filmed Entertainment, all rights reserved for A); Sally & Richard Greenhill pp 16 (E), 148 (A), 162 (B), 174 (top right), 192 (bottom), 205 (bottom); Robert Harding Picture Library p 55 (A left), 175 (top left), /©Duncan Maxwell p 174 (bottom left), /©Walter Rawlings p 162 (A); Impact/©Peter Menzel p 58 (A bottom); © Tony Jedrej p 201; Jenex Inc/www.nordixc.com p 154 (G); London Features International/Anthony Dixon p 180 (2); Paper Rose Ltd p 66 (D); ©Pictor pp 40 (top right), 50 (F), 88 (A, B, E), /Robert Llewellyn p 22(C); ©Popperfoto pp 118, 125 (bottom left), 180 (5), /Simon Bruty p 11 (D), /Paul Redding/PPP p 136 (bottom left), /Reuters pp 11 (A), 13, 136 (top right), 180 (A); Powerstock pp 55 (A right), 88 (D), 133, 148 (C); Rex Features pp 28 (A), 50 (B), 87 (C), 93 (D), 100 (bottom left), 180 (B, C, D), /Paul Brown p 58 (B top), /Stewart Cook p 180 (1), /Mike Lawn p 129, /Jeroen Oerlemans p 58 (A top), /The Sun p 136 (bottom right), /Charles Sykes p 180 (4), /Mirec Towski p 180 (3); ©Sainsbury's Archives p 166; Science & Society Picture Library/©NMPFT p 154 (D); SOA p 55 (C right); ©South West News Service p 87 (B); ©Spectrum Colour Library p 174 (bottom right); Frank Spooner Pictures p 136 (centre right); Topham/UPP p 22 (A); ©V&A Picture Library p 86 (A, B, C); VIEW/©Dennis Gilbert p 162 (E); ©John Walmsley pp 40 (bottom left), 193 (right), 206 (B); ©WENN p 180 (E); Used with permission of Whirlpool p 86 (G); World Pictures p 55 (B left).

We have been unable to trace the copyright holders for the following items and would be grateful for any information to enable us to do so: Page 87 (A, D).

The following photographs were taken on commission: Paul Mulcahy for p 27; Gareth Boden for pp 82, 111, 169; Olivia Brown for p 125 (top left); Anna Vaughan for p 125 (top right); Barbara Thomas for p 125 (bottom right); Trevor Clifford for pp 86 (D, E), 93 (B), 162, reproduced with kind permission of Argos; Abbas Hashemi for p 186. Special thanks to Jo-Ann Wheatley, Occasio Café for permission to use her premises for the photograph on p 111.

We are grateful to the following publishers for their permission to reproduce the following book front covers:
Now Wait for Last Year by Philip K. Dick 2000, Millennium, a division of The Orion Publishing Group Ltd ; *Dracula* by Bram Stoker, Oxford University Press 1998. We have not been able to reclear the cover photograph and would be grateful for any information to enable us to do so; *River Phoenix: A short life* by Brian J. Robb, 1994, Plexus Publishing Ltd; Front cover from *Echoes* by Maeve Binchy published by Arrow. Used by permission of The Random House Group Limited; *Cat's Eye* by Margaret Atwood, 1990, Virago, a division of Time Warner Books.

We are grateful to the following companies for permission to use copyright logos:
'Coca-Cola' and 'Coke' are registered trade marks of The Coca-Cola Company and are reproduced with kind permission from The Coca-Cola Company p 168 (top); 'Used with kind permission from International Federation of Red Cross and Red Crescent Societies' p 168 (top); 'Used with permission from McDonald's Corporation' p 168 (top); 'Used with permission from Mercedes-Benz UK' p 168 (top); 'Used with permission of Switch' p 168 (bottom); 'Used with permission from Virgin Atlantic' p 168 (top).

Asa Anderson p 130(t); Kathryn Baker p 118; Kathy Baxendale pp 32(m), 32(br), 65(b), 70(tl), 70(mr), 89,134(m); Debbie Boon pp 26, 187; Chris Brown p 124; Yane Christensen p 113; Tim Davies pp 65(t), 164(b); Karen Donnelly pp 15, 20, 32(t)(bl), 38, 44, 70(tr)(ml)(b), 90, 134(t) (b), 153, 178, 203; Nick Duffy pp 31, 42, 54, 68, 138(m); Alice Englander p 78; Francoise Forbes pp 80, 130(b); DTP Gecko pp 10, 11, 29, 35, 49, 66, 72, 88, 138(t), 154, 156, 202; Peter Greenwood pp 36, 37, 48,110(b), 18; David Cuzik p 110(t); Ben Hasler pp 24, 105, 117; Joanna Kerr pp 112, 171; Julian Mosedale pp 61, 81; Lisa Smith pp 51, 56, 57, 104, 164(t); David Tazzyman pp 92, 176; Andy Ward pp 23, 25; Jonathan Williams pp 74, 75, 138(b); Sam Thompson pp 97, 173.

Map of Objective PET Student's Book

TOPIC	GRAMMAR	FUNCTIONS AND VOCABULARY	PRONUNCIATION	REVISION
Unit 1 A question of sport 10–13 Sports and hobbies	Present simple/to be + frequency adverbs	Definitions and explanations; *a kind of* + *-ing*/noun; sport; attitude	/aɪ/ as in *like* /iː/ as in *steep* /ɪ/ as in *big*	*there is/are*; present simple; the alphabet; *like* + *-ing*
Exam folder 1 14–15 Reading Part 1 Speaking Part 1				
Unit 2 The meeting place 16–19 People	*like/enjoy* + *-ing*; *want/would like* + *to*; *to be* + *a(n) student*	People, personality, interests, invitations, descriptive adjectives	/ɒ/ as in *pop* /ʌ/ as in *fun* /juː/ as in *university*	Greetings; *have got*
Exam folder 2 20–21 Listening Part 3 **Writing Parts 1, 2 and 3**				
Unit 3 What's your job? 22–25 Work	Present simple vs. present continuous (for present actions); state verbs; short answers	Saying what people are doing; jobs; feelings and opinions	/æ/ as in *cat* /ɑː/ as in *cart* /ʌ/ as in *cut*	Present simple (Unit 1)
Exam folder 3 26–27 Speaking Part 3 Reading Part 5				
Unit 4 Let's go out 28–31 Entertainment	Present continuous for future plans; prepositions of time	Future plans; entertainment; time, day and date; feelings and opinions	Saying days and months	*would like* + *to?* (Unit 2); present continuous for present actions (Unit 3)
Exam folder 4 32–33 Listening Part 1 **Writing Part 2**				
Unit 5 Wheels and wings 34–37 Transport	*need*; countable/uncountable nouns; *some/any*; *a lot/several*; *a few/a little*; *a couple of*	Transport; compound nouns	Unstressed *a*, *of*, *to* and *some*	Frequency adverbs and present simple (Unit 1); compound nouns from Units 1–4
Exam folder 5 38–39 Reading Part 2				
Unit 6 What did you do at school today? 40–43 Education and history	Past simple; short answers; adjectives ending in *-ed* and *-ing*	Past events and dates; feelings and opinions; school life; school subjects; descriptive adjectives	Final sound of regular verbs in past tense: /t/ /d/ and /ɪd/	People (Unit 2); feelings and opinions (Units 3 and 4)
Exam folder 6 44–45 Listening Part 2 **Writing Part 3**				
Units 1–6 Revision 46–47				
Unit 7 Around town 48–51 Towns and buildings	Prepositions of place and direction; comparative adjectives; commands	Directions; replying to thanks; towns and buildings	/aʊ/ as in *out* /ɔː/ as in *or*	Adjectives from earlier units; spelling rules
Exam folder 7 52–53 Reading Part 3				

TOPIC	GRAMMAR	FUNCTIONS AND VOCABULARY	PRONUNCIATION	REVISION
Unit 16 **Free time 104–107** Making plans	*going to* future; present tense after *when, after* and *until* in future time	Invitations; the time; planning leisure activities	Time	Invitations (Unit 2); present continuous for future plans (Unit 4)
Exam folder 16 108–109 Listening Part 2 **Writing Part 1**				
Unit 17 **In the future 110–113** Predictions	*will* future; *will* vs. *going to; to have something done; everyone, no one, someone, anyone*	Opinions and feelings; saying what will happen; climate; soap operas	/ɑː/ as in *car* /ɔː/ as in *sore* /ɜː/ as in *third*	*need* (Unit 5); telling a story; present continuous for present actions (Unit 3)
Exam folder 17 114–115 Reading Part 4				
Unit 18 **Shooting a film 116–119** Films	Past perfect	Talking about the order of past events; cinema and films	/ə/ at the end of words	Past simple (Unit 6); saying what you like and dislike (Unit 2)
Exam folder 18 120–121 Listening Part 3 **Writing Part 2**				
Units 13–18 Revision 122–123				
Unit 19 **Happy families 124–127** Family life	Verbs followed by *to* and *-ing; make* and *let*	Agreeing and disagreeing; opinions; advice; families	/ð/ as in *their* /θ/ as in *thirsty*	Advice (Unit 9); *like* and *would like* (Unit 2)
Exam folder 19 128–129 Reading Part 5				
Unit 20 **So you want to be a pop star? 130–133** Music	Comparison of adverbs; *so* and *such; although* and *because*	Saying what you like and prefer; congratulating; music, musical instruments; jobs	Homophones	Comparative adjectives (Unit 7); superlative adjectives (Unit 11); jobs (Unit 3)
Exam folder 20 134–135 Listening Part 1 **Writing Part 3**				
Unit 21 **Money matters 136–139** Money	Reported commands and requests; possessive adjectives and pronouns	Telephoning; money	Telephone numbers	Commands (Unit 7); making plans (Unit 16); past perfect (Unit 18)
Exam folder 21 140–141 Reading Part 3				
Unit 22 **Strange but true? 142–145** The unexplained	Indirect speech	Reporting what people said; saying what you (don't) believe; describing objects, places and events	Silent consonants	*it could/might/must/ can't be* (Unit 13); present and past tenses; opinions, agreeing and disagreeing
Exam folder 22 146–147 Listening Part 4 **Writing Part 1**				
Unit 23 **Best friends? 148–151** Friendship	*which/who/that/whose/where* clauses; more adjectives and prepositions followed by *-ing*	Introductions	Linking words ending in a consonant	Clothes (Unit 14); people (Units 2 and 6); furniture (Unit 13)
Exam folder 23 152–153 Reading Part 1 Speaking Part 2				

TOPIC	GRAMMAR	FUNCTIONS AND VOCABULARY	PRONUNCIATION	REVISION
Unit 24 **I've got an idea** 154–157 Inventions	Past simple passive; future passive	Describing objects; talking about things you don't know the name of; guessing vocabulary; dates (years)	Linking words ending in *r* and *re*	*it could/might/must/can't be* (Unit 13); *a kind of* (Unit 1); present simple passive (Unit 11); centuries and decades (Unit 14)
Exam folder 24 158–159 Listening Part 3 **Writing Part 3**				
Units 19–24 Revision 160–161				
Unit 25 Shop till you drop 162–165 Shopping	Indirect questions; verbs with two objects; *too much/too many/enough* + noun	Asking for things; trying on clothes; places to shop	Stress: correcting what people say	Indirect speech (Unit 22); clothes (Unit 14)
Exam folder 25 166–167 Reading Part 3				
Unit 26 **Persuading people** 168–171 Advertising and persuasion	first conditional; *if* and *when*; *unless*	Understanding writer or speaker purpose	Stress in common short phrases	Making plans (Unit 16); agreeing and disagreeing (Unit 19)
Exam folder 26 172–173 Speaking Parts 1 and 2 **Writing Part 3**				
Unit 27 Travellers' tales 174–177 Travel experiences	Adverbs at beginning of sentences; preposition phrases; *myself, yourself,* etc. *each, every, all*	Saying why people do things; word building	/eə/ as in *chair* /ɪə/ as in *here*	Guessing unknown words; present and past simple passive (Units 11 and 24); advice (Units 9 and 19)
Exam folder 27 178–179 Reading Part 2				
Unit 28 What would you do? 180–183 Celebrities	Second conditional	Jobs; preposition phrases	Auxiliaries	*if* and *when* and first conditional (Unit 26); *it could/might/must/can't be* (Units 13 and 24); agreeing and disagreeing, opinions (Unit 19)
Exam folder 28 184–185 Listening Part 2 **Writing Part 1**				
Unit 29 What's on the menu? 186–189 Food and restaurants	*So do I, Neither/Nor do I*; polite question forms	Asking politely; restaurants; apologising; food	Unstressed words	*a kind of* (Unit 1); indirect questions (Unit 25)
Exam folder 29 190–191 Reading Part 4 Speaking Parts 3 and 4				
Unit 30 **Blue for a boy, pink for a girl?** 192–195 Boys and girls	*hardly*; *before/after* + *-ing*	Saying goodbye	Revision of /ʌ/, /æ/, /ɒ/, /ɑː/, /aʊ/, /ɔː/, /e/, /eɪ/, /ɪ/, /iː/, /ʊ/, /uː/, /ɜː/, /aɪ/, /eə/	Tenses and vocabulary from previous units
Exam folder 30 196–197 Listening Part 4 Speaking Parts 3 and 4 **Writing Parts 1, 2 and 3**				
Units 25–30 Revision 198–199				

Content of the Preliminary English Test Examination

The PET examination consists of three papers – Paper 1 Reading and Writing, Paper 2 Listening and Paper 3 Speaking. There are four grades: Pass with Merit (about 85% of the total marks); Pass (about 70% of the total marks); Narrow Fail (about 5% below the pass mark); Fail. For a Pass with Merit and Pass, the results slip shows the papers in which you did particularly well; for a Narrow Fail and Fail, the results slip shows the papers in which you were weak.

Paper 1 Reading and Writing 1 hour 30 minutes

(50% of the total marks: 25% for Reading and 25% for Writing)

There are eight parts in this paper and they are always in the same order. You write your answers on the answer sheet.

Part	Task Type	Number of Questions	Task Format	Objective Exam folder
Reading Part 1	Multiple choice (A, B or C)	5	You answer multiple-choice questions about five short texts (notices, postcards, labels, messages, emails, etc.).	1, 15, 23
Reading Part 2	Matching	5	You match five descriptions of people to eight short texts.	5, 13, 27
Reading Part 3	True/false	10	You answer ten true/false questions about a longer text.	7, 21, 25
Reading Part 4	Multiple choice (A, B, C or D)	5	You answer five multiple-choice questions testing opinion, detail and general meaning in a text.	9, 17, 29
Reading Part 5	Multiple choice (A, B, C or D)	10	You choose the correct words to fill ten spaces in a short text.	3, 11, 19
Writing Part 1	Rewriting sentences	5	You write one to three words in a gapped sentence so it means the same as the sentence given above it.	2, 16, 22, 28, 30
Writing Part 2	A short message	1	You write a short message (35–45 words) which includes three pieces of information.	2, 4, 8, 14, 18, 30
Writing Part 3	**Either** a letter **or** a story	1	You write **either** a letter **or** a story (about 100 words) in response to a short text or instruction.	2, 6, 10, 12, 14, 20, 24, 26, 30

Paper 2 Listening about 30 minutes (plus 6 minutes to copy answers onto the answer sheet)

(25% of the total marks)

There are four parts in this paper and they are always in the same order. You listen to some recordings. You hear each recording twice. You write your answers on the answer sheet.

Part	Task Type	Number of Questions	Task Format	Objective Exam folder
Listening Part 1	Multiple choice (A, B or C)	7	You answer seven multiple-choice picture questions about seven short recordings.	4, 10, 20
Listening Part 2	Multiple choice (A, B or C)	6	You answer six multiple-choice questions about a recording with one speaker or one main speaker and an interviewer.	6, 16, 28
Listening Part 3	Gap fill	6	You complete six gaps in a text by listening to a recording with one main speaker.	2, 18, 24
Listening Part 4	True/false	6	You answer six true/false questions about a conversation between two speakers.	14, 22, 30

Paper 3 Speaking 10–12 minutes for a pair of students

(25% of the total marks)

There are four parts in the speaking test and they are always in the same order. There are two students taking the examination and two examiners.

Part	Task Type	Time	Task Format	Objective Exam folder
Speaking Part 1	The examiner asks both students some questions.	2–3 minutes	You are asked to give information about yourself.	1, 12, 26
Speaking Part 2	The students have a discussion together.	2–3 minutes	You are given some pictures about a situation and you discuss it with the other student.	9, 23, 26
Speaking Part 3	Each student talks in turn to the examiner.	3 minutes	You are each given a different colour photograph which you talk about for up to a minute.	3, 8, 29, 30
Speaking Part 4	The students have a discussion together.	3 minutes	You have a discussion with the other student about a topic connected with the photographs in Part 3.	8, 29, 30

UNIT 1 | A question of sport

Introduction

1.1

1 The words below are all names of the sports round the page but the letters in the words are in the wrong order. Write the sport and the number of the picture that goes with it.

a _athletics, 3_ b _cycling_ c _basketball_ d _football_ e ....

f _hockey_ g .... h _rugby_ i _sailing_ j _surfing_

k _table tennis_ l .... m .... n .... o _skiing_

2 Which sports do you like playing or doing?
Which sports do you like watching?
Does anyone in the class not like sport?
What does he/she do or watch instead?

3 Work with a partner. Look below at the names of equipment used in sport. Match the equipment to the sports in Exercise 1 and write the name of the sport(s) next to the equipment. Some equipment matches more than one sport. Use your English–English dictionary if necessary.

basket _basketball_   bat ....   bike ....
board ....   boat ....   helmet ....
net ....   racket ....   sail ....
skis ....   stick ....

4 Make a vocabulary tree of words for a sport that you enjoy.

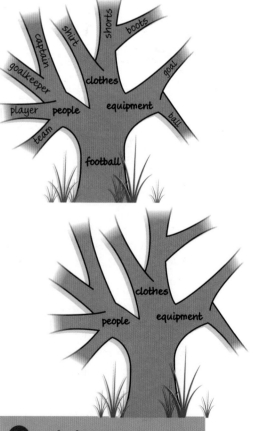

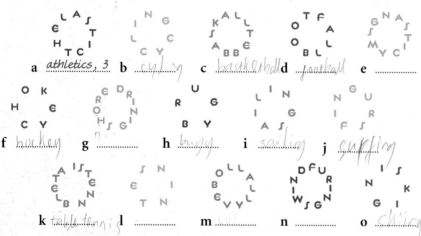

Vocabulary spot

Word trees are a useful way to learn and remember word families.

Listening

1.2

1 Look at the photographs. They show some unusual sports – street hockey, mountainboarding, snowfering and karting. Can you guess which sport is in each photograph?

a 4

b 1

c 3

d 2

2 🎧 Listen to four people talking about these sports. Which one is each person talking about? Write 1, 2, 3 or 4 next to each sport.

3 🎧 Listen to some more information about these sports. Write the answers to these questions.

Mountainboarding
a What sometimes happens? *They sometimes fall.*
b What do they always wear? They wear helmet

Street hockey
c What do they use? Street hockey
d When do they usually play this? In the summer

Karting
e How fast can you go indoors? 45
f What is a kart?

Snowfering
g What do they use? snowfering
h Where do they do this? in canada

4 🎧 Listen again. The speakers say how they feel about these sports. Which words do they use?
Can you suggest any more words like these?

Language focus

1.3

Answer these questions. Use *It's a kind of* and the words in the list below.

a What's a helmet? *It's a kind of hat.*
b What's a racket?
c What's windsurfing?
d What's table tennis?
e What's rugby?
f What's a kart?
g What's snowfering?

tennis
hat
team game
car
windsurfing on the snow
bat
surfing on water

1.4

never	sometimes	often
usually	always	

1 Rewrite each sentence below, adding one of the words in the box in the correct place. Do other people agree with your answers?

a Basketball players are tall.
  Basketball players are often tall.
b Cyclists go very fast.
c Footballers are very rich.
d Surfers get wet.
e Gymnasts wear helmets.
f There are two people in a tennis match.
g Good athletes smoke.

2 Work with a partner. Use the words in the box. Ask and answer questions like these:

Do you often finish your homework?
Yes, always!
Does your dad sometimes play tennis?
Yes, often.
Are you always tidy?
No, never!

3 Complete these sentences about yourself and other people. Use the words in the box. Use *not* in some sentences.

a _____ I don't often eat _____ cheese for breakfast.
b _My brother usually plays_ football after class.
c _____ very tired in the morning.
d _____ a sleep in the afternoon.
e _____ in the spring.
f _____ quiet in English lessons.
g _____ sport on television.

4 Now write three true sentences using the words in the box with your own ideas.

1.5 PRONUNCIATION

1 Think about the words *like* and *big*. Do they have the same sound as *wheel* and *please*?

2 Say these words aloud and put them into the correct column.

steep quite hill field like knee kind people ice little stick line big street ride rich wheel bike team

/aɪ/	/iː/	/ɪ/
quite, little, kind ice, line, ride, bike	steep, knee, stick big, street, wheel team	hill, field, people little, rich

3 🎧 Listen to the recording and check your answers.

4 Write four ways we can spell the sound /iː/ in English:
....

1.6 ACTIVITY

1 Work with a partner. Choose a sport or hobby (it's better if it's unusual!). Write down some information about it. Write sentences like these:

You play in a team. / You can do this alone.
You play in a field. / You usually do this in a swimming pool.

2 Now talk to another pair of students. Don't tell them the name of your sport or hobby. Try to guess their sport or hobby and let them try to guess yours. Ask questions like these:

Do you usually do this in summer?
Do you use a kind of board?
Do you always play with friends?
Do you often fall over?
How many people are there in the team?
Is it sometimes dangerous?

You can answer:

Yes, No or *We don't know.*

Make a poster about a sportsman or sportswoman you admire. Put their picture on it if you can. Write this kind of information on it:

What sport does he/she play?
What does he/she usually wear?
What equipment does he/she use?
What does he/she often/sometimes/ never do?
How do you feel about this sport?

LANGUAGE SUMMARY

Present simple

		Frequency adverbs		
I/you/we/they		always/usually/often/	**play**	football.
He/she/it		sometimes/never	**plays**	
I/you/we/they	**don't**	always/usually/often	**play**	football.
He/she/it	**doesn't**			
Do	I/you/we/they	always/usually/often/	**play**	football?
Does	he/she/it	sometimes/never		

To be

		Frequency adverbs	
I	**am**	always/usually/often/	happy.
You/we/they	**are**	sometimes/never	
He/she/it	**is**		
I'm	not	always/usually/often	happy.
You're/we're/they're	(aren't)		
He's/she's/it's	(isn't)		
Am	I	always/usually/often/	happy?
Are	you/we/they	sometimes/never	
Is	he/she/it		

Vocabulary

athletics basket basketball bat bike board boots champion clothes cycling cyclist elbow engine equipment field footballer goalkeeper gymnastics helmet hobby hockey horse riding ice kart knee kph match net racket rollerblades rugby sail skates skiing skis space spring stick surfing table tennis team tennis volleyball wheel windsurfing

to admire to cover to fall over to jump to smoke to wear

dangerous fun great quiet quite racing real steep strong tidy tired unusual wet windy wonderful

alone indoors

It's *a kind of* hat.

Exam folder 1

Reading Part 1

1 Look at these texts. Before you read them, guess which is:
- an email.
- a postcard.
- a post-it note.
- a telephone message.
- a notice.

The food is great but my hotel room is very small and dark. The sea is dirty so I swim in the hotel pool.

Maria

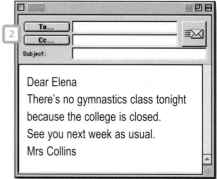

To...
Cc...
Subject:

Dear Elena
There's no gymnastics class tonight because the college is closed.
See you next week as usual.
Mrs Collins

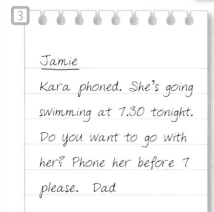

Jamie
Kara phoned. She's going swimming at 7.30 tonight. Do you want to go with her? Phone her before 7 please. Dad

The sports centre closes at 9.30 pm except Sundays when it closes at 6 pm.

Paolo Here's the information about the sports centre.
I always go on Tuesday evenings.
Ring me if you can come with me next Tuesday.
Marco

2 Now read the texts. Were you right?

Exam Advice

Look at the texts and decide what they are, e.g. a postcard, an email, etc. It will help you to answer the questions.

3 Read text 1 again. Look at these three sentences about it. Which one says the same as the postcard?

A Maria likes swimming in the sea.
B Maria likes the food.
C Maria likes her room.

B is correct. Underline the words in text 1 which tell you about the food.

Why are A and C wrong? Underline the words in text 1 which tell you about the sea and the room.

4 Now choose the correct answers for the other texts.

2 A The gymnastics class is cancelled tonight.
  B The gymnastics class is at a different time tonight.
  C The gymnastics class is in a different place tonight.

3 A Dad wants Jamie to phone him.
  B Kara wants to meet Jamie at 7.
  C Kara wants to go swimming with Jamie.

4 A The sports centre shuts at 6 pm every day.
  B The sports centre shuts early on Sundays.
  C The sports centre shuts at 9.30 pm on Sundays.

5 A Marco goes to the sports centre every week.
  B Paolo and Marco often go to the sports centre together.
  C Paolo sometimes goes to the sports centre on Tuesdays.

Speaking Part 1

Pablo

Cristina

1 Ask Pablo and Cristina some questions, using these words.

Where / come from?
Where / live?
How / old?
What / like doing?

2 Read these texts and answer your questions.

My name is Pablo. I'm Spanish. I live in a village near a large city called Seville.
I usually drive to college. I'm 19 years old.
I like playing football and going to the cinema.

My name is Cristina. I'm Mexican.
I live in the centre of the capital, Mexico City. I usually walk to school. I'm 16 years old. I like shopping, reading and going out with friends.

3 Work with a partner. One of you is Pablo and the other is Cristina.
Ask your partner the questions in Exercise 1. Then your partner asks you.

4 Think of the answers you can give about yourself to the questions in Exercise 1.

5 Now ask your partner the same questions. Your partner answers about himself or herself. Then your partner asks you. Answer about yourself.

6 Write a text about yourself.

Exam Advice

The examiner asks you questions about yourself. Learn how to talk about your age, where you live and what you like doing.

Exam folder vocabulary
message
(post-it) note
notice
capital (city)
dark (room)
dirty

Introduction

2.1

1 Colleges often give identity cards to their students. Look at these cards. What can you say about the people they belong to? What do they look like?

a
Name
.... Mandara
Age
17
Department
Modern languages student

b
Name
.... Mike
Age
19
Department
Business student

c
Name
.... safan
Age
21
Department
Music student

d
Name
.... Julia
Age
16
Department
Science student

e
Name
.... Nundang
Age
21
Department
Medical student

f
Name
....
Age
18
Department
Art student

2 🎧 When a new student arrives, another student goes to meet them. They talk on the telephone before they meet.
Listen to two conversations and write each speaker's name on the correct card. The students' names are in the box below. Which two don't you hear?

Anastasia	Julia	Kurt
Mandana	Mike	Stefan

3 Work with a partner.
Imagine you are Kurt (a boy) and Anastasia (a girl). Describe yourselves to each other.

4 Write a short description of yourself on a piece of paper. Don't write your name. Don't show it to anyone. Fold the paper.
Put all the descriptions together.
Take them out in turn and read them aloud.
Who do you think wrote each description?

> **G rammar spot**
>
> Remember to use *a/an* when you say someone is a student, or what their job is.
>
> *He's an art student. She's a singer.*

5 Complete these notes about someone you admire (e.g. a singer, a film star, a sportsman or sportswoman or a politician). Don't say the name. Describe the person and see if other students can guess who it is.

Height
Hair
Eyes
Other information

Reading

2.2

1 *The Meeting Place* is a club for young people. Here is the members' notice board. Read the advertisements and write *Travel*, *Contacts* or *Accommodation* above each one to show what it is about.

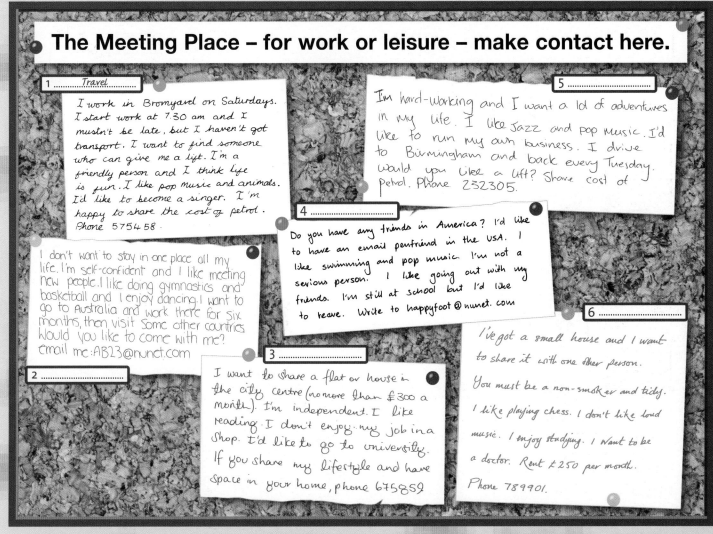

The Meeting Place – for work or leisure – make contact here.

1 Travel

I work in Bromyard on Saturdays. I start work at 7.30 am and I mustn't be late, but I haven't got transport. I want to find someone who can give me a lift. I'm a friendly person and I think life is fun. I like pop music and animals. I'd like to become a singer. I'm happy to share the cost of petrol. Phone 575458.

2 ....

I don't want to stay in one place all my life. I'm self-confident and I like meeting new people. I like doing gymnastics and basketball and I enjoy dancing. I want to go to Australia and work there for six months, then visit some other countries. Would you like to come with me? email me: AB23@nunet.com

3 ....

I want to share a flat or house in the city centre (no more than £300 a month). I'm independent. I like reading. I don't enjoy my job in a shop. I'd like to go to university. If you share my lifestyle and have space in your home, phone 675852

4 ....

Do you have any friends in America? I'd like to have an email penfriend in the USA. I like swimming and pop music. I'm not a serious person. I like going out with my friends. I'm still at school but I'd like to leave. Write to happyfoot@nunet.com

5 ....

I'm hard-working and I want a lot of adventures in my life. I like jazz and pop music. I'd like to run my own business. I drive to Birmingham and back every Tuesday. Would you like a lift? Share cost of petrol. Phone 232305.

6 ....

I've got a small house and I want to share it with one other person. You must be a non-smoker and tidy. I like playing chess. I don't like loud music. I enjoy studying. I want to be a doctor. Rent £250 per month. Phone 789901.

2 Complete this table about the advertisements by ticking the boxes.

Who	1	2	3	4	5	6
a knows what job he/she wants in the future?	✓					
b has a job now?						
c offers to pay for something?						
d wants to go to another part of the world?						
e wants to find somewhere to live?						
f enjoys sport?						
g likes quiet hobbies?						

3 Would you like to meet any of the people who wrote the advertisements? Why?/Why not?

Language focus

2.3

Work with a partner. Read the quiz together. Mark your partner's answers. Look at the bottom of page 19 to find the result.

What kind of person are you?

1 What kind of music do you like?
- **A** pop
- **B** jazz
- **C** classical

2 Do you like studying?
- **A** no
- **B** some subjects
- **C** yes

3 Would you like to travel round the world?
- **A** yes – with my friends
- **B** yes – alone
- **C** no, I wouldn't

4 You're free this evening. What do you want to do?
- **A** go to a disco
- **B** go to the cinema
- **C** stay at home and read

5 You want to find a new hobby. What would you like to learn?
- **A** to ride a horse
- **B** to paint
- **C** to make bread

6 You'd like to celebrate your birthday. What would you like to do?
- **A** have a big party on the beach
- **B** try a new restaurant
- **C** invite some friends to dinner

2.4

Complete the spaces with the correct form of *would like*, *like* or *have got*.

a Waiter: Good morning, madam. What _would you like_ to order?
Woman: Fish please, with peas and chips.

b Boy: .... Sophie .... to have a book for her birthday?
Girl: I think a CD is a better present for her because she .... pop music.

c Girl: My parents .... to go to the cinema with me on Saturday but I .... going out with my friends at the weekend.

d Man: How many brothers and sisters .... you ....?
Woman: Three sisters, but I .... any brothers.

e Girl: .... your dad .... jazz music?
Boy: Oh yes, he .... 200 CDs.

f Boy: What .... you .... doing on holiday?
Girl: Oh, I .... swimming in the sea.

g Mother: Go and visit your aunt in London. She .... to see you.

h Man: .... you .... to come to the zoo with me this weekend?
Woman: No, thank you. I .... seeing animals in cages.

i Brother: I .... to meet your boyfriend.
Sister: Oh, he's very busy. He .... going sailing at weekends so he studies hard all week.

j Girl: I .... to buy some running shoes. What .... you ....?
Shop assistant: Sorry, we .... any. We only sell football boots.

2.5

Write a notice for *The Meeting Place* notice board. Choose travel, contacts or accommodation. Say what kind of person you are and explain what you want.

2.6 **PRONUNCIATION**

1 Look at this sentence. Do the words have the same vowel sound in them?

Stop studying students!

2 Say these words aloud and put them into the correct column.

university fun pop music become some Tuesday other club long you above doctor discuss want cost future

/juː/	/ʌ/	/ɒ/
university	fun	pop

3 🎧 Listen to the recording and check your answers.

4 🎧 Read these sentences and underline the sounds /juː/, /ʌ/ and /ɒ/. Listen to the recording and repeat.

I want to become a doctor.
Some university students have a lot of fun.
I run a music club above a shop.
His other brother's got long hair.

2.7 **ACTIVITY**

1 Write down four things you like doing in your free time.

2 Now talk to other people in the class. Find out their interests.
Ask: *What do you like doing?*
When you meet someone who shares one of your interests, ask him/her: *Would you like to … with me this weekend?*
Answer: *Yes, that'd be great/fun/interesting*
or *No, I'm afraid I'm busy.*

2.8 **ACTIVITY**

1 Look at these pieces of writing from *The Meeting Place* notice board. A handwriting specialist gives her opinions about the writers. Can you guess which opinion is about each writer? Are her opinions correct?

2 Look at some handwriting with a group of people in your class. Do you think the styles of handwriting give any information about the people who wrote them?

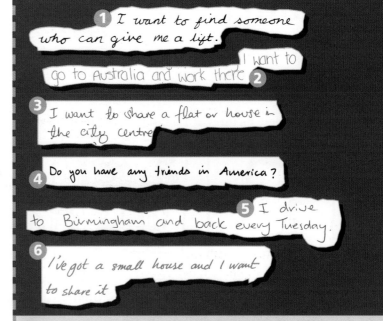

1 I want to find someone who can give me a lift.

2 I want to go to Australia and work there

3 I want to share a flat or house in the city centre

4 Do you have any friends in America?

5 I drive to Birmingham and back every Tuesday.

6 I've got a small house and I want to share it

a This is a shy, intelligent person. He/she hasn't got many friends, but is very kind and likes helping people.

b This writer enjoys life, has got lots of friends and big ideas about the future too. This young person is always busy, but perhaps doesn't understand that it's sometimes necessary to think before you act.

c This writer is a serious person and has got very clear ideas about the future. He/she enjoys trying something new.

d This person enjoys having fun, and has got lots of friends. The writer probably doesn't enjoy studying but has he/she got any ideas about the future?

e This person becomes bored very quickly and doesn't like sitting quietly at home. The writer enjoys many different activities and making friends with all kinds of people but hasn't got a lot of close friends.

f This handwriting shows a quiet person who is not very happy now and would like to change his/her life. The writer doesn't often listen to other people's opinions.

Results

Mainly As: You think life is fun. You're never serious. You have lots of friends.

Mainly Bs: You are independent. You like new experiences and ideas. You wouldn't like to stay in one place all your life.

Mainly Cs: You like a quiet life. You don't want a lot of adventures. You'd like to have an interesting job.

A mix of As, Bs and Cs: You are a happy mix!

Describing people
I've **got** long hair. (= *I have …*)
She **hasn't got** long hair.
Have they **got** long hair?
He's **an** art student.
She's **a** singer.
I'm tall and slim **with** short hair.
I've **got** brown hair/blue eyes.
I'm friendly.
I'm a friendly **person**.

like(s) enjoy(s)	**going** to the cinema films
want(s) would ('d) like	**to go** to the cinema

I'm afraid I'm busy.

Vocabulary
accommodation adventure advert(isement) art boyfriend CD chess club contact cost dancing description film star flat future hair handwriting height home idea information interests jazz life lifestyle lift member meeting mix modern languages moustache non-smoker opinion parent penfriend petrol politician quiz rent science specialist transport travel

to become to belong to to celebrate to describe to discuss to enjoy
to invite to leave to offer to order to paint to run (a business) to share

average bored broad-shouldered classical clear close curly dark fair friendly hard-working independent intelligent kind loud medical necessary pop self-confident serious shoulder-length shy slim tall wavy

perhaps probably quickly quietly

Exam folder 2

Listening Part 3

1 Look at these pictures of Dan. What does he do every day?

2 🎧 Listen to what Dan says. Does he use exactly the same words as below?
Underline the words which are different from what you hear.

a I always <u>cycle there</u>.
...............*go there by bicycle*.............................8 30......

b I have a huge breakfast at about half <u>past eight</u>.
....

c I'm studying <u>geography</u>.
....

d I usually study in my room in the afternoon.
....

e I enjoy spending time with my friends.
....

f I would like to travel round the world.
....

3 🎧 Listen again and look at the recording script.

4 Write the words Dan uses under the ones you underlined in Exercise 2.

5 Look at these pictures of Katy. What does she do every day?

6 🎧 Listen to Katy talking about her day and complete
the spaces in the sentences below. Remember she may
use different words from the ones you see here.

> At 6.30 am she goes to the (1) ......*gym*............... on foot.
> At (2) .....*7.30*.......... she has breakfast.
> Her subject is (3) .....*arts*............. .
> In the afternoon she usually goes to the (4) .....*cafellb*.......
> There is always a match on (5) .... afternoons.
> In the evening, she likes (6) .....*watching*...*TV*.
> When she finishes her course, she wants to be a
> (7) .....*nurse*........ .

Exam Advice

The words you write **in the spaces** are
always the **same** as the words you hear. But
the words **around the spaces** are sometimes
different from the words you hear.

7 🎧 Look at the recording script.
   Listen again and check your answers.

Writing folder

Writing Parts 1, 2 and 3

Exam Advice

Correct punctuation is important in your writing. Understanding punctuation also helps you when you read.

1 Work with a partner. Look at the conversation below and answer the questions.

'What's your name and how old are you?'

'My name's Azadeh and I'm seventeen.'

'What do you do?'

'I'm a student now, but I want to be a lawyer.'

a How many capital letters are there? Why are they there? Can you think of other places where English uses capital letters?

b Find the quotation marks. Mark them in colour. Why are they there?

c How many apostrophes are there? Mark them in a different colour. Why are they there? Can you think of another place where English uses an apostrophe?

d How do we end a statement?

e Where do we use a question mark?

f Where do we use a comma?

g Do you know any other punctuation marks?

2 What's the difference between *the student's books* and *the students' books*?

3 These sentences need apostrophes and capital letters. Can you correct them?

a My brother and ~~i~~ I usually watch football matches at my grandparents flat because their televisions very big.

b On thursday im going to the match between italy and scotland with dad and uncle ian.

c Were travelling in my uncles car to edinburgh and after the match, were staying at the norton hotel.

d Then on friday morning my uncle and i are visiting edinburgh castle and my fathers going to the national gallery and a museum.

4 Correct the punctuation mistakes in this note.

dear Nell,

Thank you for your email. mums computer isnt working so im sending you this note

Im going to london on saturday to do an english course at harrison college.

please write to me when im there.

Im staying with mr and mrs price at 59, esmond street. My mum and i are going shopping now to buy books warm clothes and an umbrella

Love

emilia

Exam folder vocabulary
biology canteen captain disco geography
laboratory lecture match nurse shower
fresh (air) huge national popular
on foot

Writing folder vocabulary
apostrophe castle comma computer course
gallery museum punctuation question mark
statement umbrella
to stay
It isn't working

UNIT 3 What's your job?

3.1

1 🎧 Look at the photographs and listen to eight people talking about their jobs. Match the speakers to the photographs.

a 3

b 1

c 6

d 8

e 5

f 2

g 4

h 7

2 What do the people do? Write the names of their jobs.

3 Look at the photographs again. What are the people doing?

Grammar spot

Do you know the spelling rules for -ing forms? See the Language Summary.

These rules are also useful for regular past tenses (Unit 6) and comparative adjectives (Unit 7).

4 Would you like to do any of these jobs? Why?/Why not?

Listening

3.2

1 Look at this picture. What are the people doing?
Can you guess what their jobs are?

2 🎧 Listen to the man talking on the phone. What is his job? Who is he talking to?

3 🎧 Listen to the conversation again.
Write the names of the people's jobs in the order he describes them.

1 _artist_ 2 _model_ 3 _journalist_ 4 _security_ 5 _housewife_

Language focus

3.3

1 Look again at the picture of the street. Decide what the people are doing and what they do. Put the verbs in the correct form.

a The detective __is talking__ to his boss.
b The model .... (stand) by a fountain.
c The photographer .... (sell) her photographs to magazines.
d The thief .... (walk) across the road.
e The thief .... (steal) things from cars and offices.
f The security guard .... (not look) at the thief.
g The security guard never .... (do) anything.
h The photographer .... (take) a photograph of the model.
i The artist .... (sell) her pictures to tourists.
j The thief .... (not steal) anything at the moment.
k The journalist .... (write) something in his notebook.

2 Work with two other students. Take turns to ask and answer questions. Then listen to the other two students and check their grammar.

Do you play volleyball? Yes, I do.
Are we speaking Spanish? No, we're not.

3 Work with two other students. Write five questions, using one word from each box in each question. Pass your questions to the student on your right. Now write the answers to the questions you receive. Pass your answers to the student on your left. Check the answers you receive.

design	enjoying	looking
playing	work	

I	you	he	she	they

EXAMPLE: *Do I design bridges?*
No, you don't. / Yes, you do.

3.4

Sonia is an English schoolgirl. She's fifteen.
This week she's doing work experience in a hotel.

1 Look at the activities below. Make sentences about Sonia under the headings A and B.

cycle to school
work in a hotel
study French grammar
make new friends
play volleyball with friends
not meet new people
wear her best skirt every day

not go to school
not go to the city centre
have meals with her colleagues
speak French with hotel guests
eat sandwiches for lunch
do homework in the evening
not do any homework

A What does Sonia usually do or not do?

She cycles to school.

B What is Sonia doing or not doing this week?

She isn't going to school.

2 Look at this telephone conversation Sonia had with her granny and complete the spaces using the verbs in the box.

| do do do ~~not go~~ get up help like not like prefer |
| look forward to start stay understand work not work |

Granny: Hello, dear, how are you this week?
Sonia: I'm fine thanks, Granny. How are you?
Granny: Oh, not bad. How's school?
Sonia: (a) *I'm not going* to school this week.
Granny: Why not? Are you ill?
Sonia: No, I (b) ....doing....... work experience.
Granny: What's that?
Sonia: At my school, everyone (c) .....starts..... a week of work experience when they're fifteen to learn about having a job. I (d) ...working... in a hotel.
Granny: What (e) ..are you doing in the hotel? I hope you ...
(f) ..not work.... in the kitchen. That's very hard.
Sonia: No, not in the kitchen. I (g) ....help.......... the receptionist and the manager.
Granny: Is that nice?
Sonia: Yes. Well, I (h) ......like...... working with the manager, she's really friendly. But I (i) ..prefer to helping the receptionist because I can talk to the guests. I can practise my French because some French people (j) ...are staying.. in the hotel. I (k) ..understand.almost everything they say. Isn't that great?
Granny: Yes, that's very good.
Sonia: Yes. But I am tired. When I go to school, I (l) ....get up.. at half past seven, but this week I (m) ....work at seven o'clock. I (n) ....not like.. waking up early!
Granny: Oh, well, you can have a good rest at the weekend.
Sonia: Oh, yes. I (o)..looking..forward..it.

3 🎧 Now listen to the recording and check your answers.

4 Do school students do work experience in your country? Would you like to do it?

Grammar spot

Some verbs are not normally used in continuous tenses in English. These are state (or stative) verbs. Keep a list (see the Language Summary) and add to it when you meet new ones.

5 Can you find the mistakes in these sentences and correct them?

a ~~I'm not believing~~ you can fly a plane. *I don't believe*

b Are those jeans new? I'm liking them very much.

c We're thinking this CD is very expensive.

d Are you wanting some coffee?

e I can't phone you because I'm not knowing your number.

f The teacher is speaking quickly and I'm not understanding what she's saying.

g My friends are watching a pop group on TV but I'm not liking it so I'm listening to my Walkman.

3.5 PRONUNCIATION

1 🎧 Listen to the recording and mark these words in the order in which you hear them.

a cat .... cart .... cut .....*1*.....
b bag .... bug ....
c carry .... curry ....
d match .... March .... much ....

2 🎧 Listen again and repeat each sentence.

3 🎧 Now repeat these words after the recording and decide which have the same vowel sound in them as cat /æ/, cart /ɑː/ and cut /ʌ/.

does   doesn't   can   can't
must   mustn't   are   aren't

3.7 ACTIVITY

Work with a partner.
Don't look at page 23.
Try to find all the differences between this picture and the one on page 23.
Say what the people are doing and what they are not doing now.

EXAMPLE: *The photographer isn't taking a photo now, she's talking to the artist.*

When you finish, check your memory by looking at page 23.

3.6 ACTIVITY

Work in a group. One person mimes an activity which is part of a job. The others guess what his or her job is.

Ask questions like these about the activity:

Are you making something?
Are you mending something?
Are you opening a door?
Are you answering a telephone?

The answers can only be

Yes, I am or *No, I'm not.*

Ask questions like these about the job:

Do you make things?
Do you talk to other people?
Do you work indoors?
Do you use special equipment?

The answers can only be

Yes, I do, No, I don't
or *Sometimes.*

Present continuous

I	am (not) painting	
You/we/they	are (not) painting	a picture.
He/she/it	is (not) painting	
Am I		
Are you/we/they	painting	a picture?
Is he/she/it		

Spelling -ing
Verbs ending in one consonant (e.g. *put*) double it and add *-ing* (e.g. *putting*)
Verbs ending in *e* (e.g. *prepare*) drop *e* and add *-ing* (e.g. *preparing*)
Verbs ending in two or more consonants (e.g. *paint*) or *y* (e.g. *tidy*) add *-ing* (e.g. *painting* or *tidying*)

Short answers
Present simple
Do I **teach** English?   Yes, you **do.**/No, you **don't.**
Do you **live** near the school?   Yes, I **do.**/No, I **don't.**
Does s/he **paint** pictures?   Yes, s/he **does.** No, she **doesn't.**
Does this school **open** on Sundays?   Yes, it **does.**/No, it **doesn't.**
Do we **play** football at weekends?   Yes, we **do.**/No, we **don't.**
Do they **like** ice cream?   Yes, they **do.**/No, they **don't.**

Present continuous
Am I **sitting** in the right place?   Yes, you **are.**/No, you **aren't.**
Are you **studying** English?   Yes, I **am.**/No, I'm **not.**
Is s/he **working**?   Yes, s/he **is.**/No, s/he **isn't.**
Is the sun **shining**?   Yes, it **is.**/No, it **isn't.**
Are we **speaking** Spanish?   Yes, we **are.**/No, we **aren't.**
Are they **working**?   Yes, they **are.**/No, they **aren't.**

State verbs (not continuous)
to believe   to hate   to know   to like   to love   to prefer
to think (*when it means* believe)   to understand   to want

Vocabulary
artist   boss   bridge   case   colleague   criminal   detective
disc jockey   engineer   fountain   granny   guest   hairdresser
housewife   journalist   librarian   magazine   mechanic   meal
model   notebook   pavement   photographer   receptionist   rest
salesman   security guard   shop assistant   skirt   thief   tourist
tyre   van   work experience

to arrest   to cut   to design   to get up   to lend
to look forward to   to make friends   to mend   to prefer   to sell
to stand   to steal   to wake up

ill   lazy   carefully

Exam folder 3

1   Look at this picture of a young man. Can you match these questions to their answers?

   a Where is he?
   b What does he look like?
   c What is he wearing?
   d What kind of person is he?
   e What is he doing?
   f How do you feel about doing this kind of thing?
   g Why?

   1 He's painting something.
   2 Because I don't like the smell of paint.
   3 He's not a tidy person.
   4 I wouldn't like to do this.
   5 He's wearing white shorts and a blue T-shirt.
   6 He's in a garden.
   7 He's tall and he's got short dark hair.

2   Look at this picture of a young woman. Can you answer these questions?

   a Where is she?
   b What does she look like?
   c What is she wearing?
   d What kind of person is she?
   e What is she doing?
   f How do you feel about doing this kind of thing?
   g Why?

3   Now shut your book. Can you remember all the questions?

Exam Advice

Learn these questions. They do not all fit every exam photograph, but they help you to think of what to say.

4 Work with a partner. One of you talks about Photograph A below and then the other talks about Photograph B below. Before you start, look at the seven questions on page 26. Think about your answers for your photograph. Don't say anything now.

Now cover page 26. Imagine your partner wants to know the answers to all seven questions. Tell your partner about your photograph. Are you giving your partner all the answers?

When your partner is speaking, listen carefully. Look at the questions on page 26. Tick the questions when you hear the answers.

messy person

Reading Part 5

1 Look again at the picture in Exercise 1 on page 26. Choose the correct word to go in these spaces.

1 Tom is _A_ .
   A tall   **B** long   **C** high   **D** great

2 Tom .... wearing a T-shirt.
   A do   **B** does   **C** is   **D** be

3 Tom doesn't .... to paint the fence.
   A like   **B** want   **C** enjoy   **D** prefer

2 Look again at the picture in Exercise 2 on page 26. Choose the correct word to go in these spaces.

1 Irena's .... long hair.
   A has   **B** got   **C** is   **D** wears

2 Irena usually .... a sandwich for lunch.
   A eats   **B** eating   **C** have   **D** having

3 Irena's a ....
   A hairdresser   **B** shop assistant   **C** nurse   **D** secretary

UNIT 4 Let's go out

a

Introduction

4.1

1   What do these photographs show?

b

c

d

e

f

2   🎧 Listen to the pieces of music and match them with the photographs.

3   Say what is happening in each photograph.

4   Which of these would you like to go to? Why? Which would you not like to go to?

Reading

4.2

1 Here is the contents page from an entertainment magazine.

Texts A–H are inside the magazine. Read each one quickly and decide which page it is on.

Contents

	Page
Theatre	1
Cinema	2
Music	3
Clubbing	4
Children	5
Dance shows	6

WHAT'S ON > Monday 24 – Sunday 30 August

A

FOR ONE NIGHT ONLY on Tuesday 25 August, the four prize-winning musicians who play in the Chelsea Quartet are performing outside in the Palace Gardens. They're playing music by Vivaldi and Haydn and some more modern music. Interval refreshments are included in the price of the ticket. **Concert starts at 7.30. Tickets £6.50.**

B 2

Set in San Francisco, *Meet my Family* stars Jamie Glazer and Francesca Nolte and tells the story of a family who run a restaurant. Their lives are changed by an unexpected visitor.

This year's best comedy film. 12 certificate.
Every evening this week at the Arts Picture House at 7.45 pm. Tickets £5.50.

C 5

Don't miss the excitement, the comedy, the music and the fun of the

CIRCUS OF THE CITY

The Big Top is in Central Park from 26 until 29 August. Afternoon shows start at 2.30 and evening shows start at 7. Tickets £8–£15. Book early.

D 1

The Final Choice is a new play at the Drama Studio which has a great story line.
It begins on a dark night on a city street but it is only in the last five minutes that we learn what really happens.

Two evening performances on Friday 28 and Saturday 29. Tickets £10–£24.

E

PLUS SIX, a local rock band who are now well-known and appear in concerts all over the world are returning to their home town to play their best songs in a concert on Saturday evening (29 August at 8 pm) in the Riverside Buildings. Book tickets early as they are very popular. £16.

F 6

An exciting new group called *Motari* present African and Western dances with some flamenco and jazz added. They are 15 young people, mostly African but some European and South American. They are doing two performances in the Town Hall on Sunday at 4 pm and 8 pm. All tickets £9.

G 4

Nojo's is the best place to enjoy yourself at weekends. Dance the night away on Fridays and Saturdays with DJs Simon and Dave.

For over 16s only. Open 9 pm–2 am. Arrive before 11 and pay only £4, after 11 £5.50.

H 3

Tickets are still available for a weekend festival of rock music in the gardens of Kingston Manor. Begins at midday on Saturday 29 and finishes at midnight on Sunday 30. Camping available. Tickets £30 weekend, £16 day.

2 Read each text quickly again to answer these questions. Don't worry about any words you don't know.

a Which events may make you laugh? *B and C*
b Which events are outdoors? H, C, P
c Which events cost £6 or less? G B
d Which events are only on one day? A, F E
e What can you go to on Monday evening? B
f What can you go to on Saturday afternoon? G, H

3 Underline the words you don't know in each text. Think about what they mean.

Vocabulary spot

When you read, try to understand the words you don't know before you check them with your teacher or in a dictionary.

Language focus

4.3

🎧 Listen to some conversations and decide where the people are going.

1 ....
2 ....
3 ....

4.4

🎧 Now listen again and fill in the missing words.

1

Laura: I know. It sounds good. I'd like to go.

Patrick: I'm taking my little brother. Would you like to come too?

Laura: That would be great. I love the noise, the music and all the excitement. The last time I went was **(a)** _in 1998_ when I was ten.

Patrick: Oh, really? Well, I like the clowns best. Are you free **(b)** _today_ or tomorrow? The afternoon show is best for my brother.

Laura: Sorry, I'm busy then. I'm going to the cinema **(c)** _this afternoon_ I've got the tickets so I can't change it – and I'm working **(d)** _tomorrow afternoon_

Patrick: Oh, well ... can you go **(e)** _at the weekend_? It finishes **(f)** _29 July_. That's Saturday.

Laura: I'm free **(g)** _on Saturday afternoon_

Patrick: Good. I'm free then, too. It only comes once a year so we mustn't miss it.

2

Sam: Hi, Juliet, it's Sam here. Have you got the tickets yet?

Juliet: Yeah, for tonight.

Sam: What time does it start?

Juliet: Just a minute. I'll look. Er, it starts **(h)** _at 8.15_ .

Sam: Oh, you know I work in a shop **(i)** _Monday_? In the city centre. Well, there's a sale **(j)** _this week_ so I'm working late. I have to tidy the shop **(k)** _at the end_ so I'm working till 7.30 this evening. I usually finish **(l)** _at 7 o'clock_ which is better.

Juliet: Don't worry. There are lots of adverts before the film actually starts.

Sam: OK. See you later then. Outside?

Juliet: See you there. Bye.

3

Max: It's so boring here **(m)** _in August_, Rachel. There's nothing to do.

Rachel: There are lots of good things on **(n)** _at the moment_. What are you doing **(o)** _next weekend_? My mum's going to see a dance show **(p)** _on Sunday_. We can go with her.

Max: Oh, boring. And I don't like going to things like that **(q)** _in the afternoon_.

Rachel: Well, there's the rock festival in the park. That looks good. I like listening to music outside **(r)** _in the summer_. But it's very expensive.

Max: Mm. I've only got £5.

Rachel: Well, would you like to go to the new nightclub? I went there last week **(s)** _on my birthday_. It's only £4 before 11. We can go **(t)** _on Saturday_

Max: I'd really like to go to the rock festival, but OK then. Shall we meet at your house?

Rachel: Yeah. About 9?

Max: See you then.

4.5

Look at Exercise 4.4 and use your answers to help you complete this table.

on	at	in	no preposition
Saturday afternoon	at the moment	1998	today
dates	at the weekend afternoon		
days	times		
my birthday	weekends		
	8.15		

Grammar spot

Write down and learn prepositions with the words that follow them, e.g. learn on Monday, in June.

4.6

Put the correct preposition (or nothing) in each space.

a My friend's taking me sailing .... next Sunday.

b My team's playing football against yours .... Friday afternoon.

c I'm visiting my grandmother in Chile .... this summer.

d Would you like to come to the theatre with me .... Saturday evening?

e Our friends are arriving .... 7.30 so we must get home quickly.

f I don't like swimming .... the winter – the water's too cold.

g I always feel tired .... the afternoon when the weather is hot.

h Jake's taking his driving test .... 23 March.

i My brother's getting married .... 2006.

j This street's very dark .... night.

4.7 PRONUNCIATION

1 How many syllables are there in these words?

Sunday ..... 2 ..... Monday ..... 2 ..... Tuesday ..... 2 .....
Wednesday ..... 2 ..... Thursday ..... 2 ..... Friday ..... 2 .....
Saturday ..... 3 .....

2 🎧 Repeat the words after the recording. Were you right?

3 Can you mark the main stress on these words?

January February March April May

June July August September October

November December

4 🎧 Listen to the recording and check your answers.

4.8

The people in the pictures are planning to do things at different times. Write a sentence about each person, choosing a time expression from the box. You do not need to use all the expressions.

Saturday morning	next Monday	the weekend
tomorrow afternoon	15th January	the summer
Thursday	6.30	

She's travelling to Moscow on Saturday morning.

4.9 ACTIVITY

Work with a partner. One of you is A and one of you is B. Fill in your diary on page 200 or page 202. You can choose some of the events in Exercise 4.2 or imagine some. Don't show your partner. Try to find a time when you can meet by asking *What are you doing on …?*

4.10 ACTIVITY

Work in a group of three. Your teacher will give you a game board. Play the game.

Prepositions of time
on is used before:
days, dates, *my birthday*

at is used before:
times, *the weekend, the end of the day, the moment, night, lunchtime*

in is used before:
months, seasons, years, *the morning, the afternoon*, etc.

There is **no preposition** before:
today, tomorrow (morning, evening, etc.), *this/that/next/last week, tomorrow (afternoon*, etc.)

Saying and writing the date
We write **1 March** or **1st March.**
We say **the first of March** or **March the first.**

Present continuous for future plans
She's travelling to Moscow on Saturday morning.
She **isn't travelling** to Moscow on Saturday morning.
Is she **travelling** to Moscow on Saturday morning?

Vocabulary
ballet circus clown clubbing comedy
concert contents diary driving test
entertainment event excitement fun
home town interval magic musical
musician nightclub noise opera park
performance play refreshments
rock festival sale show story line
theatre visitor

to book (tickets) to laugh to miss

available married modern unexpected

outdoors/outside what's on

Exam folder 4

Listening Part 1

1 Greg and Sophia are talking about something. Look at these three pictures. What do you think they are talking about?

 A ☐

 B ☐

 C ✓

2 Look at the question.

1 What do they decide to do tomorrow?

The box under picture C above is ticked because that is the answer.

🎧 Listen to Greg and Sophia's conversation and think about why C is the answer. Answer these questions.

a Are they playing tennis tomorrow? Why?/Why not?
b Are they playing hockey tomorrow? Why?/Why not?
c Are they going cycling tomorrow? How do you know?
d Do they both agree? How do you know?

3 Look at these pictures for four other conversations.
Think what the conversations are about. The questions help you too.

2 Which shop are they going to first?

A ☐   B ☐   C ☐

3 When is Tim meeting his father?

A ☐   B ☐   C ☐

4 Where are they going on Saturday evening?

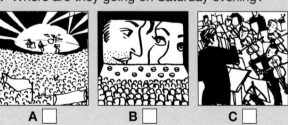

A ☐   B ☐   C ☐

5 When is Paula's birthday party?

A ☐   B ☐   C ☐

4 🎧 Now listen to conversations 2, 3, 4 and 5.
Decide which picture is correct for each one and put a tick in the box.

Exam Advice

Read the question and look at the pictures before you listen.

Writing folder

Writing Part 2

1 Look at this question. It is an example of the kind of task you will see in Part 2 of the Writing Paper. What does it ask you to do?

> You're spending a day in the capital of your country next Saturday.
> Write an email to an English friend called Helen.
> In your email you should
> • say what you would like to do in the city
> • tell her what time you are arriving
> • suggest where to meet

2 Work with a partner. Read these three answers. Only one answers the question. Which one?

a

> Dear Helen,
> On Saturday I'd like to go shopping because I want to buy a new coat and some shoes. Then I would like to go to the cinema and have an Italian meal. My father is bringing me in the car. You can come in the car with us too. We are leaving home at 9.30.
> Love Maria

b

> Dear Helen,
> I'd like to go to the cinema on Saturday and walk by the river. We can go to a café to have lunch. What do you want to do? I am arriving at 11.30. We can meet outside the station.
> Love Maria

c

> Dear Helen,
> I'd like to go to the museum on Saturday.
> I'm arriving at 11.30 so we can meet at midday.
> Love Maria

3 In Writing Part 2 you must write 35–45 words. Add *outside the museum* to answer c. Is this a good answer now?

4 Think about your own answer to the question.

　a What would you like to do in your capital city?
　b Think of different places you can meet someone.

5 Write your answer.

Exam Advice

Remember there are always three things you must write about in Writing Part 2.

6 Have you answered the three parts of the question? Count the words. Make sure you have 35–45 words.

7 How many lines of your writing is 35–45 words?

Exam folder vocabulary
chemist invitation picnic shampoo swimming costume

Writing folder vocabulary
to spend to suggest

UNIT 5 Wheels and wings

Introduction

5.1

1 Look at the photographs of different ways of travelling. These sentences describe them. Write the answers in the crossword.

Across

4 It spends a lot of time on motorways carrying people from one place to another.

5 It transports goods by road.

6 It has no roof and often goes faster than a car. ~Truck~

9 It takes people to hospital.

11 It takes lots of people to school, to work and around town.

15 It carries a few people in the air.

Down

1 It travels on top of the water.

2 It travels at about 850 kilometres per hour.

3 It is only found in cities and travels on rails.

7 Many families own one.

8 It takes people across water. It travels quite slowly. √

10 You need to be fit to travel on it.

12 It goes on long journeys across water, carrying people √ and goods.

13 It has two wheels, only carries one person and has a very small engine.

14 It runs on rails and has several carriages. *Hoa tàu*

16 You often find it outside the railway station. √

2 Work in a group. Compare your crosswords. Can you help the other people in your group?

3 How many of the different ways of travelling do you use? Count them. Write three sentences using *usually*, *sometimes* and *never*.
EXAMPLE: *I never travel by ship.*

V ocabulary spot

Write vocabulary down under a topic. Write all these words about transport together. Can you make a word tree?

Listening

5.2

1 Where do you find these signs?

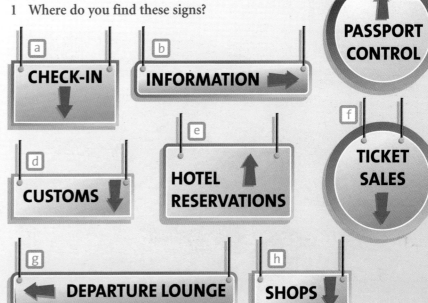

a CHECK-IN ↓

b INFORMATION →

c PASSPORT CONTROL ↑

d CUSTOMS ↓

e HOTEL RESERVATIONS ↑

f TICKET SALES ↓

g ← DEPARTURE LOUNGE

h SHOPS ↓

2 🎧 Listen to six conversations. Each conversation happens at one of the places above. Write the letter to show where the speakers are.

1 ...E... 2 ...C... 3 ...A... 4 ...H... 5 ...D... 6 ...F...

Language focus

5.3

🎧 Listen again and answer these questions.

Conversation 1
a What does the man need? *Hotel room*
b What doesn't the man need? *taxi*

Conversation 2
c What doesn't the woman need? *visa*

Conversation 3
d What does the man need to do? *goto depature*

Conversation 4
e What do they need to buy? *nothing*

Conversation 5
f Does the woman need to pay any tax? *video camera*

Conversation 6
g When does the man need to come back? *sat day evening*
h Does he need to reconfirm his return flight?

5.4

1 Joe is going to stay with a Brazilian family who live by the seaside. Here are some of the things he is planning to take. What are they?

2 Put them into the correct column.

Countable (singular)	Countable (plural)	Uncountable
a camera	some films	some shampoo
a mobifone	Some picture	Some suncreeam
a Coast	Some books	Some tea
a touchbouh	Some tea	Some money
a passport		
a bag		
an addressboule		

ⒼGrammar spot

Some uncountable nouns like *shampoo* can be countable when we add words like *bottle – a bottle of shampoo; packet – a packet of tea; bar – a bar of chocolate*.

---

3 Joe can't carry his rucksack because he has too many things. It's January in Brazil. Work in a group. What does he need to take? What doesn't he need to take?

4 Tell some other students what you decided. Do they agree with you?

5.5

Imagine you are going to stay with a friend in England for a week in January. What things do you need to take? What things don't you need to take? Write them down. Read your list to some other students.

I need to take a warm coat. I don't need to take any suntan lotion.

5.6

Complete these sentences with the correct form of *need*.

a It's very hot in the airport – I ...*need*... a drink.
b ...*You need*... (you) a new suitcase to take on holiday?
c ...*We need*... (we) book a taxi to take us to the airport?
d You ...*don't need*... (not) take the train because I can drive you home.
e Lorry drivers ...*need to*... stop for a break after a few hours on the road.
f Do ...*I need*... (I) wear a helmet on a motorbike?
g My brother ...*doesn't need to*... (not) a car because he catches the bus everywhere.
h You ...*don't need to*... (not) come to the station with me – I know where it is.

5.7 ᴀᴄᴛɪᴠɪᴛʏ

Your teacher will give you a card. Don't show it to the other students. Guess the activity on your friends' cards. Ask questions like these:

Do I need other people to do this?
Do I need good weather?
Do I need to go to a special place?
Do I need any special equipment?

Answer their questions truthfully. You can answer *Yes, No, Sometimes* or *It doesn't matter.*

5.8 ᴘʀᴏɴᴜɴᴄɪᴀᴛɪᴏɴ

1 Fill in the missing words in these sentences.

a I need ...*a*... visa.
b I've got ...*a*... couple ...*of*... suitcases.
c They need ...*to*... take their passports.
d He's got ...*a*... lot ...*of*... luggage.
e Do we need ...*to*... book a taxi?
f You need ...*some*... money.

2 🎧 Listen and repeat the sentences. What do you notice about the words you filled in?

3 Try saying these sentences. Put a circle around the words which are not stressed.

a I need ⓐ hotel room.
b You need to pay tax.
c I want some shampoo.
d I'd like to go swimming.
e He's got a few magazines.
f I've got a new pair of shoes.

4 🎧 Listen and repeat the sentences. Were you right?

5.9

1 Look at the box below. What is the difference between the two columns? Where can you put *several* and *a couple of*?

a lot of bags	a lot of luggage
not many bags	not much luggage
a few bags	a little luggage

2 At the airport, Joe meets the woman in the picture. He writes a postcard to his family. Complete the spaces with these expressions. Use some of them more than once.

a lot of a few a couple of several
much many a little

5.10 **ACTIVITY**

Sometimes we put two nouns together to make another, e.g. *address book*. Your teacher will give you some cards with nouns on them. Find the student who has a noun which goes with yours and decide which one comes first.

Dear Mum and Dad,

I'm sitting in the airport waiting for my flight. There's a woman sitting next to me who has got **(a)** ...a lot of... luggage. She's got **(b)** ...several... suitcases, **(c)** ...a few... carrier bags, and **(d)** a lot of... parcels. She's even got **(e)** ...a couple... of rucksacks. She's visiting some friends in Brazil too so I hope they meet her at the airport! I'm so pleased I haven't got **(f)** ...much... luggage. It's not busy here. There aren't **(g)** ...many... passengers waiting for my flight yet – that's probably because I got here early. I bought a book about Brazil in the airport shop. The one Uncle James gave me only has **(h)** ...a little... information about the area I'm visiting. I haven't got **(i)** ...much... English money left now. I'll ring you when I get there.
Love,
Joe

---

need

I	don't	need	a taxi.
He	doesn't		to fly to Madrid.
I/he		needn't	fly to Madrid.

Needn't is only used before a verb, not a noun.

Do	I	need	a visa?
Does	he		to buy anything?

Countable and uncountable nouns
countable
+ I've got **a lot of / some / a few / several / a couple of** magazines.
- I haven't got **any / many** magazines.
? Have you got **any / many** magazines?

uncountable
+ I've got **a little / a lot of** money.
- I haven't got **any / much** money.
? Have you got **any / much** money?

Vocabulary
address book air ambulance bicycle boarding pass break bus camera car carriage check-in chocolate coach crossword customs departure lounge ferry flight goods helicopter hospital hovercraft journey lorry luggage mobile phone moped motorbike motorway passport passport control place plane rails reservations roof rucksack ship sleeping bag suntan lotion tax tea toothbrush train tram video camera visa watch wing

to arrange   to (re)confirm

fit

by bus/train/tram

Exam folder 5

Reading Part 2

1 Look at these five people. They all want to go on holiday.
  Now look at the suitcases.
  Can you guess which suitcase belongs to each person?
  There is one extra suitcase which doesn't belong to anyone.

2 Now read some information about the five people and
  try again to match them with their suitcases. Underline
  the words which help you choose.

1 Karen likes pop music and dancing in discos and she
  would like to find a hotel where she can swim every
  day. She also wants to learn to dive on this holiday.
2 Tom is a businessman and takes his work on holiday
  with him. He needs to find a quiet hotel in the country
  which has a good restaurant.
3 Maggie would like to relax in her hotel, sunbathing,
  swimming and reading. She wants to stay somewhere
  quiet with a good restaurant.

4 John wants to stay in the mountains.
  He likes walking and is interested in flowers
  and birds. He wants to stay in a family hotel.
5 Mike wants to spend his holiday sightseeing
  in the city. He likes taking photographs of
  the places he visits and wants a hotel which
  can organise trips. He would like a hotel
  with a swimming pool.

3 Read these descriptions of places to go on holiday. Which hotel would you like to go to?

a
The Spring Hotel is a family hotel with a new swimming pool in the centre of the city. It is near all the famous buildings and art galleries. The hotel arranges coach tours to other towns.

b
Hotel Crystal is on the edge of the city with its own gardens and has 200 rooms, a first-class restaurant and three swimming pools. It is ideal for a really relaxing, quiet holiday in the sun.

c
Grand Hotel is a large hotel in the centre of the city. It has evening entertainment including a disco twice a week. There are coach trips to the mountains where visitors can walk and enjoy the flowers and the birds.

d
The Park Hotel has 300 rooms. It is in a quiet spot in the country but there are restaurants in the city which is about 10 kms away. The hotel arranges coach tours of the city for those people who do not like walking.

e
The Riviera Hotel is a family hotel in the city with its own swimming pool and the staff offer lessons in swimming and diving for guests. There is a disco every night in the hotel and it also has two restaurants.

f
The Hotel Royal is a large hotel in a village surrounded by mountains and is very quiet and peaceful. It has a gym and a good restaurant. Fax and computer facilities are available.

g
The Hotel Regent is very old and beautiful and is suitable for business conferences. Visitors can use fax and email. It is in the middle of the city and is close to lots of good restaurants.

h
The Palace Hotel is a quiet family hotel in the mountains so it is very easy to go for walks without needing to use a car. There are flowers and birds to enjoy all year round and restaurants in the village.

Exam Advice

When you choose an answer, check the text has *all* the things the person wants.

4 Look at page 38 and read the text about Karen again. Underline any more information which will help you to match her to a holiday.

5 Now find a hotel for Karen. Look at the table. Read the hotel texts again and tick which hotels have a disco. Can Karen swim and learn to dive at any of the hotels which have a disco? Tick the boxes. Which hotel is best for Karen?

Hotels	a	b	c	d	e	f	g	h
disco?	✗	✗	✓	✗	✓	✓	✗	✗
swimming?	✓	✓	✗	✗	✓		✓	✓
learn to dive?	✓		✗	✗	✓	✗	✗	✗

6 Read the text about Tom again and underline any other important information.

7 Now find a hotel for Tom. Read the hotel texts again and tick which hotels are in the country. Which one has a good restaurant?

Hotels	a	b	c	d	e	f	g	h
in the country?	✗	✗	✗	✓	✗	✓	✗	✓
restaurant?	✗	✓	✗	✗	✓	✓	✓	✗

8 Now do the same for Maggie, John and Mike.

Maggie

Hotels	a	b	c	d	e	f	g	h
quiet?	✗	✓	✗	✓	✗	✓	✓	✓
swimming?	✓	✓	✗	✗	✓	✗	✗	✗
restaurant?	✗	✓	✗	✗	✓	✓	✗	✗

John

Hotels	a	b	c	d	e	f	g	h
family hotel?	✓	✗	✓	✗	✓	✗	✗	✓
walking?	✓	✗	✓	✗	✗	✗	✗	✓
flowers and birds?	✓	✗	✓	✗	✗	✗	✗	✓

Mike

Hotels	a	b	c	d	e	f	g	h
city?	✓	✓	✓	✗	✓	✗	✓	✗
swimming pool?	✓	✓	✗	✗	✓	✗	✗	✗
organises tours?	✓	✗	✓	✓	✗	✗	✗	✗

Exam folder vocabulary
computer   conference   fax   gallery
guidebook   mountains   sightseeing
spot   sunglasses   tour   walkman
to dive   to relax
peaceful

Introduction

6.1

1   Look at the photographs. How do you think these students feel about their classes? Which class you would like to attend? Why?

2   Work in a group. Look at this student message board on a school website. Do you agree with these teenagers' opinions?

3   What opinion would you add to the message board?

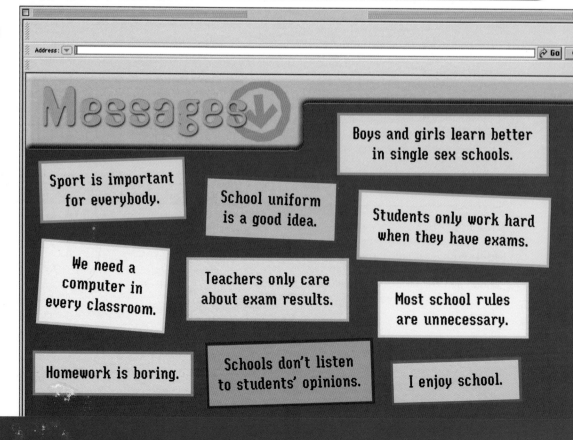

Address: ▼ | | Go

Messages ▼

Boys and girls learn better in single sex schools.

Sport is important for everybody.

School uniform is a good idea.

Students only work hard when they have exams.

We need a computer in every classroom.

Teachers only care about exam results.

Most school rules are unnecessary.

Homework is boring.

Schools don't listen to students' opinions.

I enjoy school.

Reading

6.2

Anita Green

Mavis Carver

Neil Johnson

1 Look at the three photographs of people, then read the magazine article quickly. Which photograph do you think matches each text?

2 Write the names above the texts and add the year you think the people started secondary school.

My first day

A ....

On my first day at secondary school I was very excited. My father walked to the school with me – he was very proud of me. A teacher took me into the hall with the other girls. She gave us some books and told us which rooms to go to. She used our surnames and we felt very important. My first lesson was in the science laboratory. Of course, very few schools had labs in those days. I was nervous of doing something wrong, but I was very interested and I soon stopped feeling worried. I became a scientist that day! I studied hard because I wanted to go to university to do science. And I went when I was eighteen.

B ....

I remember my first day at secondary school very well. I was eleven years old. When I arrived at the school, the playground was full of big boys, some of them looked like men to me. I was frightened. I asked some boys where to go, but no one helped me. When I found my classroom, the teacher was angry because I was late. I was miserable. I wanted to go home. Of course, I soon made friends and began to enjoy some of the lessons. But those first days were terrible.

C ....

My first day at secondary school was fun! I was with my friends from primary school, so I wasn't nervous. In the morning, some of the older students took us on a tour of the school. They showed us the different departments like the art rooms, the computer rooms and the sports ground. Then we met our teachers and they gave us our timetables. Everyone was very friendly and we all felt quite happy. Of course, when we started lessons, we realised that the work was difficult. I could understand the science, but I couldn't understand the maths at all. At the end of the day I was very tired! And we got lots of homework. I didn't feel so confident then.

6.3

1 Read the texts again. Underline the adjectives which tell you about people's feelings.

2 Look at the adjectives you underlined. Which are about good feelings and which are about bad feelings? Make two lists. Can you add any other words to these lists?

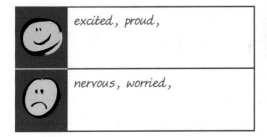

🙂	excited, proud,
🙁	nervous, worried,

3 Think about your first day at a school. How did you feel? Were you excited, frightened or proud?

Language focus

6.4

Look at these photographs. How do the people feel? Complete the sentences with adjectives from the box.

amused   bored   frightened   interested   ~~tired~~   worried

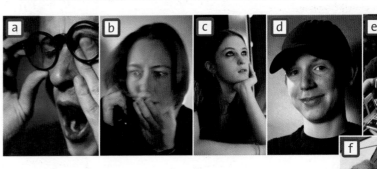

a This man is ...*tired*.. .
b She's ....
c This is a .... teenager.
d This boy is ....
e These boys are ....
f They're ....

6.5

Look at these pictures. Complete the sentences with adjectives from the box.

amusing	boring	~~frightening~~	interesting
tiring	worrying		

a
That's a *frightening* film.

b
Some people think that programme is ....

c
I think this is .... news.

d
Lots of my friends say this is an .... magazine.

e
He's got a .... job.

f
We all think that book is ....

6.6

1   Who can write the past tense of these verbs most quickly? (They are all in the magazine article.)

List A		List B	
arrive	*arrived*	be	*was/were*
ask	....	become	....
help	....	begin	....
look	....	can	....
realise	....	feel	....
show	....	find	....
start	....	get	....
stop	....	give	....
study	....	go	....
use	....	make	....
walk	....	meet	....
want	....	take	....
		tell	....

2   What is the difference between the verbs in List A and the verbs in List B?

Grammar spot

The spelling rules for the past simple of regular verbs ending in *-e* or one consonant are like the spelling rules for *-ing* forms (see the Language Summary and Unit 3 Grammar spot). Look at page 208 for a list of irregular verbs you need to know.

3   Answer these questions about the past simple.

   a   What verb do you use to make negatives and questions in the past simple?
   b   How do you make negatives and questions of the verb *to be* in the past simple?

4   Ask and answer questions like these about Mavis:

   Was Mavis excited on her first day at secondary school?
       Yes, she was.
   Were there any boys in the hall?
       No, there weren't.
   Did she walk to school alone?
       No, she didn't.
   Did the teacher give the girls any books?
       Yes, she did.
   Was Mavis's first lesson in the classroom?
       No, it wasn't.

5   Now ask and answer questions about people in your class.

6   Work with two other students. Look at the texts about Neil and Anita. Write three questions, using *was*, *were* or *did* in each question. Give your questions to another student. Answer the other student's questions. Check their questions and answers and let them check yours when you finish.

6.7

1   Complete this interview with a historian by putting the verbs in the box into the past simple.

attend	be	be	become	believe	get
~~go~~	go	have	not learn	make	need
not need	stay	teach	work		

Our reporter Zari Ahmed talked to Dr Jim Bennett about the history of education in England.

Z: What was education like in England in the nineteenth century?

JB: Before 1876, many children in England never **(a)** .*went*. to school. These children **(b)** .... from poor families and their families **(c)** .... money.

Past simple

Verb	Past	Negative		Question	
be	was	wasn't		was	he?
	were	weren't		were	they?
have	had		have	I	have?
take	took	didn't	take	you	take?
					did	it	
arrive	arrived		arrive	we	arrive?
				they	

Spelling regular past tenses
Verbs ending in *e* (e.g. *arrive*) add *d*.
Verbs ending in one consonant (e.g *stop*) double it and add *ed* (e.g. *stopped*).
Verbs ending in consonant + *y* (e.g. *study*) change *y* to *i* and add *ed* (e.g. *studied*).
Verbs ending in two or more consonants (e.g. *help*) or vowel + *y* (e.g. *stay*) add *ed* (e.g. *helped*, *stayed*).

Short answers
Yes, I **did**.	No, I **didn't**.
Yes, I **was**.	No, I **wasn't**.
Yes, we **were**.	No, we **weren't**.

Adjectives with *-ing* and *-ed*
amusing boring frightening interesting tiring worrying

amused bored frightened interested tired worried

Vocabulary
adult century department evening class exam factory feeling hall historian maths playground primary school single sex school science sports ground subject surname teenager timetable uniform website

to attend to care about to study

angry confident frightened full important interesting miserable nervous proud terrible worried

---

2 Do you think education was like this in your country in the nineteenth century?

Z: Where **(d)** .... they ....?
JB: Oh, in different places, for example, on farms or in factories. So they **(e)** .... to read or write.
Z: **(f)** .... anyone .... to evening classes?
JB: Yes, some men went when they **(g)** .... adults. They **(h)** .... better jobs and **(i)** .... more money. Some **(j)** .... engineers or writers or politicians. Some **(k)** .... other working men in their free time.
Z: **(l)** .... women .... evening classes?
JB: Very few. In the nineteenth century many people **(m)** .... that women **(n)** .... education.
Z: **Really? That's terrible.**
JB: Yes, but after 1876, all children **(o)** .... some education. They **(p)** .... at school until they were at least ten years old.
Z: **That's not very old.**
JB: No, but it was a start.

6.8

1 Look quickly at text A on page 41 again. Complete the questions for these answers.

a How *was Mavis's first day at secondary school* ? *Very exciting.*
b Who ....? *Her father.*
c What ....? *Some books.*
d Where ....? *In the science laboratory.*
e Why ....?
Because she wanted to go to university.

2 Now write four questions like the ones above about Neil or Anita. Exchange questions with another student. Answer each other's questions.

6.9 PRONUNCIATION

1 Make three cards with /t/, /d/ and /ɪd/ on them.

2 🎧 Listen to some verbs in the past simple. Raise the card which shows the sound at the end of each verb. Does everyone in the class agree?

3 Put the verbs into the correct column.

arrived /d/	helped /t/	started /ɪd/

6.10 ACTIVITY

Play past simple bingo. Who is the first to cover a line of verbs?

6.11 ACTIVITY

Work in a team. Which team can make the longest list of school subjects in three minutes?

Exam folder 6

Listening Part 2

1 Look at the picture. Who are the people and how do they feel?

2 🎧 Listen to a taxi driver talking. Does the picture match what you hear?

3 🎧 Listen again and answer these questions.

  a What did the woman need to do at 10.30?
  b What happened at 10.15?
  c What time was the flight to New York?
  d Did the woman have the wrong plane ticket?
  e Were they at the right airport?

4 Now answer these questions. They are like the questions in the PET exam.

> **1** What time did they arrive at the airport?
>
>   **A** 10.15
>   **B** 10.30
>   **C** 12.20
>
> **2** Why was the woman angry?
>
>   **A** The taxi was very expensive.
>   **B** Her plane ticket was wrong.
>   **C** She was at the wrong airport.

5 Look at the recording script. Underline the sentence which gives you the answer to question 1. Underline the sentence which gives you the answer to question 2.

Exam Advice

The questions often use different words from the recording.

6 Look at the picture. What is happening?

7 🎧 Listen to a woman talking about her first day working in a restaurant kitchen. Choose the correct answer A, B or C.
Read the questions before you listen.

> **1** How did she feel on her first morning?
>
>   **A** excited
>   **B** worried
>   **C** frightened
>
> **2** Why didn't she enjoy her first day?
>
>   **A** She didn't feel well.
>   **B** She didn't like the chef.
>   **C** She was alone in the kitchen.
>
> **3** What happened when she made mistakes?
>
>   **A** The customers complained.
>   **B** The customers were happy.
>   **C** The waiters were angry.

Writing folder

Writing Part 3

1 Read this question. It is an example of the kind of task you will see in Part 3 of the Writing Paper.

> • This is part of a letter you receive from an English friend.
>
> > I'm coming to your school for one term. In your next letter, tell me about the school. What do you like about it?
>
> • Now you are writing a letter to this friend.
>
> • Write your **letter** in about 100 words.

2 Read these three answers. Which one answers the question?

A

> I'm coming to your school for one term and I'd like to know more about it. How big is it? What are your favourite lessons? I'd like to know how many computer rooms there are because I want to study computing after I leave school. My best subject is maths but I also like science. The science teachers in my school are very good. I hope you do lots of different sports. I enjoy rugby and athletics and I'm in my school team. I know you have lots of friends so I hope I'm in the same class.

B

> My school is quite small. It's in the city centre. I walk there every day. The building is old and in winter it's very cold. After school my friends and I sometimes go to the city centre. There are three cinemas and lots of coffee bars. I like playing tennis and basketball and I go to the sports hall in the city centre at weekends. I think school is boring. I want to travel round the world and I'm looking forward to leaving school soon.

C

> My school is in the city centre. It has 1000 students aged 12-18. We have lessons from 8.30 until 4.30 except Wednesday afternoons. On Saturdays we have lessons from 8.30 until 12. My favourite lessons are science and sport. We have very good laboratories and I enjoy those lessons. I also like sport – we play basketball, football, hockey and tennis. There's a really good swimming pool too. I often go to the computer room after school and do my homework. I've got a lot of good friends here. It's a very friendly school. We often meet after school and at weekends.

3 Make a list of the topics students A, B and C wrote about. Can you think of any other things to write about in your answer?

buildings
position
favourite subjects

4 What do you like about your school? Write some notes next to each heading like this.

buildings – new, clean, lots of windows
position – near railway station
favourite subjects – English, drama

5 Now answer the question. Write about your school. Count the words. Are there 90–110?

Exam Advice

You lose marks if you write under 80 words.

6 How many lines of your writing is 90–110 words?

Exam folder vocabulary
boot (of car)   passenger   purse   tip   traffic jam
to feel ill   to refuse
annoyed   delicious   lucky   in a hurry

Writing folder vocabulary
drama   favourite   position   term

UNITS 1–6 Revision

Speaking

1 Work with a partner. Look at these sentences. Say if each sentence is true for you and give your partner some extra information.

   a I've got brothers and sisters.
   Yes, that's true. I've got two brothers and three sisters. My brothers are students. Their names are Alex and Paul. My sisters … OR No, that's not true. I've got one brother but no sisters. My brother …
   b I've got green eyes and long dark hair.
   c There are several tall boys in this class.
   d Football matches are exciting.
   e My parents and I like different kinds of music.
   f I often watch sport on television.
   g I usually enjoy school.
   h I saw a great film last weekend.
   i I walked to school yesterday.
   j My friends and I like going to pop concerts.

Vocabulary

2 Think about the meaning of these words. Mark the odd one out in each of these lists.

   a bat (flat) net racket
   b engineer helicopter lorry tram
   c confident lazy shy slim
   d ferry nightclub theatre zoo
   e guest helmet shorts skirt
   f century flight journey tour
   g boss colleague joke person
   h diary factory magazine notebook
   i performance playground subject timetable

Reading

3 Read this email and answer the questions using short answers.

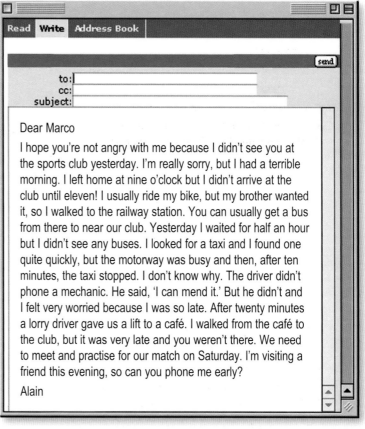

Read **Write** Address Book

send

to:
cc:
subject:

Dear Marco

I hope you're not angry with me because I didn't see you at the sports club yesterday. I'm really sorry, but I had a terrible morning. I left home at nine o'clock but I didn't arrive at the club until eleven! I usually ride my bike, but my brother wanted it, so I walked to the railway station. You can usually get a bus from there to near our club. Yesterday I waited for half an hour but I didn't see any buses. I looked for a taxi and I found one quite quickly, but the motorway was busy and then, after ten minutes, the taxi stopped. I don't know why. The driver didn't phone a mechanic. He said, 'I can mend it.' But he didn't and I felt very worried because I was so late. After twenty minutes a lorry driver gave us a lift to a café. I walked from the café to the club, but it was very late and you weren't there. We need to meet and practise for our match on Saturday. I'm visiting a friend this evening, so can you phone me early?

Alain

   a Did Alain go to the club yesterday? *Yes, he did.*
   b Did Alain arrive at the club early?
   c Does Alain often cycle to the club?
   d Do buses go from the railway station to near the sports club?
   e Were there many buses near the railway station yesterday?
   f Did Alain get a taxi?
   g Were there many cars on the motorway yesterday?
   h Does Alain know why the taxi stopped?
   i Did the taxi driver mend his taxi?
   j Was Alain happy?
   k Did Alain and the taxi driver walk to the café?
   l Are Marco and Alain playing in a match this weekend?
   m Is Alain going out this evening?

Grammar

4 In each group of the sentences below, only one is correct. Tick the correct sentence and put a cross by the incorrect ones.

1 A Are you like horse riding? ✗
   B Do you like horse riding? ✓
   C Would you like horse riding? ✗

2 A Does often your brother play volleyball with you?
   B Does your brother often play volleyball with you?
   C Does your brother play often volleyball with you?

3 A We needn't book our tickets today.
   B We needn't to book our tickets today.
   C We don't need book our tickets today.

4 A I want some informations about what's on this weekend.
   B I want some information about what's on this weekend.
   C I want an information about what's on this weekend.

5 A Do you enjoy meeting new people?
   B Do you enjoy to meet new people?
   C Do you enjoy meet new people?

6 A My sister's a medical student.
   B My sister she's a medical student.
   C My sister's medical student.

7 A How many students there are in your class?
   B How many students have your class?
   C How many students are there in your class?

8 A I'm going shopping in lunchtime.
   B I'm going shopping on lunchtime.
   C I'm going shopping at lunchtime.

9 A We've got several luggage in the car.
   B We've got lots of luggage in the car.
   C We've got a couple of luggage in the car.

10 A They didn't find any good CDs in that shop.
   B They didn't found any good CDs in that shop.
   C They weren't find any good CDs in that shop.

11 A Do they serve any refreshment on the train?
   B Do they serve a refreshment on the train?
   C Do they serve any refreshments on the train?

12 A Were any journalists at the concert?
   B Was any journalists at the concert?
   C Went any journalists at the concert?

5 Read this conversation and put the verbs into the correct tense.

Vicky: Hi, Zara, (a) _you're_ (you/be) late today.

Zara: Hi, Vicky. Yes, (b) .... (I/can/not) wake up this morning.

Vicky: Why? (c) .... (you/go) to bed late?

Zara: Yes, (d) .... (I/go) to a concert with my sister.

Vicky: (e) .... (it/be) good?

Zara: Oh, (f) .... (it/be) wonderful. (g) .... (we/see) a pop group called *Travelling People*. (h) .... (I/usually/not/like) pop music, but (i) .... (I/enjoy) this. But (j) .... (the concert/begin) at nine o'clock and (k) .... (there/be) two local groups before *Travelling People*. (l) .... (it/end) at midnight and then (m) .... (we/meet) some friends.

Vicky: Well, (n) .... (you/have) a good time. (o) .... (I/not/do) anything exciting.

Zara: What about next weekend? (p) .... (you/go) out then?

Vicky: Yeah. (q) .... (my cousin/give) a party. (r) .... (you/want) to come? (s) .... (he/always/have) very good music and (t) .... (he/know) lots of interesting people. His name's Glen Jarvis.

Zara: Is Glen your cousin? (u) .... (I/not/realise) that. Yes, let's go together.

Vicky: OK. I can phone you on Friday.

Vocabulary

6 Use one word from the box to complete each space.

> became   boring   describe   design   excited
> exciting   finished   helped   job   hard-working
> share   summer   take   ~~teenagers~~   tired

Penny is twenty-one. She's a journalist on a magazine for (a) _teenagers_ .

I (b) .... a journalist when I (c) .... college last (d) .... I saw an advert for this (e) .... in the local newspaper and I was really (f) .... when I got it. There's a lot to do every day, but I'm a (g) .... person, so I'm happy. I am often (h) ...., but life is never (i) .... I travel to some (j) .... places and I go clubbing in different cities. I (k) .... photographs and I (l) .... my adventures for the magazine. We are a small team on this magazine, so we (m) .... all the work with our colleagues. Last week I (n) .... my boss to (o) .... some pages. That was fun.

UNIT 7 Around town

Introduction

7.1

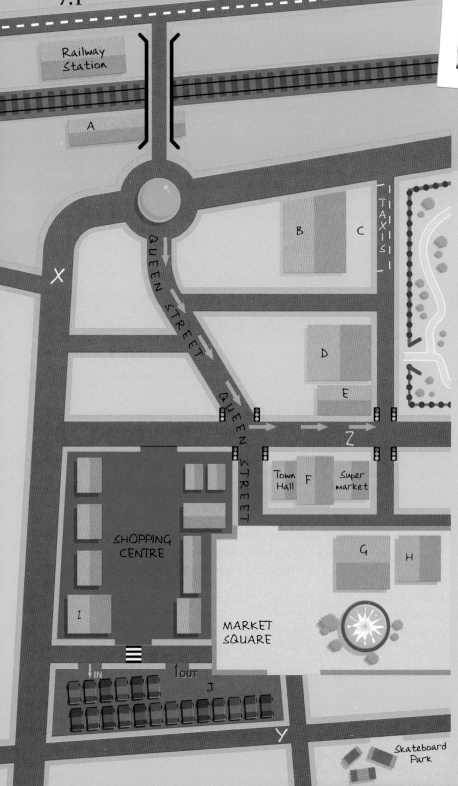

Notes

Go to

Greengrocer – on left inside Greenwood Shopping Centre. Entrance to shopping centre by pedestrian crossing. Large car park opposite entrance.

Nightclub – behind railway station, entrance under the bridge.

Museum – in market square (fountain in front of museum).

Library – in corner of market square next to museum.

Sports stadium – in one-way street between supermarket and town hall.

Newspaper kiosk – outside bus station (taxi rank in front of kiosk so sometimes difficult to stop).

Swimming pool – opposite park gates.

Petrol station – next to swimming pool and opposite supermarket by some traffic lights.

1 Shane needs to do some deliveries but he is new to the town. His boss gave him some notes. Look at the notes. Match 1–10 below with A–J on the map.

1 greengrocer ......I......
2 car park ....
3 nightclub ....
4 museum ....
5 library ....
6 sports stadium ....
7 bus station ....
8 newspaper kiosk ....
9 swimming pool ....
10 petrol station ....

2 Can you think of any other important buildings in your town which aren't on this map?

Listening

7.2

1 🎧 Find X, Y and Z on the map. Listen to three conversations. For each one, follow on the map the directions you hear and decide where each person wants to go. For Conversation 1 start at X, for Conversation 2 start at Y and for Conversation 3 start at Z.

2 Can you guess the question each person asks to get directions? What can you say when you don't understand? How do English people usually reply to *thank you*?

🎧 Listen again to check your answers.

Language focus

7.3

Write the directions next to these diagrams.

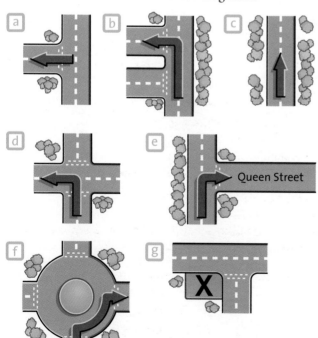

a ....*Turn*......... left.
b Take the .... the left.
c Go ....
d .... the ....
e .... right .... Queen Street.
f .... at the ....
g It's .... the ....

7.4 **PRONUNCIATION**

1 Say these words aloud. Can you hear the sound /aʊ/ or /ɔː/? Put the words into the correct column.

out   or   round   sports   town   course   corner
about   hall   board   down   how   walk

/aʊ/	/ɔː/
out	or

2 🎧 Listen to check your answers. Repeat the words after the recording.

3 Find the /aʊ/ or /ɔː/ sound in these sentences. Underline them in different colours.

a It's on the <u>corner</u>.
b Walk down the road.
c Of course.
d Turn right at the roundabout.
e Go past the town hall.
f Where's the skateboard park?
g It's outside the sports stadium.

4 🎧 Repeat the sentences after the recording.

7.5

Look at the map on page 48.
You are in the market square. Write on a piece of paper the place you want your partner to go to. Don't show the paper to your partner. Give directions to your partner. At the end, your partner can tell you where he or she is. Show him or her what you wrote on the paper. Is your partner in the right place?

7.6

Look at the photographs and write a sentence for each one using one of these prepositions.

> up ~~down~~ on off along around through over

EXAMPLE: *He's skateboarding down the steps.*

7.7

1 Read these sentences about skateboards and bikes and underline the comparative adjective in each.

 a A skateboard is <u>lighter</u> than a mountain bike.
 b A skateboard is cheaper than a mountain bike.
 c A mountain bike is bigger than a skateboard.
 d Cycling is safer than skateboarding.
 e Skateboarding is more exciting than cycling.
 f Mountain bikes are more fashionable than skateboards.
 g A mountain bike is noisier than a skateboard.
 h Skateboards are more popular than mountain bikes.
 i Skateboards are more common than mountain bikes.

2 What grammar rules about comparative adjectives can you make from the sentences in Exercise 1?

 a One-syllable adjectives ending in ....*two*.... consonants, add *er*.
 b One-syllable adjectives ending in two vowels and a consonant, add ....
 c Most adjectives ending in a .... and a consonant, double the consonant and add ....
 d Most adjectives with more than one ...., use *more*.
 e Adjectives of one and two syllables ending in *y*, usually change *y* to .... and add ....
 f Short adjectives ending in *e*, usually add ....

3 Rewrite the sentences in Exercise 1 using *not*.

 a A mountain bike *isn't as/so light as a skateboard*.
 b A mountain bike ....
 c A skateboard ....
 d Skateboarding ....
 e Cycling ....
 f Skateboards ....
 g A skateboard ....
 h Mountain bikes ....
 i Mountain bikes ....

4 Do you agree with the sentences in Exercise 1?

7.8

Write the comparative of these adjectives in the correct column.

> friendly thin steep famous popular nice
> strong old lazy wet busy rich difficult tidy
> miserable wide

Add *er*	Double the last letter and add *er*	Use *more*	Change *y* to *i* and add *er*	Add *r*
			friendlier	

Grammar spot

Can you remember which tenses have spelling rules which are like the rules for making comparative adjectives? Can you think of any irregular comparative adjectives?

7.9

Look at each pair of pictures and write a sentence comparing them, using the words given.

a Tom / Edward
Edward / cold
Edward isn't as/so cold as Tom. or *Edward is less cold than Tom.*

b Steve / John
Steve / hot

c Jack / Sue
Sue's homework / bad

d school bus / taxi
taxi / slow

e The Thames / The Amazon
The Amazon / wide

f Liz / Jill
Jill / sad

g watch / ring
ring / expensive

h shorts / T-shirt
shorts / dirty

7.10 ACTIVITY

Your teacher will give you some cards.
Match the words on the cards with their endings.
The winner is the person who collects the most cards.

7.11 ACTIVITY

Work with a partner. Your teacher will give you a maze. Find your way through it. Now join another pair of students and tell them how to get through your maze. Then they do the same for you.

LANGUAGE SUMMARY

Asking for directions
Can/Could you help me, please? I need to find a petrol station.
Excuse me, can/could you tell me the way to the skateboard park, please?

Giving directions
Turn right at the roundabout.
Turn left at the crossroads.
Take the first turning on the left.
Go straight on.
Go/walk straight down this road.
Go/walk down Queen Street to the Market Square.
Walk/Go past the town hall.
Walk across the square.
It's a one-way street.
It's a pedestrian area.

Saying you don't understand
I'm sorry, I don't understand.
Can/Could you repeat that, please?

Prepositions of place
inside outside opposite by behind
under in front of in in the corner of
next to between near

Prepositions of direction
up down on off along around under
through over

Comparative adjectives
One-syllable adjectives
cold + **er** = **colder**
nice + **r** = **nicer**
big + **ger** = **bigger** [ending in one vowel + consonant]

Two- and three-syllable adjectives
famous + **more** = **more famous**
fashionable + **more** = **more fashionable**
BUT
dirt(y) + **ier** = **dirtier** [two syllables ending in **y**]

Irregular
good / **better**
bad / **worse**

Cycling is **more** dangerous **than** skateboarding.
Skateboarding is **less** dangerous **than** cycling.
Skateboarding is **not so/as** dangerous **as** cycling.

Vocabulary
area car park corner crossroads
entrance gate greengrocer library
market square mountain bike
newspaper kiosk one-way street
pedestrian area pedestrian crossing
petrol station roundabout shopping centre
side sports stadium square supermarket
taxi rank town hall traffic lights turning

cheap expensive far fashionable light
next nice noisy safe wide

to reach to turn

you're welcome

Exam folder 7

Reading Part 3

1 Look at the photograph of Lincoln, a city in the east of England. What can you say about Lincoln from the photograph?

2 Read the text. Don't worry if there are some words you don't understand. Does it say what you expected from the photograph?

3 Mark the parts of the text which tell you about:

   a the cathedral
   b The Lawn
   c walking tours
   d the Waterside Centre
   e the river
   f the railway station

4 Now look at this sentence:

> **1** The cathedral is near the castle.

Read the part of the text about the cathedral again. Is the cathedral near the castle? Underline the answer. Is the statement correct or incorrect? Write A for correct or B for incorrect.

5 Now look at these sentences. For each one, find the right part of the text. Decide if the text says the same as the question. Is each sentence correct or incorrect? Write A for correct or B for incorrect.

> **2** The Lawn is a hospital.
> **3** It takes an hour to walk from the Tourist Information Centre to the castle.
> **4** The Waterside Centre is older than St Mark's Shopping Centre.
> **5** The river goes through the centre of the city.
> **6** You need to cross the road to go from the bus station to the railway station.

Exam Advice

For each question, find the right part of the text then read it slowly.

Exam folder vocabulary
attraction cathedral toy trip

Lincoln

The city of Lincoln is 2,000 years old and there are a lot of interesting buildings to see. The cathedral is in the north of the city just outside the main city centre. You can walk to many of Lincoln's other attractions from the cathedral. It's not far from the castle. There is a wonderful view of the city from there. Behind the castle is The Lawn, an old hospital, which is now a museum with shops and a café. You can sit in the beautiful gardens to have lunch or a coffee.

During the summer, walking tours leave from the Tourist Information Centre, which is next to the castle. They are not expensive, last about an hour and visit all the main attractions. There are some very interesting museums. The Toy Museum is not far from the Tourist Information Centre and has children's toys and games from the last century.

There are shops and a market in the old city centre. There are two shopping centres – one is the Waterside Centre opposite the market and the other is St Mark's Shopping Centre. St Mark's is newer than the Waterside Centre and is just south of the main city centre. Go straight down the High Street from the city centre and it is on the right.

In the middle of the city centre, there are some beautiful spots away from the crowds. For example, you can walk by the river or take a boat trip. Trips leave from Bayford Pool.

You can travel to Lincoln by train, bus or car. It is 216 km from London. The bus station is beside the river and the railway station is a few minutes' walk from the bus station on the other side of St Mary's Street.

UNIT 8 Let's celebrate

Introduction

8.1

1 Look at the photograph. What is happening?

2 Do people celebrate like this on special days in your country?
Which dates do they celebrate?
What do they do?

3 Work with a partner. Look at the pictures. What is happening? What do you think the people are saying?

4 🎧 Listen to the recordings. Write what the people are saying in the spaces. Did they say what you thought?
Repeat the words after the recording.

5 Can you use any of these phrases at other times?

6 Write three dates that you celebrate. They can be public festivals or family days.
What do you do on these days? What do people say?

Reading

8.2

1 Look at these pairs of photographs. They tell us something about the weddings of four different couples. What can you guess about them?

2 Read the newspaper article and match one pair of photographs to each of the couples.

What style of wedding do people in the UK want these days? Our reporter Suzy Hill talked to four couples who have some very different wedding plans.

We're getting married ...

in the Caribbean.

Anna: 'We're having a romantic wedding on the beach at sunset. I've bought a new bikini and some sunblock.'

Jay: 'I've just been to the travel agent to book our plane tickets and our hotel. We've told our family and friends and they're organising a barbecue to celebrate with us when we come back.'

in secret.

Lorne: 'Do you promise you aren't putting this in the paper until next week? OK. We're both very famous so we often have problems with our fans. We've bought the rings and we've rented a cottage in the mountains for our honeymoon. No one can disturb us there.'

Esmerelda: 'We're very much in love and want to be alone together. We haven't planned a party. We haven't even told our families or friends. We haven't told our secretaries or our agents, and we certainly haven't told any journalists except you. I hope we're not making a mistake now. Please don't tell anyone before next week!'

in our local church.

Nigel: 'We got engaged last year and we're having a family wedding in the village where we live. We've invited all our friends and our parents and all our relations.'

Fiona: 'My parents have organised a big party. It's taken months! They've booked a band to play in the evening and they've hired a special car to take me to the church. We've planned our honeymoon, but we haven't told anyone where we're going because some people aren't good at keeping a secret – we'll tell them on our wedding day.'

in our lunch hour.

Dawn: 'We're both very busy people. We run a successful business. Our secretaries have organised everything and they've sent invitations to our friends. I don't know who's accepted or who's refused.'

Gary: 'My secretary has made the appointment at the registry office and she's already booked a table at a good restaurant for lunch – we're taking an extra long lunch break. Then we're going back to work! We haven't planned a honeymoon yet because we're too busy to go away. Perhaps next year ...'

3 Work with a partner. Answer these questions together.

   a Where are Anna and Jay getting married? *in the Caribbean*

   b What has Anna bought?

   c Who have they told?

   d When are they having a party?

   e Why do Lorne and Esmerelda have problems?

   f What have they bought?

   g Why have they rented a cottage in the mountains?

   h Who have Nigel and Fiona invited to their wedding?

   i Who has organised a party for them?

   j Who is doing the music?

   k Why haven't they told anyone where they're going for their honeymoon?

   l Why doesn't Dawn know who is coming to her wedding?

   m Where are Dawn and Gary going after the wedding? And then where?

   n Why haven't they planned their honeymoon?

4 Can you match these words from the newspaper article? Check your answers in the text.

a	take	1	an appointment
b	keep	2	a band
c	book	3	a barbecue
d	organise	4	a break
e	refuse	5	a car
f	make	6	a cottage
g	rent	7	an invitation
h	hire	8	a mistake
i	make	9	a secret

5 Which couple has made the best wedding plans, in your opinion? Why?

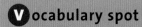

Vocabulary spot

Learn verb + noun pairs together when you meet them.

Language focus

8.3

Put the verbs into the present perfect, then look at the newspaper article on page 55 to check your answers.

   a I ...*'ve bought*... (buy) a new bikini and some sunblock.

   b We .... (tell) our family and friends.

   c We .... (rent) a cottage in the mountains for our honeymoon.

   d We .... (not plan) a party.

   e We .... (not tell) our secretaries or our agents.

   f They .... (book) a band to play in the evening.

   g They .... (send) invitations to our friends.

   h I don't know who .... (accept) or who .... (refuse).

   i My secretary .... (make) the appointment at the registry office.

8.4

1 Look at the pictures below. It's Wednesday. Jeff and Paul are having a party, but there have been a few problems.
Make sentences about the pictures using the present perfect.
Use your dictionary to check the past participles if necessary.

burn / pizza

They've burnt the pizza.

a break / chair

b drop / glass

c lose / key

d eat / all the food

e spill / juice

f drink / fizzy drinks

g make / terrible mess

2　It's Thursday. Jeff has gone to work, so Paul is clearing up. Jeff wants to be sure that Paul remembers everything. Write the questions Jeff asks when he phones Paul, and then write Paul's answers.

　a clean / floor *Have you cleaned the floor yet?*
　　　　　　　Yes, I've just cleaned it.
　b wash / glasses
　c tidy / sitting room
　d find / key
　e throw away / rubbish
　f buy / food
　g mend / chair

3　Complete the spaces with *already* or *yet*.

> **Paul:** Have you planned your weekend (a) ....*yet*.... ?
> **Jeff:** Oh, yes. I'm taking Samantha to see *Golden Boy*. I've (b) .... booked the tickets.
> **Paul:** Oh, right, the new film. Have you invited her (c) .... ?
> **Jeff:** Well, I haven't phoned her (d) .... But she said last week she wants to see it.
> **Paul:** It's very good.
> **Jeff:** Have you seen it (e) .... ? That's quick!
> **Paul:** Yes, I have. And Samantha's (f) .... seen it, too.
> **Jeff:** How do you know?
> **Paul:** We went together last night.

8.5 PRONUNCIATION

1　How do you say these dates?

　3 July　　1 January　　25 March
　24 October　　2 February

2　🎧 Listen to the recording and repeat them.

3　🎧 Write down the dates you hear.

4　Work in a group. Think about important events in your country, your school and your own lives.
　Find one event for each of these dates below (they can be in any month). Which group finishes first?

　1st　2nd　6th　15th　25th　31st

8.6 ACTIVITY

Make a list of all the things you need to do to plan a party. Then play the memory game round your class or group. Your teacher will give you the instructions.

Present perfect

I/you/we/they	have (not)/haven't	finished/eaten.
He/she/it	has (not)/ hasn't	
Have/haven't	I/you/we/they	finished/eaten?
Has/hasn't	he/she/it	

Regular verbs have the same form for the past simple and the past participle:

open	opened	opened
plan	planned	planned
organise	organised	organised

Some irregular verbs have the same form for the past simple and the past participle:

| send | sent | sent |
| tell | told | told |

Some irregular verbs have a different form for the past simple and the past participle:

be	was/were	been
go	went	been/gone
take	took	taken

just, already and yet + present perfect
I've **just** booked the tickets.
She's **already** booked a table.
Have you finished your work **already**? (surprise)
We haven't planned a honeymoon **yet**.
Have you booked the hotel **yet**?
Haven't you booked the hotel **yet**? (= why not?)

Vocabulary
agent anniversary appointment barbecue bikini church cottage couple fan fireworks honeymoon juice mess registry office relation reporter ring rubbish secret sunblock sunset travel agent wedding

to accept to burn to disturb to drop to get engaged to get married to hire to lose to organise to promise to spill to throw away

fizzy public romantic

in love

Congratulations! Enjoy your meal! Good luck!
Happy anniversary! Happy birthday! Have a good journey!
Have a nice weekend! Well done!

Exam folder 8

Speaking Part 3

1 Here are some festivals that people celebrate in the UK. Can you match the photographs to the festivals?

1 Christmas – on 25th December
2 St Valentine's Day – on 14th February
3 Easter – in March or April
4 Notting Hill Carnival – at the end of August

2 Here are two photographs of people taking part in celebrations. Work with a partner. Choose one photograph each. Look back at the questions you answered in Exam folder 3 (page 26). Think about your photograph.

3 Tell your partner about your photograph. While you are listening to your partner, think about the questions from Exam folder 3. At the end, tell your partner if he/she has answered all the questions. Are there any questions you can add to the ones on page 26?

Exam Advice

Learn expressions you can use when you don't know the word for something.
I don't know the word in English. It's a kind of X.

Speaking Part 4

Do you have any festivals in your country like the ones in the photographs?
Work with a partner. Ask and answer these questions about festivals in your country.

What / do?
What / celebrate?
When / happen?
Go out / friends / family?
How / prepare?
Wear / special clothes?
Eat / special food?

Exam Advice

Speaking Part 4 is a discussion. Say what you think, but ask your partner some questions too.

Writing folder

Writing Part 2

1 Read these questions. Underline the three things you must do in each task. Check that you understand the verbs in the Exam Advice box.

1 You are having a birthday party next Friday.
You want to invite your English friend, Matthew.
Write a card to send to Matthew.
In your card, you should
- invite him to the party
- tell him who is coming
- suggest how to get there

2 Your English friend, Catherine, has invited you to her birthday party next week but you can't go.
Write a card to send to Catherine.
In your card, you should
- thank her
- apologise
- explain why you can't go

3 It was your birthday last week.
Your English friend called Ben sent you a present.
Write a card to send to Ben.
In your card, you should
- thank him for the present
- describe what you did on your birthday
- ask him when his birthday is

Exam Advice

In Writing Part 2 you need to understand the following verbs – *apologise, ask, describe, explain, invite, say, suggest, tell, thank.*

2 Put the correct name at the beginning of each card.

a
Dear ....
I'm having a birthday party next Friday. Would you like to come? All our friends from school are coming and some of my family. I live in the city centre. Take a bus to the bus station, then you can walk from there.

b
Dear ....
Thank you very much for the book you sent me for my birthday. I spent the day with my family and I went to a nightclub in the evening with my friends. Can you tell me when your birthday is?

c
Dear ....
Thank you for inviting me to your birthday party next week. I'm sorry but I can't come because my brother and his wife are visiting us with their new baby. I hope you enjoy the party.

3 Look at card a. Underline *Would you like to come?* These words invite Matthew to the party. Now underline in different colours the words which tell him who is coming and the words which suggest how to get there.

4 Do the same with cards b and c.

5 Write the answers to these questions. Write 35–45 words.

Your English friend called Emily has invited you to go to a concert next Saturday but you can't go.
Write a card to send to Emily. In your card, you should
- thank her
- apologise
- explain why you can't go

You spent last Saturday in the city centre with some friends.
Write an email to your English friend called Tim. In your email, you should
- tell him how you got there
- describe what you did
- invite him to go with you next time

Exam folder vocabulary
crowd   egg
Writing folder vocabulary
present   to apologise   to explain

a ....

b ....

c ....

d ....

e ....

f ....

g ....

h ....

i ....

j ....

k ....

Introduction

9.1

1 What are these people doing? Which parts of their bodies are they exercising?

2 Write down the parts of the body (a–q) in the photographs.

3 Do you go to a gym? Is it a good way to keep fit? What do you do to keep fit?

l ....

m ....

n ....

o ....

p ....

q ....

r ....

9.2

1 🎧 In some places when people feel ill, they can phone a medical helpline and talk to a nurse. Listen to some people talking to a nurse. Why are they phoning?

2 🎧 Listen again. What advice do you think the nurse gives each one?

- go to the hospital
- call an ambulance
- go to the doctor's
- stay at home

3 Work in a group. Compare your answers with other students.
If you disagree, decide which answer is the best.

4 🎧 Listen to the nurse's answers. Compare her answers with your group's answers. Were they the same or different?

Language focus

9.3

How do you say what is wrong with you? Complete these sentences and write them under the pictures.

My arm ....   I've got a .... in my chest.
I've got ....   I feel ....
I've got a ....   I've got a .... eye.
I've got a ....

I've got a temperature.

....

....

....

....

....

....

....

9.4

1 🎧 Listen to the nurse's answers again. Write down what she says when she gives advice.

a You _should take_ him to the hospital.
b Why .... some cough mixture?
c You .... an ambulance.
d She .... any more food today.
e Why .... your eyes in warm water?
f You'd .... the doctor.

2 Give the people in Exercise 9.3 some advice. You can use some of these expressions.

- take some cough mixture/antibiotics/ paracetamol/aspirin
- have a warm drink
- stay in bed
- call an ambulance
- go to the doctor's

9.5

Look at these sentences from the conversations in Exercise 9.2. They all contain expressions with *at*. Can you complete the spaces?

| night   home   ~~school~~   last   least   the moment |
| all   lunchtime   once   the weekend |

a My son fell over at _school_ .
b He can't move his fingers at ....
c I cough at ....
d Have you got a cold at ....?
e She had a burger and chips at ....
f I'm relaxing at ....
g He's just stopped at ....
h I don't want to ring the doctor at ....
i Sleep with at .... two pillows.
j You'd better dial 999 at ....

Vocabulary spot

Learn prepositional phrases in groups.

9.6

Match these questions and answers.

a Did he hit his head?
b Have you got a cold?
c Does he feel sick?
d Does she have a headache?
e Has she eaten a lot today?
f Are you tired?
g Do you wear glasses or contact lenses?
h Is he hot?
i Has he taken any aspirin?

1 Yes, he has.
2 Yes, she does.
3 No, I'm not.
4 No, he didn't.
5 Yes, he is.
6 No, I don't.
7 No, she hasn't.
8 Yes, he does.
9 No, I haven't.

9.7

Write short answers for these questions. Exchange answers with a partner and check your partner's work.

a Have you completed the exercise above? _Yes, I have._
b Do you understand it?
c Is your teacher in the room?
d Are your friends working?
e Are you working?
f Is this exercise easy?
g Have you finished it yet?
h Has your partner checked your answers?
i Do you want to take a break soon?

9.8 ACTIVITY

Work in a group. Your teacher will give you a card. Mime what it says on the card. The other students guess what's wrong with you and give you advice.

9.9 ACTIVITY

Read the problem your teacher gives you. Below the problem is some advice but it isn't the right advice for your problem. Someone else has the right advice for you. Listen to other students' problems and tell your problem to other students. Give your advice to the right person.

9.10 PRONUNCIATION

1 Which letters complete the spaces – *a, ay, ai, e, ie* or *ea*? You need to use some of the letters more than once.

   a My son f.*e*.ll over.
   b Can I h......lp you?
   c My fr......nd t......kes the tr......n to college.
   d I eat a h......lthy br......kfast every d...... .
   e I hit my h......d and now I've got a p......n.
   f Don't br......k that glass.
   g I saw a gr......t pl...... tod...... .

2 Look at the letters you have filled in. Which ones make the sound /eɪ/ (as in *say*)? Underline them in a colour. Which ones make the sound /e/ (as in *tell*)? Underline them in a different colour.

3 🎧 Listen and repeat the sentences. Were you correct? Make any corrections.

4 Which letters spell the sound /eɪ/? Which letters spell the sound /e/?

9.11 ACTIVITY

1 How healthy are you? Answer these questions about yourself.

a	Do you and your friends enjoy dancing?	YES/NO
b	Are you keen on computer games?	YES/NO
c	Do you love chocolate?	YES/NO
d	Have you got a bicycle?	YES/NO
e	Are you a member of a sports club?	YES/NO
f	Have you got more than one TV in your house?	YES/NO
g	Do you and your family go for walks together?	YES/NO
h	Do your parents exercise every week?	YES/NO
i	Did you eat any vegetables yesterday?	YES/NO
j	Have you got a car?	YES/NO
k	Did you eat two or more burgers last week?	YES/NO
l	Do you eat fresh fruit every day?	YES/NO
m	Do you sleep at least seven hours every night?	YES/NO
n	Do you exercise three times a week?	YES/NO

2 Your teacher will give you a board with the questions on it. You can use your answers above as you play.

3 Do you agree with the results of the game? Can you think of other things you can do to stay healthy and keep fit?

Saying what's wrong with you

My arm hurts.
I've hurt my arm.
I've broken my arm.
I've got a pain in my chest.
I've got a cold / a cough / a sore throat / a temperature /
   (a) stomach ache / (a) backache / (an) earache / a headache /
   (a) toothache.
I feel sick.

Vocabulary

advice ankle antibiotics aspirin backache burger chest chin chips contact lenses cough cough mixture
ear earache eye finger glasses headache heart lip neck nose pain paracetamol pillow popcorn
stomach stomach ache temperature throat thumb toe tongue toothache vegetable wrist

healthy sore

to advertise to break to complain to dial
to feel sick to hurt to move to sneeze

Sorry to bother you

Expressions with at

at all at night at the moment at lunchtime at home at last at school at the weekend at least at once

Giving advice

Why don't you take some cough mixture?
You should go to bed.
You shouldn't eat any more food.
You'd better phone the doctor.

Short answers

Have you finished? Yes, I have. / No, I haven't.

LANGUAGE SUMMARY

Exam folder 9

Reading Part 4

1 In Reading Part 4, the first question always asks you what the writer is trying to do. Read these four texts and match them to A, B, C and D below. Underline the words in each text which helped you to find the answers.

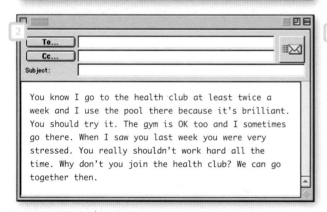

1 I joined your health club last week. The equipment is up-to-date and easy to use but when I came in for the first time on Thursday I was very surprised that there were no instructors in the gym. Nobody checked my heart before I started using the equipment. I am not happy about this because it is very dangerous. I am coming back next week to use your pool and I hope you have a lifeguard there.

3 *Blacks Health Club is opening next week and we are offering a special discount to the first 100 members. You can join the club for half the normal price. Just come along or phone me, Mick Smith, the manager, on 983546.*

Don't miss the chance to join and use our gym and pool. There is no other club in town which is as good as this one.

2
To...
Cc...
Subject:

You know I go to the health club at least twice a week and I use the pool there because it's brilliant. You should try it. The gym is OK too and I sometimes go there. When I saw you last week you were very stressed. You really shouldn't work hard all the time. Why don't you join the health club? We can go together then.

4 I was very surprised to see you in the health club last week because you always say that you hate doing exercise. It was very rude of me to laugh at you when you tried to ride the exercise bike in the gym. I'm really sorry. The equipment in the gym is old and is sometimes difficult to use so it wasn't your fault. But the club is cheap! I hope we can be friends again. I go to the club every Sunday afternoon – shall we meet there?

What is the writer trying to do?
A advise someone
B apologise to someone
C advertise something
D complain about something

2 There is always a question asking you about the writer's opinion.
Match the texts above to A, B, C and D below. Underline the words in each text which helped you to find the answers.

Which of the following opinions does the writer have?
A The equipment in the club isn't very good.
B The club is the best in town.
C The pool in the club is better than the gym.
D The club needs more staff.

3 There are always two questions about the details in the text. This may be about something very small.
Match the texts above to A, B, C and D below. Underline the words in each text which helped you to find the answers.

Which of the following is stated in the text?
A The writer works at the club.
B The writer is a new member of the club.
C The writer always goes to the club on the same day.
D The writer goes to the club several times a week.

Exam Advice

For some questions you need to read part of the text. For other questions you need to read all of the text.

1 Look at the picture. Where is Andy? How does he feel?

2 You want to visit Andy and take him a present. Look at the things in the pictures below. Think about which ones Andy can use and which ones he can't use. Which things does he need? Which would he like to have?

Exam Advice

Ask the examiner to repeat what he or she said if you don't understand what to do. You can say *Please can you repeat that?*

3 Work with a partner. Discuss which present to take Andy. Explain why you think some things are better than others. Try to agree on what to take him.

Say what you think:
I think …
In my opinion …

Make suggestions:
We'd better take him X because …
Why don't we take him X?

Agree and disagree:
I (don't) agree (that) …
That's (not) a good idea.

Exam folder vocabulary
discount fault instructor lifeguard staff
to advise   to agree   to disagree   to join
brilliant   (to work) hard   normal   rude   stressed

4 See if the rest of the class agrees with you.

UNIT 10 I look forward to hearing from you ...

a

The Edge School of English
105, Redcoats Road, Birmingham, B15 4LB UK

Ms Maria Schmidt
Landhutstr. 384
3427 Utzenstorf
Switzerland

Dear Ms Schmidt,

Thank you for your application form for our summer course
(15th–30th July).

I have arranged accommodation for you with Mrs Susan Miller
at Lime Trees, 15, The Grove, Birmingham B14 2AJ. Please can
you write to her and tell her the date and time of your arrival.

We look forw...

Yours sincere...

J H Ell...

John Elling...
Office Mana...

b

Dear Delia,

This is a lovely place
and the hotel is great.

See you when I get back.

Love T.

D. Green
102 Finsbury Road
Topcross
Hants

c

Happy Anniversary!

d

Happy Birthday

e

From:
Date:
To:
Subject:

Thanks for your email. I can't see you on
Saturday, so what about Sunday?
Tim

f

phone bookshop
before 4.30

g

Dear Granny,

It was very kind of you to send
me the CD for my birthday. How
did you guess I wanted that one?

h

I hope you can write to me
soon. Please tell me about
the town where you live.
I guess it's very different
from towns in this country.

i

Closed
for lunch.
Open 2.15

j

I feel very sad when we're not together.
I think about you all day every day.
Do you think about me?

k

✉ CU L8r

Introduction

10.1

1   Look at the messages. What are they? *A is a business letter.*

2   Work with a partner. Discuss what kind of person probably
    wrote each one and who read it.

3   🎧 Listen to the recording. Match each speaker to a message.
    There is no speaker for two of the messages. Are your
    answers the same as the ideas you had in Exercise 2?

    1 .....c.....   2 ....   3 ....   4 ....   5 ....
    6 ....   7 ....   8 ....   9 ....

4   Do you write letters or cards? Which of a–k have you written
    or read recently?

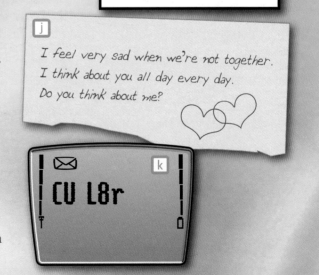

Reading

10.2

1 Work with a partner. Quickly read these letters and emails. There are two groups of four, but they are mixed up. Put them into two groups: Group a and Group b. Decide which three belong with a and which three belong with b. Then put them in the correct order.

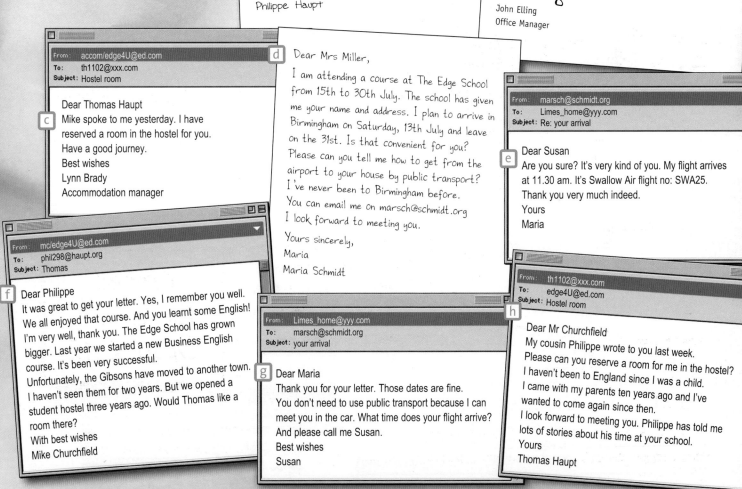

a

Dear Mike,

Do you remember me? I was in your class five years ago. We had a lot of fun and I learnt a lot of English. And you see I haven't forgotten it. Isn't that good? I hope everything is OK with you and the other teachers at The Edge School.

I'm writing now for my cousin, Thomas. He is coming to your school next month. He's twenty-two. He hasn't studied English since secondary school so he isn't very confident. Have there been many changes to the school since I was there? I stayed with a very friendly family five years ago - the Gibsons. Do they still take students?

You can email me on phil298@haupt.org

With many thanks for your help,

All the best,
Philippe Haupt

b

The Edge School of English
105, Redcoats Road, Birmingham, B15 4LB UK

Ms Maria Schmidt
Landhutstr. 384
3427 Utzenstorf
Switzerland

Dear Ms Schmidt,

Thank you for your application form for our summer course (15th–30th July).

I have arranged accommodation for you with Mrs Susan Miller at Lime Trees, 15, The Grove, Birmingham B14 2AJ. Please can you write to her and tell her the date and time of your arrival.

We look forward to seeing you in July.

Yours sincerely,

J H Elling

John Elling
Office Manager

c

From: accom/edge4U@ed.com
To: th1102@xxx.com
Subject: Hostel room

Dear Thomas Haupt

Mike spoke to me yesterday. I have reserved a room in the hostel for you.
Have a good journey.
Best wishes
Lynn Brady
Accommodation manager

d

Dear Mrs Miller,

I am attending a course at The Edge School from 15th to 30th July. The school has given me your name and address. I plan to arrive in Birmingham on Saturday, 13th July and leave on the 31st. Is that convenient for you? Please can you tell me how to get from the airport to your house by public transport? I've never been to Birmingham before.

You can email me on marsch@schmidt.org

I look forward to meeting you.

Yours sincerely,
Maria
Maria Schmidt

e

From: marsch@schmidt.org
To: Limes_home@yyy.com
Subject: Re: your arrival

Dear Susan
Are you sure? It's very kind of you. My flight arrives at 11.30 am. It's Swallow Air flight no: SWA25.
Thank you very much indeed.
Yours
Maria

f

From: mc/edge4U@ed.com
To: phil298@haupt.org
Subject: Thomas

Dear Philippe
It was great to get your letter. Yes, I remember you well. We all enjoyed that course. And you learnt some English! I'm very well, thank you. The Edge School has grown bigger. Last year we started a new Business English course. It's been very successful. Unfortunately, the Gibsons have moved to another town. I haven't seen them for two years. But we opened a student hostel three years ago. Would Thomas like a room there?
With best wishes
Mike Churchfield

g

From: Limes_home@yyy.com
To: marsch@schmidt.org
Subject: your arrival

Dear Maria
Thank you for your letter. Those dates are fine. You don't need to use public transport because I can meet you in the car. What time does your flight arrive? And please call me Susan.
Best wishes
Susan

h

From: th1102@xxx.com
To: edge4U@ed.com
Subject: Hostel room

Dear Mr Churchfield
My cousin Philippe wrote to you last week.
Please can you reserve a room for me in the hostel? I haven't been to England since I was a child. I came with my parents ten years ago and I've wanted to come again since then.
I look forward to meeting you. Philippe has told me lots of stories about his time at your school.
Yours
Thomas Haupt

2 Answer these questions.

a How has The Edge School changed?
It's grown bigger.

b Why hasn't Mike seen the Gibsons for two years?

c Why isn't Thomas very confident?

d Has Thomas been to England before?

e What has Lynn done for Thomas?

3 Answer these questions.

a When did Mike teach Philippe?
Five years ago.

b When did the Business English course start?

c When did the school open a student hostel?

d Who did Philippe stay with in England?

e When did Thomas first visit England?

Language focus

10.3

1 Work with a partner. Ask and answer questions like these beginning with *When* and *How long*.

   When did you learn to swim?
   How long have you known your best friend?

2 Choose the correct tense, present perfect or past simple. When you have finished, check your answers with a partner.

> **Thomas:** Hi. I'm Thomas. Are you a new student?
> **Maria:** Yes. (**a**) *I arrived/I've arrived* on Saturday. My name's Maria.
> **Thomas:** (**b**) *Did you have/Have you had* a good journey?
> **Maria:** Yes, it (**c**) *was/has been* very easy. My landlady (**d**) *met/has met* me at the airport. (**e**) *Were you/Have you been* here long?
> **Thomas:** (**f**) *I was/I've been* here for two weeks. (**g**) *I learnt/I've learnt* quite a lot of English.
> **Maria:** (**h**) *Did you go/Have you been* to England before?
> **Thomas:** Yes, (**i**) *I did/I have*. But that (**j**) *was/has been* ten years ago. What about you?
> **Maria:** (**k**) *I visited/I've visited* London last year. But (**l**) *I didn't come/I haven't come* to Birmingham.
> **Thomas:** (**m**) *I found/I've found* some good shops and cafés since (**n**) *I arrived/I've arrived*. Would you like to look round the city centre with me later?
> **Maria:** Yes, sure. But we'd better go to our classes now.
> **Thomas:** OK. See you later.

3 After her language course, Maria got a job. She wrote this email to Thomas. Put the verbs into the present perfect or past simple.

Dear Thomas
I'm having my lunch break and I want to tell you about my summer job at the telephone sales office.
I (**a**) *'ve been* here for one week and I (**b**) .... (already earn) £100! When I (**c**) .... (begin), the manager (**d**) .... (give) me a list of people to phone. I (**e**) .... (tell) them about our cheap holidays but they (**f**) .... (not want) to buy one. Then I (**g**) .... (get) a new list of people to phone. I (**h**) .... (sell) fifteen holidays since Wednesday. Yesterday I (**i**) .... (buy) two new CDs, a coat and some shoes. In fact I (**j**) .... (spend) £99 since the manager paid me. I'd better start work again!
Love Maria

10.4

Complete the second sentence in each pair of sentences so that it means the same as the first. Use *ago*, *for*, *in* or *since*.

   a My boyfriend has been away since January.
   My boyfriend went away ......*in*...... January.

   b This restaurant has been here for six months.
   This restaurant opened six months ....

   c I started this job in June.
   I've worked here .... June.

   d We bought this car five months ago.
   We've had this car .... five months.

   e Ali left here on Tuesday.
   I haven't seen Ali .... Tuesday.

   f I haven't worked in that office for two years.
   I left that office two years ....

10.5

Work with a partner.
Ask your partner some questions about the pictures using *Have you ever* and the words below.
Answer your partner's questions truthfully, saying *Yes, I have*, or *No, I haven't*. If you say *Yes*, tell your partner when you did it.

EXAMPLE: *Have you ever played volleyball on the beach?*
Yes, I have. I played in a match last year.

a play volleyball

b send an email

c go to Bangkok

d go to a pop concert

e ride a bike

f go to a wedding

Grammar spot

Remember:
He's gone to Acapulco = He's there, not here.
He's been to Acapulco = He went there, but he came back.

10.6

1 How do you begin letters in English?

2 How do you end a letter to a close friend? How do you end a letter to a stranger?

10.7 PRONUNCIATION

1 🎧 Listen to the recording and put the underlined words into the correct column – /s/ or /z/.

   a Those are my <u>books</u>.
   b There are three <u>schools</u> in this street.
   c Where are the <u>shops</u>?
   d She's got really long <u>legs</u>.
   e Her <u>shoes</u> are uncomfortable.
   f We had <u>chips</u> for lunch.
   g I like <u>cakes</u>.
   h The <u>lessons</u> were boring.
   i Her <u>boots</u> are black.

/s/	/z/	/ɪz/
books	schools	glasses

2 Underline the words below ending in /ɪz/, then copy them into the table above.
   🎧 Listen to the recording and check your answers.

   a He needs new glasses.
   b There are ten bridges in the city.
   c I bought two new hairbrushes.
   d There are three football matches tomorrow.

3 🎧 Repeat these sentences after the recording.

   a My father plays tennis very well.
   b My back aches.
   c He never catches the ball.
   d She swims every day.
   e He likes travelling.
   f She stays at home on Sundays.
   g He never finishes work early.
   h He eats salad every day.
   i She always watches him when he plays football.
   j He hopes to be a scientist.
   k The hotel arranges everything.

10.8 ACTIVITY

Your teacher will give you the name of a famous person. Don't show it to anybody. Answer the questions other people ask you and ask questions to find out who the other people are. Ask and answer questions like these:

Did you write books? No, I didn't.
Did you live in England? No, I didn't.
Did you live in Europe? Yes, I did.
Did you die in the last century? Yes, I did.
Did you paint pictures? Yes, I did.
Have I seen any of your pictures? Yes, you have.
Were you Picasso? Yes, I was!

If you don't know the answer to a question, say *I can't remember* and check with your teacher.

10.9 ACTIVITY

What do these email shortcuts mean?

:) :(:{ :o CU 4U 2U CUL8R RUOK?

Present perfect and past simple

verb	present perfect		past
go		gone/been	went
be		been	was/were
start	have/has	started	started
grow		grown	grew
write		written	wrote

ever

Have you **ever** been to Bangkok? Yes, I have./No, I haven't.
Has she **ever** ridden a bicycle? Yes, she has. /No, she hasn't.

Vocabulary

application form   arrival   cousin   form   hostel   landlady   shortcut

to forget   to grow   to look round (a place)   to reserve   to spend (money)

convenient   fine   sure

ago   since   sincerely   unfortunately

for since ago in/at

| I've lived here | for two years. |
| | since 2003. |

I moved to this house	two years **ago**.
	in 2003.
	at Christmas.

←——— I've worked here since 2001. ———→
←——— I've worked here for two years. ———→

↑2001   NOW = 2003 ↑

↑ I **started** this job in 2001.
↑ I **started** this job 2 years **ago**.

Exam folder 10

Listening Part 1

> In this part of the exam, you listen to seven short recordings and decide which of three pictures answers the question. You hear the recording twice.

1 Look at the question and pictures for question 1 in Exercise 3. What is the question about? Think of some vocabulary which is useful before you listen.

2 Work with a partner. Look at questions 2–5 in Exercise 3. Write down some useful vocabulary.

3 🎧 Listen to the recordings.

- For each question there are three pictures and a short recording.
- Choose the correct picture and put a tick (✓) in the box below it.

1 How did the woman travel?

A ☐   B ☐   C ☐

2 Where did the man stay?

A ☐   B ☐   C ☐

3 Which is the girl's brother?

A ☐   B ☐   C ☐

4 Which job is Alice doing now?

A ☐   B ☐   C ☐

5 What has the boy bought his mother?

A ☐   B ☐   C ☐

Exam Advice

The answer is sometimes at the beginning, sometimes in the middle and sometimes at the end of the recording.

Writing folder

Writing Part 3

1 Look at the task below and think about these questions.

   a What does *What about you?* mean here?
   b What kind of places can you write about?
   c What kind of things can you do to keep fit?

   - This is part of a letter you receive from an English penfriend.

   > Dear Alice,
   > I've just joined a fitness centre. What about you? Is there a place where you can do sport near your home? Tell me how you keep fit.

   - Now you are writing a letter to your penfriend.
   - Write your **letter** in about 100 words.

2 Look at this answer. Does it answer the questions in the task? Is it a good answer?

   > I don't go to a fitness centre. I prefer to do sport outdoors. There's a sports ground near our house. I go swimming quite often.
   >
   > All the best,
   > Mirza

Exam Advice

In Writing Part 3, it is important to answer the question and to give extra information to make your answer interesting.

3 Which of these sentences can you use to improve Mirza's letter? Decide where to put them. Why can't you use the other sentences?

   a Thanks for your letter.
   b I live near the station.
   c There's one near our house and my brother joined it last year. He says it's good.
   d I often go to the cinema with my brother.
   e I go there on Saturdays and play football with my friends.
   f On Sundays we have matches against other teams.
   g I usually go to the big pool in the city centre, but sometimes we go surfing in the sea.
   h Do you go to a fitness centre?
   i I really like that and I think it's a great way to keep fit.

4 Now look at this answer. Make up some sentences to add to it. Compare your ideas with those of other students.

   > I go to our local fitness centre every week. There's also a tennis club near our house, but I don't go there. I sometimes play volleyball after school.
   >
   > Love,
   > Liz

5 Write your own answer to the task in about 100 words.

Exam folder vocabulary
campsite   floor   view
to train   to wait
lovely
Writing folder vocabulary
fitness centre

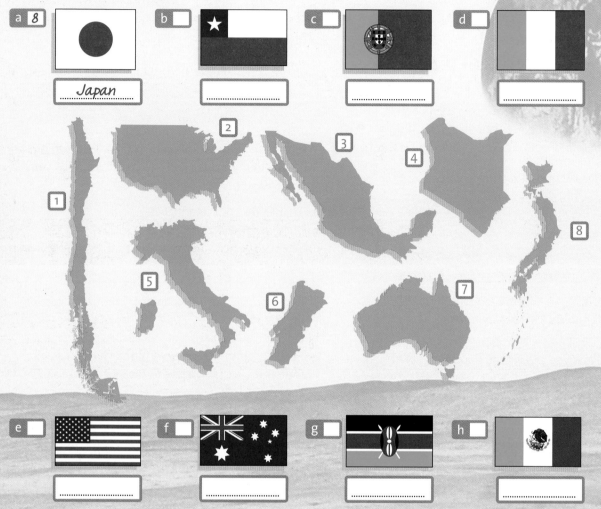

a 8 ....Japan....

b ....

c ....

d ....

e ....

f ....

g ....

h ....

Introduction

11.1

1   Work in a group. Match the flags of the countries to their shapes and write the names underneath.

| Chile | ~~Japan~~ | the USA | Portugal |
| Australia | Kenya | Mexico | Italy |

2   In your group, complete these sentences about the countries above. Who finishes first? Who got them all correct?

   a   _Chile_ is in South America.
   b   .... is in the same continent as Italy.
   c   .... and .... share a border.
   d   .... is on the equator.
   e   .... and .... are islands.

3   In your group, draw the flag and shape of two other countries on a piece of paper. Write a sentence about the country.

   EXAMPLE: *It is an island and it is in Asia.*

   Pass your piece of paper to another group. Look at the flags, shapes and information from other groups and decide which countries they are.

Listening

11.2

1 Look at the questions on the right.
Do you know any of the answers? Tick what you think is the correct answer.

2 🎧 Listen to a radio quiz. Mark the answers that Rory gives in a different colour. Does he choose the same answers as you?

3 Work in a group. Three of Rory's answers are wrong. Which are they?

4 🎧 Now listen to the answers and check which ones Rory got right. Did you find his three wrong answers in Exercise 3?

1 Which is the smallest ocean in the world?
A the Atlantic Ocean
B the Indian Ocean
C the Arctic Ocean

2 Which is the longest border in the world?
A between the USA and Canada
B between the USA and Mexico
C between Argentina and Chile

3 Where is the wettest place in the world?
A in India
B in Colombia
C in Nigeria

4 Which planet is the largest?
A Earth
B Venus
C Jupiter

5 In which country is the busiest airport in the world?
A in the USA
B in Japan
C in Greece

6 Which island is the biggest?
A Great Britain
B Greenland
C Cuba

7 Which continent has the most people?
A Asia
B Australasia
C Africa

8 Which city is the most expensive to live in?
A Geneva in Switzerland
B Paris in France
C Tokyo in Japan

9 Where is the deepest valley in the world?
A in the USA
B in China
C in Kenya

10 Which country is the farthest from the equator?
A Portugal
B Australia
C Peru

Language focus

11.3

1 Complete this table.

small	....	....
long	....	....
wet	....	....
....	larger	....
....	....	the busiest
big	....	....
expensive	....	....
....	deeper	....
far	....	....

2 Look at these people and write three sentences about each person using the words in the box to help you.

William

Charlie

Michael

| happy confident interesting friendly angry |
| kind frightening serious hard-working shy |

EXAMPLE: *William is the happiest.*

3 Compare your sentences with a partner.

11.4

1 Write these abbreviations in words.

mm cm m km km^2

2 Listen to some numbers your teacher will read to you. Write them down (in figures, not words).

3 🎧 Now listen to the answers to the radio quiz again and write the answers to these questions in figures.

    a How large is the smallest ocean? *14,351,000 km^2*
    b How long is the longest border?
    c How much rain falls every year in the wettest place?
    d How wide is the largest planet?
    e How many people go through Atlanta airport every year?
    f What is the area of Greenland?

11.5

1 Look at these pieces of writing in different languages. Do you know which languages they are?

  a Είμαι μαθητης και μου αρέσουν όλα τα αθλήματα
  b Jag är elev och jag tycker om alla slags sporter
  c Jestem studentką i lubię różne sporty
  d 私は学生で、スポーツは何でも好きです。
  e Sou um estudante e gosto de todo tipo de esportes.
  f Ich bin Studentin und ich mag Sport.

	Language	Nationality	Country
a	....	....	....
b	....	....	....
c	....	....	....
d	....	....	....
e	....	....	....
f	....	....	....

2 Now complete this table for other countries.

Language	Nationality	Country
....	....	Spain
....	Mexican	....
Italian	....	....
....	Russian	....
....	....	Australia

3 How many languages do you speak? How many languages do you think there are in the whole world? How many can you think of?

11.6

1 Look at these sentences, then make some similar sentences about other languages.

Australians **speak** English.

English **is spoken by** Australians.

> ### **G**rammar spot
>
> The passive uses the same past participle as the present perfect. Make sure you learn the irregular past participles. See the Irregular verb list on page 208.

2 Work with a partner. Ask and answer the questions below using the verb *grow*.

  a oranges / Spain / England?
    Are oranges grown in Spain or England? They're grown in Spain. They aren't grown in England.

  b coffee / Kenya / France?
  c pineapples / Canada / Mexico?
  d tea / Italy / India?
  e rice / Switzerland / China?

11.7

1 Look at these pictures. What is happening? Put the pictures in the correct order.

1 *d*   2 ......   3 ......   4 ......   5 ......   6 ......   7 ......

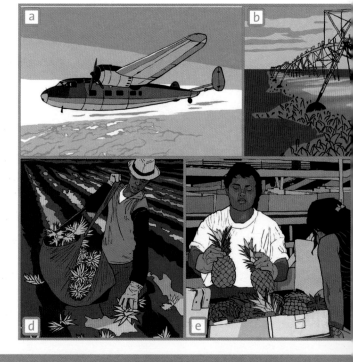

Superlative adjectives

adjective	comparative	superlative	formation
kind	kinder	the kindest	Most one-syllable adjectives add **est**
sad	sadder	the saddest	One-syllable adjectives ending in vowel + consonant double the last consonant and add **est**
frightening	more frightening	the most frightening	Most two- and three-syllable adjectives use **the most**
angry	angrier	the angriest	Adjectives ending in y drop the y and add **iest**
bad	worse	the worst	irregular
good	better	the best	irregular
far	farther	the farthest	irregular

Present passive

to be + past participle

Australians **speak** English. (active)

English **is spoken by** Australians. (passive)
Coffee **isn't grown** in England.
Is tea **grown** in Italy?

Numbers and measurements

a billion	mm (millimetre)
a million	cm (centimetre)
a thousand	m (metre)
a hundred	km (kilometre)

Countries, nationalities and languages

Spain, Spanish, Spanish

What to say when you don't know or you need to think

Oh, just a moment.
Er, I'm sorry, could you repeat that please?
I think …
Mm. I'm not sure …
No, let me try again.
Let me think.
I'm sorry, I don't know.
Just a moment.

Vocabulary

border continent country the equator
figure flag ground island lake
language machine nationality ocean
orange pineapple planet rice score
shape trolley valley world

to compare to pack to pick to plant
to transport to water

deep

underneath

---

2 Write a sentence in the present passive about each picture using a verb from the box. Use *by* if you need to.

pick	transport	eat	~~plant~~
water	buy		pack

EXAMPLE: d *The pineapples are planted in the ground.*

11.8 **PRONUNCIATION**

1 What sounds are at the beginning of these two words?
<u>ch</u>eese <u>sh</u>ampoo

2 Look at the underlined letters in these words. How do you say them? Which sound do you hear? Some words are in the wrong column. Which are they?

3 🎧 Listen and repeat the words. Were you right?

<u>ch</u>eese	<u>sh</u>ampoo
Chinese	<u>sh</u>y
tea<u>ch</u>er	spe<u>ci</u>al
mu<u>ch</u>	informa<u>ti</u>on
<u>ch</u>eap	o<u>c</u>ean
bru<u>sh</u>	lun<u>ch</u>
ques<u>ti</u>on	pi<u>ct</u>ure
tempera<u>tu</u>re	ma<u>ch</u>ine

11.9

🎧 Can you remember what Rory says when he wants to think about his answer? What does he say when he doesn't know the answer? Listen to the recording again and mark what he says on a copy of the recording script.

11.10 **ACTIVITY**

Look at the quiz again on page 73. Work in two or three teams. Write six similar questions about your town, school, region or country. Read your questions to the other team(s). Who gets the highest score?

11.11 **ACTIVITY**

Your teacher will give you a card with a number on it. Think how to say it in English and try to remember it. Listen to other students say their numbers and decide which order they come in.

Exam folder 11

Reading Part 5

> In this part of the exam, you have to choose the correct word to go in each space in a text.

1 In some questions, the answer is correct because of its meaning.
Look at these four words and fit each one into the correct sentence below.

A birthday **B** wedding **C** celebration **D** anniversary

1 Yesterday was the .... of when we first met.
2 I was 19 on my last ....
3 After the .... they went on their honeymoon.
4 They had a huge .... when he arrived home.

2 In some questions, both the meaning and the grammar are important.
Look at these four words and fit each one into the correct sentence below.

A realised **B** watched **C** looked **D** saw

1 She .... at the painting for a long time.
2 When I .... my friend, I shouted to her.
3 I .... the football match until the end.
4 The man .... he was lost.

How did you decide for sentence 1?
How did you decide for sentences 2, 3 and 4?

3 Some questions just test grammar.
Look at these four words and fit each one into the correct sentence below.

A Did **B** Have **C** Was **D** Has

1 .... Carmen invited me to her house at the weekend?
2 .... Carmen invite you to her house last weekend?
3 .... Carmen working when you visited her?
4 .... you ever been to Carmen's house?

4 In some questions, you need to choose the correct word to join two parts of the sentence.
Look at these four words and fit each one into the correct sentence below.

A because **B** so **C** but **D** although

1 The food was disgusting .... he didn't eat it.
2 The food was disgusting .... my sister isn't a good cook.
3 The food was disgusting .... everyone ate it.
4 .... the food was disgusting, everyone ate it.

5 Look at the photograph and answer these questions.

  a Where are these people?
  b What are they doing?
  c What is in the background?
  d What's the weather like?
  e What are they wearing?
  f How do they feel?

6 Now read the text opposite and answer these questions. Don't look at Exercise 7 yet.

  a Where did Alan Chambers and Charlie Paton go?
  b How did they get there?
  c Where did they spend one day? Why?
  d How did they get home?
  e What did Alan give Charlie?

Exam Advice

Read the text before you answer the questions so you have an idea of what it says.

TO THE TOP OF THE WORLD

The coldest walk in the **(0)** ....A.............. is probably the one Alan Chambers and Charlie Paton did a few years **(1)** .... when they walked to the North Pole. To prepare for the trip they **(2)** .... a day in a freezer at a temperature of −30°C. But they were more comfortable there than at the North Pole **(3)** .... they weren't tired or hungry!

They began their 1,126 km walk **(4)** ....
8 March 2000 and **(5)** .... at the North Pole 70 days later. A plane took them straight home from there.

Charlie had his 30th **(6)** .... during the trip and he was amazed when Alan gave him **(7)** .... small cake with a candle on it. Alan said the **(8)** .... moment for him was Charlie's face when he **(9)** .... that cake.

The strange thing is that more men **(10)** ....
walked on the moon than to the North Pole.

7   You now know what the text is about.
    Look at the questions below. Read the text again and choose the correct word for each space. Look carefully at the words around the space.

0	**A** world	**B** country	**C** planet	**D** earth
1	**A** then	**B** ago	**C** since	**D** after
2	**A** passed	**B** stayed	**C** spent	**D** put
3	**A** because	**B** but	**C** therefore	**D** so
4	**A** in	**B** at	**C** on	**D** for
5	**A** got	**B** reached	**C** went	**D** arrived
6	**A** celebration	**B** anniversary	**C** wedding	**D** birthday
7	**A** the	**B** a	**C** much	**D** some
8	**A** greater	**B** good	**C** best	**D** better
9	**A** saw	**B** looked	**C** watched	**D** realised
10	**A** did	**B** have	**C** was	**D** has

Exam folder vocabulary
background freezer
moon
to realise
disgusting

UNIT 12 | A good read

a

Introduction

12.1

1 🎧 Listen to the recording.
At the end, say what you think happened.

2 Which of these books do you think the story comes from?

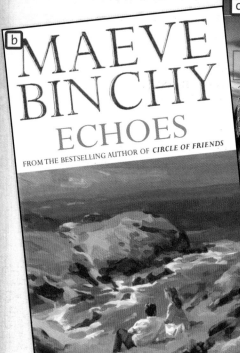
b

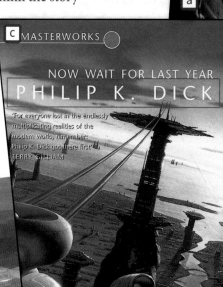

c MASTERWORKS
NOW WAIT FOR LAST YEAR
PHILIP K. DICK
'For everyone lost in the endlessly multiplicating realities of the modern world, remember: Philip K. Dick got there first' TERRY GILLIAM

d Cat's Eye
'Gripping...irresistible... Read it' THE TIME

e OXFORD WORLD'S CLASSICS
BRAM STOKER
DRACULA

Kelly's Luck f
M. L. Inder

3 Here are some kinds of books. Match them to the pictures of covers above.

1 a modern novel *d*
2 a horror story
3 a biography
4 a science fiction novel
5 a thriller
6 a love story

4 Which of the books are fiction and which are non-fiction?

5 What kinds of books do you like reading?

Ⓥocabulary spot

Learn the names of the kinds of books you like and the kinds you don't like so that you can talk about what you like reading.

Reading

12.2

1 Below is part of a book called *The Double Bass Mystery* by Jeremy Harmer.

Penny is a double bass player. She and her boyfriend Simon play in an English orchestra. They are in Barcelona. Last night they gave their first concert there. Penny was tired after the concert and fell asleep quickly.

Read on and find out what happened next.

Chapter 5   *Screams in the night*

I was asleep, but my head was full of pictures and stories. I was dreaming about double basses and violinists and parties on the beach. Simon was in my dream. Our conductor was in it. So was my old teacher, playing a double bass on the sand. Then I heard a different sound.

Somebody was shouting. No, it was worse than that. Somebody was screaming, screaming very loudly. I opened my eyes. I woke up. It was five o'clock in the morning.

Somebody screamed again. And again. And again. This time I wasn't dreaming.

I got out of bed. I put on a T-shirt and some jeans and went out of my room. Doors were opening on the left and the right. Adriana came out of her room. She ran up to me. She was half asleep, still in her night-dress. 'What is it?' she asked sleepily. 'What's going on?'

'I don't know,' I answered.

Martin Audley (a trumpet player) came up to us. 'Who screamed?' he asked.

'Nobody knows,' I told him. 'But it sounded terrible.'

There was another scream. It came from outside.

We ran back into my room and looked out of the window, down at the street. There was a police car there, some people, more and more people. And something else.

'Come on,' I said. We got the lift to the ground floor. When it stopped we ran out of the hotel and pushed to the front of all the people.

Marilyn Whittle, the harp player, was already there. Her face was white and her eyes were large and round.

'Look! Look!' she said. She was pointing in front of her. She screamed again.

We looked. She was pointing at the person at her feet. It was Frank Shepherd. His mouth was open. There was blood all over his head.

Martin spoke first. 'My God!' he said. 'He's dead!'

2 Now answer these questions.

a Why did Penny wake up?
b What did she do next?
c Who did she talk to?
d What did they see out of the window?
e Why was Marilyn screaming?

3 Work in a group. What do you think happened next?

Language focus

12.3

What was happening? Match the sentences a–c with the sentences 1–3.

a Penny woke up.
b Penny went out of her room.
c Marilyn said, 'Look! Look!'

1 She was pointing at Frank.
2 Doors were opening.
3 Somebody was screaming very loudly.

12.4

1 Put the verbs in the story below into the past continuous.

The spy

When I left the nightclub it (a) <u>was raining</u> (rain). When I reached the underground station, a lot of people (b) .... (wait) for trains. While I (c) .... (walk) along the platform, I noticed a girl with long hair. She (d) .... (stand) beside a chocolate machine. She looked worried. Suddenly, she screamed and fell to the ground. A man came forward. He (e) .... (carry) a bag. 'I'm a doctor,' he said. I watched her carefully while the doctor (f) .... (help) her.

A train came into the station. While the passengers (g) .... (get) onto the train, I saw the girl give the doctor a piece of paper. I thought she was ill. The doctor (h) .... (read) something on the paper. I watched his face. Then I looked for the girl. She (i) .... (not lie) on the ground. She (j) .... (sit) in the train. The doors closed. When the train started to move, I saw that she (k) .... (laugh).

2 What do you think was happening? Answer these questions.

a Who was the spy?
b What was wrong with the girl?
c What was the doctor reading?
d Why was the girl laughing?

12.5

Georg is a university student. His twin brother Kurt is a disc jockey in a club. Write sentences about what they were both doing last Saturday, using the words in the table.

Time	Georg	Kurt
6.30	get up	drive home from work
7.00	cook breakfast	have shower
11.00	play basketball	sleep
1.30	have lunch	still sleep
3.00	work in library	buy some new CDs
7.00	walk home	listen to music
9.00	watch television	still listen to music
11.00	go to bed	drive to work

a *While Georg was getting up, Kurt was driving home from work.*
b ..... cooking breakfast ..... having shower.
c playing ba .....
d .....
e .....
f .....
g .....
h .....

12.6

What were Georg and Kurt doing when the phone rang? Why didn't they answer? Complete the sentences. Use the past continuous.

a When the phone rang, Georg *was listening to music.*

When the phone rang, Georg and Kurt were playing tennis.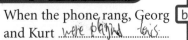

c When the phone rang, Kurt was cooking .....

When the phone rang, Georg and Kurt were driving

e When the phone rang, Kurt was putting out petrol. Petrol.

12.7

Work with a partner. Look at the picture on page 23. Don't look at page 25. Try to remember all the differences and write them down. Use the past continuous.

EXAMPLE: *In the second picture, the journalist wasn't writing in his notebook, he was talking to the model.*

12.8

1 Think about the recording you listened to in Exercise 12.1. Choose the correct tense for each verb.

Dyson (a) ~~was entering~~/entered the office quietly and (b) was shutting/shut the door. First, he (c) was pulling/pulled the blind. Next, he (d) was switching/switched on his torch. Then he (e) was taking/took some papers out of the desk. While he (f) was reading/read them, he (g) was hearing/heard a car door outside the building.

  The police? No, not yet. Kelly – it must be Kelly!

  Quickly, Dyson (h) was switching/switched off his torch and (i) was listening/listened. What (j) was happening/happened? Kelly (k) was looking/looked in other rooms. She (l) was walking/walked along the corridor. Dyson was ready. He (m) was standing/stood behind the door with his gun in his hand when Kelly (n) was coming/came into the room.

  And then . . .

2 Put the verbs in the past simple or past continuous.

Kelly (a) ..... *hit* ..... (hit) Dyson's arm and (b) .... (try) to take the gun. A bullet (c) .... (hit) Dyson's foot and he (d) .... (fall) to the floor. Kelly (e) .... (try) to decide what to do when she (f) .... (hear) the police car. She (g) .... (run) out of the building, (h) .... (jump) into her car and (i) .... (drive) away.

  Dyson (j) .... (still lie) on the floor of the office when the police (k) .... (arrive).

12.9 PRONUNCIATION

1 Practise the sounds /uː/ as in *two* and /ʊ/ as in *took*. Can you find them in these two sentences?

Don't shoot! Put the gun down!

2 🎧 Listen and repeat these sentences. Which words have the sound /uː/? Which words have the sound /ʊ/? Mark them in different colours.

a The pool is too full.
b Would you like to come too?
c The school rules are in this blue book.
d Look at that cool suit.
e It's true he's a good cook.
f Put your hand on the rope and pull.
g You stood on my foot.

3 When you have checked your answers, put the words into the table.

/uː/	/ʊ/
pool	full

4 Work with a partner. Take turns to say the sentences again.

12.10 ACTIVITY

What can you say about a book?
Work in a group and put these sentences into four lists.
Use the headings your teacher gives you. You may decide that some sentences belong with more than one heading.

a These stories are really fantastic.
b This book has had great reviews.
c These are my favourite poems.
d This thick book is expensive, but it has lots of up-to-date diagrams.
e My friends have enjoyed this book.
f The descriptions are terrible.
g Everybody wants to borrow this book from the library.
h It's a stupid story.
i I think this is a brilliant and original book.
j It's a perfect book for a long journey.
k This story is similar to others in the same series.
l The hero is horrible and the heroine is silly.
m This book is very popular in America.
n This book is depressing.
o This amusing story takes place in Athens.
p This is an amazing story with wonderful descriptions.
q This book is a translation.
r This book has had an astonishing success.
s The writer tells a traditional story in simple language.

12.11 ACTIVITY

Think of a book you have read. Write a short review of it for the other people in your class. Write 50–60 words. Use language from Exercise 12.10 to help you. Try to answer these questions in your review:

What is the book called and who is it by?
Is the book fiction or non-fiction?
If it's non-fiction, what is it about?
If it's fiction, what kind is it and where does the story take place?
What is your opinion of it?

Past simple
When I woke up . . .

Past continuous

I/he/she/it	was (not) screaming.
You/we/they	were (not) screaming.
Was I/he/she/it Were you/we/they	screaming?

When I left the nightclub, it **was raining**.
While you were sleeping, I **was cooking** lunch.

Vocabulary
biography blood conductor (music) diagram dream fiction God gun horror lift night-dress novel orchestra platform poem review sand science fiction scream series sound spy thriller torch translation

Come on! (= hurry up) to enter to go on (happen) to hit to lie (on floor) to point to pull to put on to sound to switch

amazing asleep astonishing dead fantastic ground (floor) original perfect simple sleepily stupid traditional underground

(to run) back out of still

Exam folder 12

Speaking Part 1

In this part of the exam, the examiner talks to each student and asks a few questions. The students say a number and also spell a word for the examiner.

1 🎧 Listen to the recording. The students are taking PET in England. What kind of information does the examiner want to know?

2 🎧 Listen again and complete the questions which the examiner asks.

Examiner: Hello. Now, (a) *Can I check your name?*
You're Luca?
Luca: Yes.
Examiner: And you're Monica?
Monica: That's right.
Examiner: And what's (b) *your candidate number,*
Luca?
Luca: 1307.
Examiner: Thank you. And yours, Monica?
Monica: 1328.
Examiner: Thank you. So, Luca,
(c) *where do you come from?*
Luca: I'm from Italy.
Examiner: Really? (d) *What part of* Italy?
Luca: The north, near Brescia. Have you heard of it?
Examiner: Yes, I think so. And (e) *how long have you been London?*
Luca: About three months. I'm at the Regional College in Highland Road.
Examiner: I don't know that. (f) *Is it a big college*
Luca: Oh, yes. It's got five hundred students in the English department.
And there are lots of students who study other subjects.

Examiner: Oh, I see. Now, you said your college is in Highland Road. (g) *How do you spell Highland Place?*
Luca: H-I-G-H-L-A-N-D.
Examiner: Thank you. Now, Monica, what about you? (h) *Are you in the Highland? School.*
Monica: I'm at the English Academy, a language school. Do you know it?
Examiner: The English Academy? Yes, I think so. Is it quite small?
Monica: That's right.
Examiner: And (i) *and when did you start*
Monica: In January.
Examiner: Oh, yes? (j) *Is your first time visit? here*
Monica: Yes.
Examiner: (k) *Are you enjoy here* ?
Monica: Well, I like the school and I'm living in a house with some friends, so we have a lot of fun together. But the weather hasn't been very good.
Examiner: Yes, it's been very wet, hasn't it? Now, you said you're at the Academy. (l) *Can you spell it for me* .
Monica: Er, A-C-A-D-E-M-Y.
Examiner: Thank you.

Exam Advice

Learn these useful questions. You can use them in the exam.
Could you speak more slowly, please?
Could you repeat that, please?

3 Can you spell the name of your school and your address?

4 Work with a partner. Take turns asking questions like the examiner and answering them about yourself.

Writing folder

Writing Part 3

1 Read these titles of stories.

    1 The unwanted present.
    2 A wonderful surprise.
    3 The lost key.
    4 The wrong house.
    5 A dangerous plan.
    6 A difficult journey.

2 Below are the beginnings and endings of the stories. Match each one to its title.

3 Work in a group. Write the middle of one of the stories on a piece of paper.

4 When you have finished, pass your piece of paper to another group. They decide which story it belongs to.

Exam Advice

Make sure your story has a good beginning and ending.

5 Choose one of the titles and write your own story. Write about 100 words.

a
Last Friday the weather was good so I walked to school. While I was going across the park I saw something metal on the ground.

....

The businessman gave me €100. I was really amazed. He said, 'I was looking for it all round town. Thank you for finding it.'

b
Last summer, we moved to a big city. A few days later, I went to the city centre on my own.

....

I phoned home. I said, 'I know we live in Oxford Road, but what number is it?'
When I arrived, all my family were laughing about me. I've been careful not to forget our address since then.

c
When we looked out of the tent, it was snowing hard. We packed our rucksacks and put on our coats.

....

At last we saw the lights of the city. Half an hour later we were sitting in a café with a hot drink in front of us.

d
It was John's birthday, but he was sitting alone in his room. He usually met his friends on Saturday evenings, but this week they were all busy. He was miserable.

....

'It's been a great evening,' he said.

e
I work in a café on Saturdays. One man who often comes in is a journalist. A fortnight ago, when I brought him his coffee, he said, 'I'm going to meet someone.'
'Who?' I asked.

....

'I hope you'll return safely,' I said.
'I hope so, too!' he answered.

f
I like my cat. Her name is Sheba and she is black, beautiful and very intelligent. At night she explores the garden.

....

I wrapped it in newspaper and put it in the dustbin before Sheba woke up. I don't think she knows.

Writing folder vocabulary
dustbin   fortnight   metal
to explore   to look for   to wrap
amazed

Speaking

1 Work with a partner. Look at these sentences. Say if each sentence is true for you and give your partner some extra information.

   a In my town the swimming pool is next to a supermarket. *Yes, that's true. The swimming pool is in the city centre near the market square.* OR *No, that's not true. The swimming pool is next to a petrol station.*
   b The weather today is warmer than last week.
   c Football is less popular than basketball.
   d I am younger than my partner.
   e I sometimes have a headache after school.
   f I've never been to a wedding.
   g My family often have barbecues in summer.
   h I visited the USA two years ago.
   i My country has lots of mountains.
   j I like reading science fiction stories.

Grammar

2 Read this postcard and complete each space with one of the words from the box.

already	yet	for	since	~~ago~~
in	ever	while	on	never

Dear Fiona,

Nick and I arrived in London two days
(a) ..*ago*.. . Have you (b) .... been to London?
I've (c) .... been before but Nick came here
(d) .... 2001. I've wanted to come (e) I
was a little boy. We've (f) .... been on a river
trip and on a bus around the city – I enjoyed
them both. I haven't been to any museums
(g) .... but Nick went to one yesterday
(h) .... I was looking round the Tower of
London. We're staying in London (i) ....
a week and we're going to Edinburgh (j) ....
Friday. See you soon.

Mark

Reading

3 Read these reviews of four books, then look at the sentences below. Decide which book each sentence matches.

a
I have read several books by Darren McGough and this novel is as good as all his others. Most of McGough's stories happen in Australia because that is where he comes from. This one starts on a beach in Spain and finishes up a mountain in China. It is very exciting and the ending is a surprise.

b
Like all Sergio Sanchez's books, this one is very popular in South America and Spain. I've wanted to read it for a long time and now I can because it is available in English. It is about a journey which a group of people made across Argentina at the beginning of the last century.

c
This is the third book Colin Wesley has written about animals but I enjoyed this one the most. It is easier to read than the others and the photographs are beautiful. Wesley spent a year living in Australia taking photos and writing about Australian animals. It costs a lot (€30).

d
Ruth Rawlings takes 400 pages to write about the life of Maria Cornwell. She was an opera singer in the 1920s and she travelled all over the world. The book is very long but is not expensive at €10. Rawlings has not written a book before and I hope this is not the last one as it is very good.

	A	B	C	D
1 The story takes place in South America.		✓		
2 It is the writer's first book.				
3 It is expensive.				
4 It is fiction.				
5 It is translated from another language.				
6 The writer is Australian.				
7 It is a biography.				
8 It is a thriller.				
9 It is already successful in some countries.				
10 It is better than the last book by this writer.				

Grammar

4   There is one mistake in each of these sentences. Correct it.

   a   I lived here since last May.
       I've lived here since last May.
   b   This is the sadest film I've ever seen.
   c   Coffee is growed in Brazil.
   d   This car park is less expensive as the one by the library.
   e   The taxi rank is outside of the supermarket.
   f   You better take an aspirin.
   g   The supermarket is busyest on Saturdays.
   h   This is the worse rugby match I've ever watched.
   i   Could you repeating that, please?
   j   My shoes aren't as fashionable than my sister's.
   k   Carlos is from Mexican.

Vocabulary

5   Look at the map on page 48 and complete these directions.

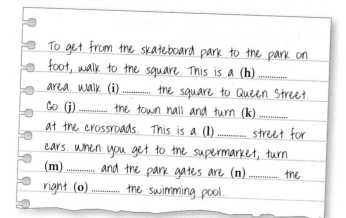

To get from the skateboard park to the railway station by car, (a) *turn* left when you come out of the skateboard park, go (b) .... on until you get to a (c) .... Turn right here and go (d) .... this road until you get to a (e) .... Turn left and go (f) .... a bridge. The railway station is (g) .... the left.

To get from the skateboard park to the park on foot, walk to the square. This is a (h) .... area. Walk (i) .... the square to Queen Street. Go (j) .... the town hall and turn (k) .... at the crossroads. This is a (l) .... street for cars. When you get to the supermarket, turn (m) .... and the park gates are (n) .... the right (o) .... the swimming pool.

6   Think about the meaning of these nouns. Divide them into four groups.

ankle anniversary birthday border carnival continent corner cough desert entrance festival honeymoon island neck ocean roundabout stadium thermometer throat tongue fountain turning valley wedding

UNIT 13 A place of my own

Introduction

13.1

1 Look at the photographs. What are these things called? Which of the words in the box can you use to describe each of them?

antique	beautiful
cheap	comfortable
crazy	expensive
glass	modern
old-fashioned	plastic
traditional	ugly
unusual	useful
wooden	

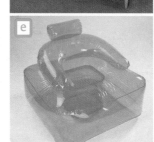
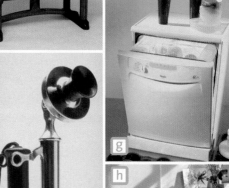

2 Read what these people say about them. Match the things in the pictures to their owners.

1 I think this is great because I like unusual furniture. Some people say it's not very comfortable in hot weather but I don't mind.

2 This is useful, it's modern and it was cheap. It's not beautiful, but it's not ugly and I can keep all my clothes in it.

3 I was walking down a side street when I saw this in a shop window, and I decided to buy it that day. I don't have any other antiques, but this is the kind of thing which looks good in any big room.

4 I've had it for two years now. It was expensive, but in my opinion, it was worth it because it's the most useful thing in the kitchen.

5 I don't really like it at all because it's old-fashioned, and I prefer modern furniture. But I can't afford to change it and it's quite useful – I can keep lots of things in it.

6 This matches the other furniture in the room because it's traditional – we've had it since we got married. We all like it because it's very comfortable.

7 My parents gave it to me for my birthday. I know it was expensive, but I love modern design, and really beautiful things are always fashionable.

8 It's crazy, isn't it? Everyone laughs when they see it, but it works OK, and it makes me happy.

3 Work with a partner. Tell each other what kind of furniture you like.

Listening

13.2

1 🎧 Listen to four people called Neil, Ian, Adam and Patricia talking about where they live. Write the name of the speaker next to each photograph.

a ....

b ....

c ....

d ....

2 🎧 Listen again. Who talks about these things? Mark your answers in the table.

	Ian	Patricia	Adam	Neil
dining room				
bathroom	✔			
shower				
roof				
towers				
windows				
curtains				
carpets				
hi-fi				
central heating				
solar power				

3 Answer these questions.

a How does Ian save money?
He doesn't pay rent.
b What does Ian do when he gets bored with the view?
c What were Patricia and her husband doing when they found their unusual home?
d Where is Patricia's sitting room?
e What did Adam use to make his house?
f Why isn't Adam worried about his house?
g Why doesn't Neil mind the noise?
h Why is Neil's house perfect for him?

Language focus

13.3

1 Work with a partner. Talk about the things in the pictures below. Can you guess what they are? Use the language in the box below.

I'm sure it's not …	**Perhaps it's …**	**I'm sure it is …**
It can't be …	*It could be …*	*It must be …*
	It might be …	

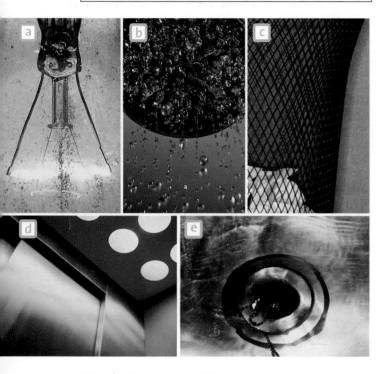

2 Choose the correct verb.

1 A Who's that man? Isn't he a well-known actor?
   B I don't know, but he *could*/*must* be. He's very handsome.

2 A I've just tried to phone Toni at her aunt's house, but she's not there.
   B But she *must*/*might* be there. She's babysitting her cousins.

3 A I want to buy a computer like your brother's. Do you know how much they cost?
   B No, but they *can't*/*must* be very expensive because I know he hasn't got much money.

4 A Where's the orange juice?
   B I'm not sure. Probably in the fridge, or it *must*/*might* be on the table in the other room.

5 A Are your neighbours on holiday?
   B They *can't*/*could* be. The car isn't outside the house.

13.4

Are these sentences true or false? Correct the sentences if necessary.

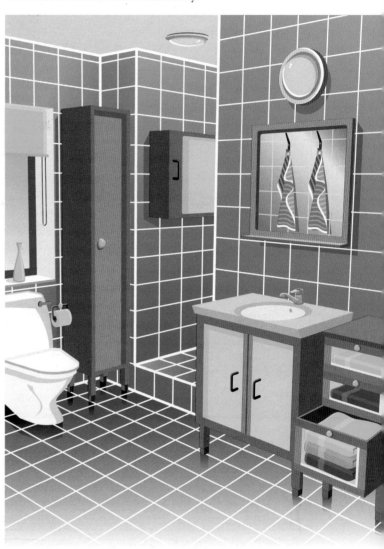

a The basin is below the mirror. *true*
b The toilet is opposite a cupboard.
c There's a light facing the window.
d The basin is on top of a cupboard.
e There's a window behind the basin.
f There's a step between the basin and the tall cupboard.
g There's a low cupboard in the corner.
h There are towels on hooks on the wall opposite the mirror.
i We can see toothbrushes inside some of the drawers.
j There's a cupboard on the wall beyond the step.

13.5

1 Work with a partner. Can you name all the rooms and furniture in this flat?

2 Now decide which rooms to put these things in. Use your dictionary if necessary.

basin	chest of drawers	cooker
cushions	desk	sink
pillows	sofa	wastepaper basket

3 The owners of this flat want to buy some new furniture. What advice would you give them?

Ⓥocabulary spot

Learning the names of things on a picture can help you to remember them. Remember the picture and the names of the things together.

13.6 PRONUNCIATION

1 Think about the sounds /ʒ/ and /dʒ/. Can you find them in this sentence?

I heard a great joke on television yesterday.

2 🎧 Listen and repeat these sentences. Which words have the sound /ʒ/? Which words have the sound /dʒ/? Mark them in different colours.

a Can you measure these jeans, please?
b He's on a journey through Asia.
c We keep the fridge in the kitchen and the TV in the lounge.
d I'm doing revision for my college exams.
e Do you go jogging for pleasure?
f He's jealous of the disc jockey's job.
g She usually pays generous wages.
h The Bridge Hotel has excellent leisure facilities.
i A giraffe is an unusual pet.
j We've just made an important decision.

3 When you have checked your answers, put the words into the table below.

/ʒ/	/dʒ/
television	joke

4 Work with a partner. Take turns to repeat the sentences in Exercise 2 again. Listen to each other's pronunciation.

13.7 ACTIVITY

Work with a partner. Your teacher will give each of you a picture. Don't look at each other's pictures.
Tell each other what you can see in your picture and where everything is. Find all the differences.
Write sentences like this:

In Picture A the TV is on the table, but in Picture B it's on the chest of drawers.

Guessing

| It | can't
could
might
must | be | a toothbrush. |

Saying where things are
above below between beyond facing inside opposite
over through under

in the corner on top of side by side

upstairs downstairs on the ground/first/second floor

Talking about the price of things
I can/can't afford it.
It's (not) worth £100.

Vocabulary
armchair basin bookshelf branch bulb carpet
central heating chest of drawers clock cooker cupboard
curtain cushion dishwasher drawer fridge furniture hi-fi
hook living room mirror nail plug poster roof rope
sink (kitchen) sitting room sofa solar power stair(s) step(s)
toilet towel tower tunnel wall wastepaper basket

to afford to blow to damage to heat to park to save

antique crazy enormous low old-fashioned plastic proper
ugly useful wooden worth

and so on

Exam folder 13

> In this part of the exam, you read five descriptions of people. For each one, you choose one text to match it.

1 Here are five texts about people who all want to do a language course at a college in England and eight advertisements for colleges. Underline the important information in 1–5 below.

1 Alma doesn't like cities and wants to live somewhere quiet with an English family. She wants to do a full-time course.

2 Kostas enjoys city life. He wants to do a part-time course and have a part-time job as well. He is not interested in going on trips or doing activities with the college after his classes. He wants to rent his own flat.

3 Margarita would like to live in a hostel with other students. She wants to do a full-time course. She likes to play sport in her free time.

4 Tomek is looking for a full-time four-week course at a college which organises social activities for students. He doesn't mind living in the city or the country but he wants to stay with a family.

5 Hiroki wants to do a part-time course at a college which can arrange his accommodation. He loves walking so he wants to be near the countryside. He doesn't enjoy organised trips and activities.

2 Look at the description of Alma again. Quickly look through the advertisements on the opposite page.

a Find the colleges which aren't in the city. Are they in quiet places?
b Which of these colleges has accommodation with a family?
c Which of these colleges have full-time courses?
d Which college is suitable for Alma?

Exam Advice

No text can be the answer to two questions.

3   Decide which college would be the most suitable for the other people.

A

Langdale College is on the edge of a small town surrounded by hills, twenty kilometres from the city. It offers English lessons in the mornings with activities, sports and trips to other towns and places of interest in the afternoons and at weekends. Courses last six or twelve weeks. All students live with local families.

B

Anderson College is in the centre of the city. Students can choose from a range of part-time courses – either mornings only, afternoons only or three mornings/ afternoons and two evenings. The college has sports facilities, a drama centre, library and club which students can use if they wish. The college does not arrange accommodation.

C

The Park School is ten kilometres from the city. It is surrounded by woods and there are lots of footpaths through attractive countryside. All students live in a hostel next to the school. There are classes in the mornings and the rest of the time students are free for private study.

D

Highcliff College is in the city near the university. It runs four-week and eight-week full-time courses. Students live with families. They spend evenings and weekends with their families learning about English family life and practising their English.

E

The Milburn Academy is in the city centre. It offers full-time twelve-week courses. Students are also expected to join in the social and sports events organised for evenings and weekends. The college owns several large houses nearby where students live and prepare their own meals.

F

The Waterside College is a large city college which has part-time English courses all year round. All students live in college hostels in different parts of the city. The college has its own sports hall and swimming pool and at weekends there are trips to other cities.

G

The Marlowe School offers two-week and four-week courses all year, full-time. It is situated in a quiet part of the city but there are buses both into the centre and to the nearby countryside. Students stay with local families if they wish. Every evening during the week there is a social event for students and there are trips at weekends.

H

The Beechwood Academy is in a village about 15 km from the city. It offers full-time courses. Students live with families in the village and are encouraged to join in family life as much as possible. The village has a leisure centre.

Exam folder vocabulary
edge   facilities   footpath   range   wood
to encourage   to join in   to last   to (not) mind   to prepare   full-time
part-time   private   situated   social

UNIT 14 What's in fashion?

a   b   c   d

Introduction

14.1

1 Look at the picture. What is happening?

2 🎧 Listen to some people in the audience.
   Decide which model each speaker is
   talking about. Circle A, B, C or D.

   1 A B C D   7 A B C D
   2 A B C D   8 A B C D
   3 A B C D   9 A B C D
   4 A B C D   10 A B C D
   5 A B C D   11 A B C D
   6 A B C D   12 A B C D

3 🎧 Listen again for these adjectives. Write down the nouns
   they describe.

   high   *heels*   fashionable   *jackets*
   leather   ....   striped   *suit*
   enormous   *shirts*   comfortable   ....
   grey   *shirt*   dark blue   *hat*
   awful   *baseball cap*   sleeveless   *shirts*
   silk   ....   orange   *shirt*

4 Would you like to wear any of these clothes?
   Who will buy them, do you think?

Reading

14.2

1 Read this magazine article about fashion in Britain during the last century. Match each paragraph to one of the photographs.

Do you think you're
fashionable?

What did your granny or your dad use to wear?

fashion went mad in Britain in the ....s. Clothes were made from exciting new materials like shiny plastic and even paper. Women used to wear very short skirts and long shiny black plastic boots. Sometimes the boots went over their knees. Young men used to wear bright colours. They wore wonderful patterned shirts with wide collars and big ties. Their hair was quite long.

Very full skirts were in fashion for young women in the ....s. They often used to wear gloves, sometimes even indoors. Teenage girls sometimes used to wear short white cotton socks and flat shoes. Some young men, who were known as 'teddy boys', used to wear very narrow ties and narrow trousers. Their shoes or boots sometimes had high heels and pointed toes.

Women used to wear long straight dresses in the ....s. They ended just below the knee and didn't have a waist. The dresses often used to have a belt around the hips. Women liked wearing scarves and beads round their necks. Their hair was very short and they always used to wear hats when they went out. Men used to wear trousers with very wide legs. They often wore sweaters and flat caps.

Very short T-shirts were the latest fashion in the ....s. Girls used to wear them with jeans. Everyone wore trainers. Teenagers used to wear a lot of jewellery – in their ears, noses and even tongues – and they painted their nails in crazy colours. Young men used to have very short hair and they used to wear baseball caps and loose trousers. Sweatshirts and jogging trousers were very popular.

2 Work in a group. Can you guess the decade (e.g. 1970s) for each paragraph and its photograph? The paragraphs are not in the correct order. Put them in the correct order.

3 Read the text again. Underline any words you don't know. Can you guess what the words mean?

4 Work in a group. Talk about the meaning of the words you don't know.

Vocabulary spot

Use the photographs to help you understand words you don't know.

5 Which of the clothes look comfortable/uncomfortable? Which look cool/warm? Which look exciting/boring? Which clothes are the most uncomfortable? Which are the most exciting?

Language focus

14.3

Match the adjectives on the left with their opposites on the right.

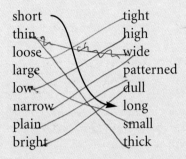

short — tight
thin — high
loose — wide
large — patterned
low — dull
narrow — long
plain — small
bright — thick

14.4

1 Look at these pairs of sentences. Finish the second one so that it means the same as the first one.

  a Her skirt is too short for her.
  Her skirt isn't _long enough_ for her.

  b The tunnel is too narrow for us to drive through.
  The tunnel isn't _wide enough_ for us to drive through.

  c The bridge is too low for the bus to go under.
  The bridge isn't _high enough_ for the bus to go under.

2 Now try these sentences. Finish the second one so that it means the same as the first one.

  a The suitcase isn't large enough for all our things.
  The suitcase _is too small_ small for all our things.

  b The material isn't thick enough to keep you warm.
  The material _is too thin_ thin to keep you warm.

14.5

Which of the clothes in Exercise 14.2 don't you like?
Write some sentences with *too* and *enough*.
Use the adjectives in the box to help you.

short	warm	large	wide	bright	long	colourful

EXAMPLE: *In C, the man's trousers are too wide.*
In D, the girl's skirt isn't long enough.

14.6

1 Here are some descriptions from the magazine article in Exercise 14.2. What do these adjectives tell us about the nouns? Put them in the correct column.

shiny   cotton   ~~wonderful~~   plastic   white   ~~long~~   black patterned   short

Opinion	Size	Description	Colour	Material	Noun
	long				boots
wonderful					shirts
					socks

2 Look back at the first and second paragraphs of the magazine article and find the words from the exercise above. Are the columns in the correct order?

3 Now put these adjectives in the correct order.

  a a blue/large sofa   *a large blue sofa*
  b a brown/warm coat
  c a(n) wooden/old/beautiful desk
  d a(n) amazing/silk/short dress
  e a new/brilliant film
  f some cotton/black/fashionable shorts
  g a glass/shiny table

> ### **G**rammar spot
>
> Learn some of the descriptions. They can help you to remember the rules for the order of adjectives, e.g. *a large blue sofa*.

14.7 PRONUNCIATION

1 Look at these lists of words. Think about the sound /f/. Which is the odd word out in each list?

    a bright light cough through
    b enough photograph telephone alphabet
    c paragraph fashion geography physics

2 🎧 Listen and repeat the words. Do you want to change your odd word out?

3 What are the different ways of spelling the sound /f/? What are the different ways of pronouncing the letters *gh*?

14.8

1 Work with a partner. Ask your partner what he/she used to do when he/she was seven years old.

    a What / wear? *What did you use to wear?*
    b What time / get up?
    c What time / bed?
    d What / weekends?
    e What / enjoy doing?

2 Now write four sentences about your partner. Write two things he/she used to do and two things he/she didn't use to do.

14.9 ACTIVITY

1 Work in pairs.
Student A: look at the photograph on page 200. It is a photograph of a street 100 years ago.
Student B: look at the photograph on page 202. It is a photograph of the same street now.

Student B: ask Student A questions beginning *Did there use to be ...?*
Student A: reply *Yes, there did* or *No, there didn't.* Give Student B some extra information by saying *There used to be ...*

2 Find at least five things which have and haven't changed. Write them down together.

14.10 ACTIVITY

Think about what you were wearing yesterday. Write a description on a piece of paper without your name on it. Give it to your teacher. Listen to everyone's description. Can you guess who they all are?

---

used to
People **used to** wear short skirts.
People **didn't use to** wear short skirts.
Did people **use to** wear short skirts?

too/enough
The dress is **too small (for her).**
The dress **isn't big enough (for her).**

It looks ...

Adjective order
opinion, size, description, colour, material
wonderful long shiny black plastic boots

Centuries and decades
in the twentieth century
in the 1960s

Vocabulary
beads belt boots (baseball) cap collar cotton decade dress fashion glass gloves hat jeans jewellery jogging trousers leather material pattern physics plastic scarf shirt silk sleeve sock suit sweater sweatshirt telephone tie trainers

dark/light (colour) black blue brown green grey orange purple red yellow white

awful bright colourful cool dull fashionable flat full horrible loose mad narrow patterned plain pointed shiny sleeveless striped thick tight wonderful

Exam folder 14

Listening Part 4

1 Read this instruction. What does it tell you about the people? What does it tell you about their conversation?

You will hear a conversation between a boy, Sandy, and a girl, Megan, about their jobs.

Exam Advice

Read the instructions. They tell you who the speakers are and what they will talk about.

2 Work with a partner. Read the six sentences in Exercise 6.
What subjects do you think Sandy and Megan talk about? Can you guess what their jobs are?

3 When you listen, you decide if each sentence is correct or incorrect. If it is correct, put a tick (✓) in the box under A for YES. If it is not correct, put a tick (✓) in the box under B for NO.

Practise with these sentences. Are they correct or incorrect?

		A YES	B NO
1	I've finished this course.	☐	☐
2	We are living in the twentieth century.	☐	☐
3	A baseball cap is a kind of hat.	☐	☐
4	The Arctic Ocean is the smallest ocean in the world.	☐	☐
5	Earth is the largest planet.	☐	☐

4 Questions 1 and 4 in Exercise 6 ask if Sandy and Megan are happy in their jobs.
They use these adjectives in their conversation.
Put them into two groups: *like* and *dislike*.

> awful   not interesting enough   miserable
> depressing   interesting   great   brilliant
> exciting   boring

5 Questions 3 and 6 in Exercise 6 ask if Megan agrees with Sandy.
They use these expressions in their conversation.
Put them in two groups: *agree* and *disagree*.

> Of course.   You're wrong there.
> I don't think so.   Exactly.
> That's not a good idea.

6 🎧 Look at the six sentences below.

- You will hear a conversation between a boy, Sandy, and a girl, Megan, about their jobs.
- Decide if each sentence is correct or incorrect.
- If it is correct, put a tick (✓) in the box under A for YES. If it is not correct, put a tick (✓) in the box under B for NO.

		A YES	B NO
1	Megan thinks her new job is perfect.	☐	☐
2	Megan takes photographs of models.	☐	☐
3	Megan agrees that bookshops are depressing.	☐	☐
4	Sandy is looking for a job in a different bookshop.	☐	☐
5	Sandy has studied photography.	☐	☐
6	Megan agrees to ask about a job for Sandy at the magazine.	☐	☐

7 🎧 Listen again and check your answers.
Which words helped you to answer the questions?

Writing folder

Writing Parts 2 and 3

1 Read this question. What kind of things are you going to write about?

> * This is part of a letter you receive from an English friend.
>
> > I'm really looking forward to hearing about your new flat. Did you find the furniture you wanted?
>
> * Now you are writing a letter to this friend.
> * Write your **letter** in about 100 words.

2 Now read the answer. How many different things did the writer buy?

> Dear Nicholas,
> I went shopping this morning and I bought some things for my flat. I got a lamp in that new shop near the station. Then I found some cushions to match my sofa. They look nice. Then I bought a mirror which I've put on my chest of drawers. It was cheap. I'd like to buy a bed but I can't afford it so I bought a cover instead. The bed I've got is old. When I was coming home I walked through the market and I saw some posters so I bought three.
> All the best,
> Dan

3 There aren't many adjectives in the letter. Add some of these adjectives to the letter to make it more interesting.

modern	large	shiny	crazy
tiny	blue	plastic	big
comfortable	red	amazing	green
colourful	cotton	leather	small
soft	wooden	new	lovely

4 Read this question.

> You are on holiday at the seaside and you buy a postcard.
> Write the postcard to your English friend called Sarah. In your card, you should
> * tell her about your journey
> * describe the place where you are staying
> * say what you like best

5 Here is an answer. Put a different adjective into each space.

> Dear Sarah,
> We had a very .... journey here because the weather was .... so the ferry was late. We are staying in a .... town. We have a .... room with a .... view. I like the sea best. The water is ....
> Love, Rosie

6 Now do this question.

> * This is part of a letter you receive from an English friend.
>
> > In your next letter, tell me what kind of clothes you like wearing. Tell me what you have bought recently.
>
> * Now you are writing a letter to this friend.
> * Write your **letter** in about 100 words.

Exam Advice

Use adjectives to make your writing more interesting.

Exam folder vocabulary
depressing
Writing folder vocabulary
to receive

UNIT 15 Risk!

Introduction

15.1

1 In Britain, the law says you can do some things when you are 16 but you can't do others. Guess which things you can do in Britain when you are 16.

When you are 16:	In Britain	In your country
you can buy a pet.	✓	
you can vote in elections.	✗	
you can get a tattoo.		
you can work full-time.		
you can buy fireworks and lottery tickets.		
you can pilot a plane.		
you can get married (if your parents agree).		
you can ride a moped.		
you can learn to drive a car.		
you can give blood.		

2 Complete the other column for your country. Put ? if you aren't sure.

3 Compare your answers with a partner.

4 Can you add any more things you can or can't do at age 16 in your country? Write them down.

5 Which things are different in your country from Britain?
Do you agree with the laws in your country about what you can do at age 16?
Which would you like to change?

The Marathon of the Sands

Seven day foot race across the Sahara Desert in Morocco. 230 km in seven days. For more information, contact

15.2

🎧 Listen to Ryan talking to his friend Martha, who did the Marathon of the Sands last year.
Decide if these sentences are true or false.

a Ryan enjoyed skydiving. *true*
b You have to be over a certain age to do the race.
c Martha thought that running on sand was the most difficult thing about the race.
d The runners have to share tents.
e The average daytime temperature is 40°.

Language focus

15.3

🎧 Martha says these things about the competition. Listen again and put them into the correct column.

a finish in seven days
b carry your own food
c carry water for seven days
d take other drinks to mix with the water
e carry your own tent
f bring your own sleeping bag
g stay in your tent after sunrise
h go into the organisers' camp
i take a Walkman

You have to	You can't	You can	You don't have to
a			

15.4 ACTIVITY

Work in a group. Your teacher will give you some cards with the names of jobs on them. Take turns to take a card. Don't tell the other students your job.

They ask you: *Do you have to …?*
You can give them one clue: *You don't have to …* or *You have to … .*
Which group guesses the jobs first?

Possible questions

get up early?
travel around in a car?
stand up most of the day?
talk a lot?

wear a uniform?
walk a lot?
work in the evening?
write lots of emails?

work regular hours?
wear a costume?
get dirty?

15.5

Can you remember what Ryan and Martha said in Exercise 15.2?
Put these words into the sentences.

up   on with   on with   off

a How did you get ...*on*.... ?
b You have to get .... quickly when the organisers call everyone.
c You need to get .... the other people.
d When you get .... the plane you can't believe how hot it is.
e I have some work that I need to get ....

Vocabulary spot

Write down phrasal verbs as you learn them. Keep them together so you can look at them when you need to.

15.6

1 Read the beginning of this letter Ryan wrote after he tried skydiving.
What did he have to do? What didn't he have to do?

> Dear Sergio,
> I went skydiving today. Someone told me about a place where you could do it and I decided to try. I had to arrive several hours before the jump so I could fill in some forms and they could give me instructions on how to jump. I didn't have to take any special clothes with me because they gave me a skysuit.

2 Look at some more photographs of people doing activities which might be risky. Have you ever done any of these things? Would you like to try?

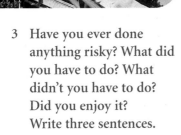

3 Have you ever done anything risky? What did you have to do? What didn't you have to do? Did you enjoy it? Write three sentences.

15.7 ACTIVITY

Ask other students these questions. How many people in your class like taking risks? Who takes the most risks?

a	Do you like travelling alone?	YES/NO
b	Would you like to do the Marathon of the Sands?	YES/NO
c	Do you always use a pedestrian crossing to cross the road?	YES/NO
d	Do you enjoy frightening rides at the funfair?	YES/NO
e	Are you always late for appointments?	YES/NO
f	Would you like to fly your own plane?	YES/NO
g	Do you throw away food when it reaches its sell-by date?	YES/NO
h	Do you arrive at a train station or bus stop ten minutes early?	YES/NO

15.8 PRONUNCIATION

1 Say these four words. They each contain the letters *ou* but *ou* is pronounced differently in each word.

ner<u>vou</u>s   <u>you</u>ng   b<u>ou</u>ght   h<u>ou</u>se

2 🎧 Listen and repeat the words after the recording.

3 🎧 Put the words below into the correct column. Listen and check your answers.

dangerous   thought   shout   enough
flavour   touch   ought   out

nervous	young	bought	house

4 Can you think of any other words to add to the columns?

15.9

1 Martha gave Ryan some information about the Marathon of the Sands. Look at the sentences below. The underlined words are adverbs. Can you make adjectives from them?

EXAMPLE: *sensible*

a You have to behave <u>sensibly</u>.
b The organisers travel more <u>comfortably</u>.
c They wake everyone up very <u>noisily</u>.

2 Now make adverbs from these adjectives.

anxious *anxiously*   cheerful ....
heavy ....   perfect ....
confident ....   loud ....
quick ....   gentle ....

3 Here is the rest of Ryan's letter. Put the adverbs from Exercise 2 in the spaces.

I was joined by a special belt to an instructor. There were three of us who did the jump with our instructors. We sat in the plane waiting (a) *anxiously* for our turn. The instructors chatted (b) .... the whole time. When the plane got to the right height, my instructor turned to me and shouted very (c) .... 'Are you ready?' If you don't answer (d) ...., they don't allow you to jump. Then I jumped and it was brilliant. You fall very (e) .... for about 40 seconds, then you pull the cord to open your parachute. And you float down very (f) .... I landed (g) .... on the ground with a bump but I didn't hurt myself. I was very pleased because I did everything (h) .... I'll write again soon.
All the best, Ryan

15.10 ACTIVITY

1 Make these adjectives into adverbs.

angry quick quiet nervous miserable lazy
happy urgent secret serious shy slow
loud sleepy excited

2 Your teacher will give each of you an adverb. To get a point for your team, you must say the sentence below so that the other team can guess your adverb. For example, if your adverb is *anxiously*, you should say your sentence anxiously.

When I was on my way here today, something strange happened to me.

Must

I/You/He/She/We/They **must** come home now.
I/You/He/She/We/They **mustn't** come here again.

We use **had to** for the past of **must**.

It is a rule	If you want	
You **have to/must**	You **can**	+
You **can't/mustn't**	You **don't have to**	–

Can

You **can** vote when you are 18.
Can you vote when you're 17?
You **can't** vote when you are 17.

Have to

Present
I/You/We/They **have to** take a tent.
He/She **has to** take a tent.

Do I/You/We/They **have to** take a tent?
Does he/she **have to** take a tent?

I/You/We/They **don't have to** take a tent.
He/she **doesn't have to** take a tent.

Past
I/You/He/She/We/They **had to** take a tent.
Did I/you/he/she/we/they **have to** take a tent?
I/You/He/She/We/They **didn't have to** take a tent.

Making adverbs from adjectives
Add *ly* (perfect → perfectly)
Change *y* to *i* and add *ly* (noisy → noisily)
For adjectives ending in *le*, take off *e* and add *y* (comfortable → comfortably)

Vocabulary

backpack bump camp chance
competition competitor cord
costume desert election
funfair instructions law
lottery marathon organiser
parachute personality risk
skydiving strength sunrise
tent temperature

cheerful gentle hard medical
ready regular risky sensible
urgent

to float   to get up   to get on with
to get on   to get off   to pilot
to set off   to shout

apart from

LANGUAGE SUMMARY

Exam folder 15

In this part of the exam, you look at short texts. There are three possible explanations – A, B or C. You have to decide which one says the same as the text.

1 Look at this sign and answer the questions.

> ## CHILDREN UNDER FIVE MUST HAVE AN ADULT WITH THEM ON THIS RIDE

   a Where is the sign?
   b What does *children under five* mean?
   c Which children can go on the ride without an adult?

2 Read the three possible explanations. Which explanation – A, B or C – means the same as the sign? Why are the other explanations wrong?

> **A** Children less than five years old cannot go on this ride alone.
> **B** Children in groups of five or more must have an adult with them.
> **C** Adults are not allowed on this ride.

3 Now look at another sign and answer the questions.

> ## ADVENTURE PARK
> ### THIS ENTRANCE CLOSED UNTIL 11 AM TODAY
> ### USE OTHER ENTRANCE BESIDE CAFÉ

   a Signs often have words missing to make them shorter.
      Add the missing words to the sign.
   b Where in the park is this sign?
   c How many entrances are open before 11 am today?
   d How many entrances are open after 11 am today?

4 Read the three possible explanations of the sign then answer the questions.

> **A** There will only be one entrance to the park after today.
> **B** This entrance cannot be used before 11 am today.
> **C** The park opens at 11 am today.

   a Does *cannot be used* mean the same as *closed* in the sign?
   b Does *until 11 am today* mean the same as *after today*?
   c Which is the correct explanation – A, B or C?
   d Why are the other explanations wrong?

5 Which words can you add to this sign?

PLEASE REMAIN IN SEATS UNTIL RIDE
STOPS COMPLETELY

6 Read the three possible explanations of the sign and decide which is the correct explanation – A, B or C. Why are the other explanations wrong?

A The ride starts when all the seats are full.
B Do not stand up when the ride is moving.
C If the ride stops, wait until it begins again.

7 Now look at this sign. What does it say? Which is the correct explanation – A, B or C?

PARK CLOSES AT 6 PM
EXCEPT IN DECEMBER
WHEN IT CLOSES AT 4 PM

A The park shuts earlier than 6 pm on some days.
B The park stays open later for one month of the year.
C The park is open all year except in December.

8 Now look at this sign. What does it say? Which is the correct explanation – A, B or C?

BUY SANDWICHES AND DRINKS HERE
HOT FOOD AVAILABLE AT LUNCHTIME
AT RESTAURANT BY LAKE

A You can buy a hot meal in two different places.
B The restaurant near the lake serves hot food in the middle of the day.
C Sandwiches and drinks are only available at lunchtime.

Exam folder vocabulary
sandwich   seat

UNIT 16 Free time

Introduction

16.1

1 Do you make good use of your free time? Try this flowchart to find out.

Start

Do you feel bad if your bedroom is in a mess?

NO → *Do you ever forget to wear your watch?*

YES ↓

Do you ever forget to wear your watch?

NO →

Do you enjoy tidying your desk? NO → If you try a new shampoo and don't like it, do you throw it away immediately?

Do you sometimes forget your mates' birthdays?

YES ↓

Have you ever forgotten to meet someone you promised to see?

Do you have lots of rubbish under your bed?

Do you ever make plans for your mates without asking them what they want to do?

Did you decide what to wear today before you went to bed last night?

Are your CDs in alphabetical order? NO

Do you keep your notes for different subjects in special files?

Do you always do your homework at the same time?

Do you often sit down to start your homework and then find you don't know what you have to do?

Do you ever do your homework on the way to class? YES → *Are you often the last person to arrive when you meet your mates?*

Have you ever lost your temper because you can't find something?

Do you have more free time than your mates?

You're wasting your time!
You're not making good use of your time at all. Your room is a mess and you can never find anything! You're probably famous among your mates for being late and never knowing what's happening. Try to learn to make a few plans and then try to keep them. You have more free time than you realise, if you only use it sensibly!

You're almost organised!
You usually manage your time quite well and you're fairly tidy. You're good at preparing for anything really important but sometimes you're careless. You often have to finish things in a hurry. Try to plan your days carefully and you'll find you don't run out of time so often.

You're totally organised!
You're so organised and tidy that your mates sometimes worry about you. You're never late and you never lose anything. That's great, but don't let it rule your life completely. We all need to relax sometimes and a little bit of mess won't hurt you. Your mates might like you better if you're not perfect!

2 Do you agree with the result? Tell other people your result. Do they agree?

3 Look at the pictures. These students have an English test tomorrow. What are they doing now? Are these good ways to use your time the day before an English test?

Reading

16.2

1 Look at this message board from a website. What is it about?

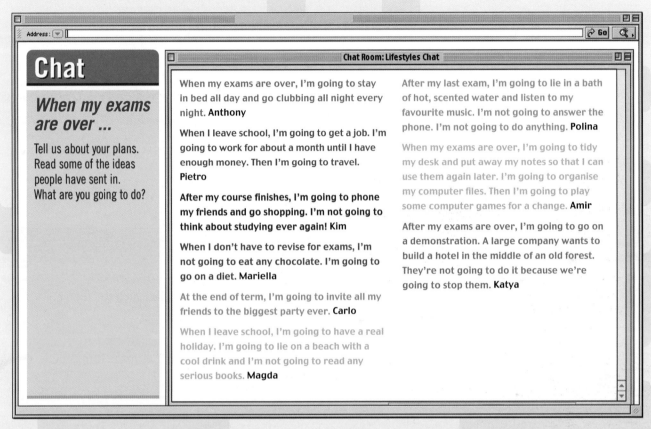

Chat

When my exams are over ...

Tell us about your plans. Read some of the ideas people have sent in. What are you going to do?

Chat Room: Lifestyles Chat

When my exams are over, I'm going to stay in bed all day and go clubbing all night every night. **Anthony**

When I leave school, I'm going to get a job. I'm going to work for about a month until I have enough money. Then I'm going to travel. **Pietro**

After my course finishes, I'm going to phone my friends and go shopping. I'm not going to think about studying ever again! **Kim**

When I don't have to revise for exams, I'm not going to eat any chocolate. I'm going to go on a diet. **Mariella**

At the end of term, I'm going to invite all my friends to the biggest party ever. **Carlo**

When I leave school, I'm going to have a real holiday. I'm going to lie on a beach with a cool drink and I'm not going to read any serious books. **Magda**

After my last exam, I'm going to lie in a bath of hot, scented water and listen to my favourite music. I'm not going to answer the phone. I'm not going to do anything. **Polina**

When my exams are over, I'm going to tidy my desk and put away my notes so that I can use them again later. I'm going to organise my computer files. Then I'm going to play some computer games for a change. **Amir**

After my exams are over, I'm going to go on a demonstration. A large company wants to build a hotel in the middle of an old forest. They're not going to do it because we're going to stop them. **Katya**

2 Who has the best idea? Who has the worst?

Language focus

16.3

1 Work with a partner. Ask and answer questions using the words in the box.

| What | When | Where | Who | Why |

EXAMPLE: *What is Anthony going to do all day when his exams are over?*
He's going to stay in bed.
When is Kim going to phone her friends?
After her course finishes.

2 What are these people going to do?

a *She's going to jump out of the plane.*

b ....

c ....

d ....

e ....

3 Work with a partner. Ask and answer questions using these phrases with *going to*. When you finish, tell the class some of the things your partner is going to do.

a after this lesson
What are you going to do after this lesson, Brigitte?
I'm going to have a coffee.
b this evening
c tomorrow morning
d next weekend
e when you finish this course
f after you complete this exercise

4 Who gave the funniest or most interesting answers? Write down three of them.

Grammar spot

When we talk about future time, a present tense follows *when*, *after* and *until*.

5 Complete these sentences using a verb in the present simple.

a When I ...*see*... my brother, I'm going to ask him for some money.
b When I .... more money, I'm going to buy some CDs.
c When my sister .... home from university, we're going to have a party.
d Our neighbours are going to move when their son .... a new job.
e After the new road .... , the bus company is going to increase fares.
f I'm not going to do any more work until you .... me.
g I'm going to listen to some music after we .... this exercise.

16.4 **ACTIVITY**

Your teacher will give you a card with an activity on it. You have to mime the preparation for the activity. Do not mime the activity. You can do this alone or with a partner. The class has to guess what you are going to do.

16.5

1 Work with a partner. Use the sentences a–h below to complete the conversation.

Liz:	Hi, Sam. What are you doing?
Sam:	1 *I'm making a poster. Do you want to help me?*
Liz:	I'm afraid I can't. I'm going to watch the football on television. Aren't you going to watch it?
Sam:	2 ....
Liz:	Why?
Sam:	3 ....
Liz:	So what's wrong with that?
Sam:	4 ....
Liz:	Another time perhaps. Anyway, I think the car park's a good idea. There isn't enough parking in the town.
Sam:	5 ....
Liz:	Why not?
Sam:	6 ....
Liz:	OK, but what are you and your friends going to do to stop it?
Sam:	7 ....
Liz:	Well, good luck. Now I'm going to watch the match.
Sam:	8 ....

a Because the council is going to build a new car park.
b But it's a really bad idea. It isn't going to make things better for teenagers.
c Because they're going to put it by the market, you know where Space Party is? The club we went to last week. That's where they're going to build it. Would you like to come on the demonstration?
d ~~I'm making a poster. Do you want to help me?~~
e We're going to stand in the shopping centre and we're going to tell people what's happening.
f Because they're going to knock down Space Party. So what are we going to do at weekends? Space Party's the only place to go to in this town.
g OK. You can tell me about it when I get home.
h No, not this time. I'm going to join a demonstration in the city centre.

2 🎧 Listen to the recording and check your answers.

16.6

1 What's your favourite time of day?

2 🎧 Listen to the recording and write down the times you hear, using figures.

a *12.50* b .... c .... d .... e .... f ....

3 🎧 Listen again and check your answers.

4 Now write the times in words.

a *ten to one* b .... c .... d .... e .... f ....

16.7 PRONUNCIATION

1 How many ways of asking the time do you know? Practise asking the time.

2 Practise saying the times in Exercise 16.6.

3 Work with a partner. Ask and answer questions about time, using the words in the list and then invent one or two more.

   a get up / last Friday
   b be / now
   c get up / next Sunday
   d arrive here / today
   e be / now in New York

   EXAMPLE: *What time did you get up last Friday? At ten to seven.*

16.8 ACTIVITY

1 🎧 Listen to three short conversations between Marco and three of his friends. Look at his personal organiser and write down his plans for Sunday.

2 What is Marco going to do on the day before his English test? Do you think this is a good plan?

3 Write down three things (real or imaginary) that you are going to do this weekend. Write down the exact time for each activity.

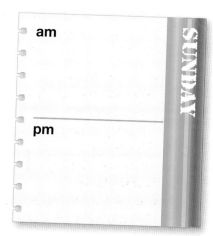

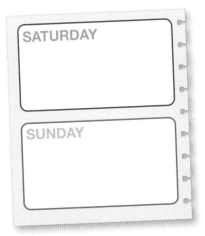

4 Go round the class. Tell other people what you are going to do and invite them to join you. Accept and refuse invitations to do things with them. You can't change the times you have chosen. Do not show your notes to other people.

5 When you finish, find out who is going to have the busiest weekend.

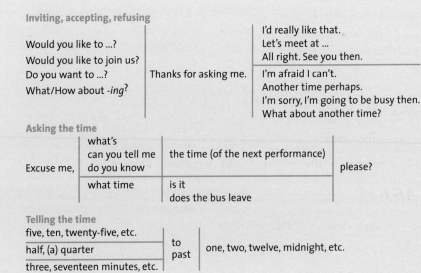

Inviting, accepting, refusing

Would you like to ...? Would you like to join us? Do you want to ...? What/How about *-ing*?	Thanks for asking me.	I'd really like that. Let's meet at ... All right. See you then.
		I'm afraid I can't. Another time perhaps. I'm sorry, I'm going to be busy then. What about another time?

Asking the time

Excuse me,	what's can you tell me do you know	the time (of the next performance)	please?
	what time	is it does the bus leave	

Telling the time

five, ten, twenty-five, etc.	to past	one, two, twelve, midnight, etc.
half, (a) quarter		
three, seventeen minutes, etc.		

Asking questions about time
What time did you get up on Friday?
What time is it now in New York?

going to future
for things we plan to do and when we can already see what is going to happen

I am you/we/they are he/she/it is	(not) going to	go.
Am I Are you/we/they Is he/she/it	going to	go?

the present tense
future time after when, after and until
When our exams **are** over we're going to have a party.
I'm going to work hard **until I have** lots of money.
After I finish this course I'm going to relax.

Vocabulary
council demonstration file mate

to send in to go on a diet to go shopping
to lose (your temper) to rule
to run out of to waste

alphabetical careless cool immediately
over (= finished) scented totally

on the way

LANGUAGE SUMMARY

Exam folder 16

Listening Part 2

In this part of the exam, you listen to a recording of one person speaking or an interview and answer six questions by choosing A, B or C. You hear the recording twice.

1 Look at the instructions at the top of the exam task on the right. What can you learn about the recording?

    a What kind of conversation is it?
    b How many people do you hear?
    c What is the conversation about?

2 Look at question 1 in the exam task. Question 1 tells us that we are going to hear about a woman called Philippa. What else does it tell us?
Now look at questions 2–6 in the exam task and make guesses about what you are going to hear. When you have finished, compare your guesses with the answers in the box at the foot of this page.

Exam Advice

Before you hear the recording, you have some time to read through the instructions and questions. You should use these to help you understand what you are going to hear.

3 Now read the options for each question in the exam task. Remember that the words you read in the questions are often different from the words you hear, although they have a similar meaning. Can you match these words from the questions with the words which have a similar meaning?

1 some poetry   a a show
2 with a group of tourists   b travelling by bus across the States
3 two weeks   c a poem
4 travelling by air   d flying
5 crossing the States   e a tour organised by a
   by bus   travel agent
6 an exhibition   f a fortnight

4 🎧 Now do the exam task.

- You will hear a radio interview with a woman called Philippa about a trip she is going to make.
- For each question, put a tick (✓) in the correct box.

1 How did Philippa win her prize?
  A ☐ by writing some poetry
  B ☐ by writing a novel
  C ☐ by describing a journey

2 Philippa is going to travel with
  A ☐ a group of tourists.
  B ☐ two friends.
  C ☐ her brother.

3 When are they going to leave the UK?
  A ☐ immediately
  B ☐ in two weeks
  C ☐ at the end of the year

4 Where are they going to stay first?
  A ☐ Amsterdam
  B ☐ New York
  C ☐ California

5 Which part of the trip is Philippa most excited about?
  A ☐ travelling by air
  B ☐ visiting famous cities
  C ☐ crossing the States by bus

6 When Philippa returns she is going to
  A ☐ have an exhibition.
  B ☐ get a job.
  C ☐ study.

5 🎧 Listen again. Use the second listening to answer any questions you were unsure about.

1 Philippa won a prize.
2 She's going to travel with some other people.
3 They are going away from the UK.
4 They are going to visit more than one place.
5 Philippa is most excited about one part of her trip.
6 She talks about what she plans to do after her trip.

Writing folder

Writing Part 1

1 Look at the two sentences below. Which word do you need to write in the space so that the second sentence means the same as the first? Below are three students' answers. Which one is correct?

> **1** We have a new swimming pool in our town.
> There .... a new swimming pool in our town.

Student A: *have*
Student B: *has*
Student C: *is*

2 Read this question and look at three students' answers. Which one is correct?

> **2** The new pool opened two days ago.
> The new pool has been open .... days.

Student A: *for two*
Student B: *since two*
Student C: *after two*

Exam Advice

Write only the missing words.

3 Now do these questions. Complete the second sentence so that it means the same as the first, using no more than three words.

> **3** The old swimming pool wasn't as big as the new one.
> The new swimming pool is .... the old one.
>
> **4** The new pool is closed on Monday mornings.
> The new pool isn't .... on Monday mornings.
>
> **5** Young children are not allowed to go in the deep end.
> Young children must .... in the deep end.
>
> **6** This is the first time I've been to the new pool.
> I .... to the new pool before.
>
> **7** I went to the old pool every week.
> I used .... to the old pool every week.
>
> **8** My old swimming costume isn't big enough for me.
> My old swimming costume is too .... for me.
>
> **9** I borrowed a swimming costume from my friend.
> My friend .... a swimming costume.
>
> **10** We stayed in the pool for three hours.
> We .... three hours in the pool.

Exam folder vocabulary
exhibition poetry prize scenery
abroad

UNIT 17 | In the future

Introduction

17.1

1 Look at the pictures on this page. Don't read the articles yet. Can you guess when these articles first appeared? Write the years in the spaces at the top of each article.

2 Read one of the articles, A or B, and discuss the questions which follow them.

A

WILL THEY REALLY LIVE LIKE THIS?

DATE: .... TWENTY-FIRST CENTURY LIFE BY PROFESSOR H. J. PEABODY.

How will our great-grandchildren live? Some people's ideas seem to me most improbable. They suggest that every family will have a house with central heating and a bathroom with hot and cold water available at all times. No one will eat meals. Instead, they will take a delicious pill every morning which will provide all the food they need for a day. Most people will travel to work in motor cars and they will listen to recorded music as they drive along. They believe life will be easier and more comfortable.

I believe that many of these ideas are typical of the nonsense we hear nowadays. Do our readers have any more sensible suggestions?

a Think about life now. Do we do the things Professor Peabody describes in the article? What don't we do?
b Did the professor feel positive about the ideas he describes?

B

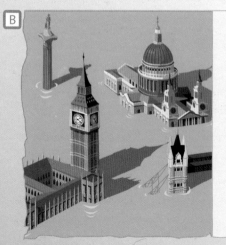

Will this really happen?

DATE: ....

How will the world change over the next two centuries?

Scientists at a recent conference in Buenos Aires warned that the ice at the North and South poles will soon melt. Sea levels will rise and there will be floods in many parts of the world. Cities such as London will begin to disappear under water. The sea will also cover many low islands, for example in the Maldives. The populations of countries with low coastal areas such as Bangladesh will have to move. The weather will change more suddenly and there will be many storms with extremely strong winds. In Europe, temperatures will rise and rainfall will increase.

c Have you heard some of these ideas before? Do you think they are correct?
d Did the scientists feel positive about the future?

3 Now answer these questions.

a What do you think life will be like in the future?
b What will change and what will be the same?
c Do you feel positive about the future?

Listening

17.2

1 *Café Europe* is a soap opera on the radio. Look at the photographs of the characters and talk about the people. Would you like to meet any of them? Who?

Meet the people at Café Europe!

Mario – the owner

Claudia – a student, works as a waitress

Karim – works as a waiter

Adam – Karim's flatmate

Nathalie – Claudia's flatmate, a student

2 Look at what happened last week in *Café Europe*. What will happen this week? Discuss your ideas. Write down your predictions.

LAST WEEK

First, Mario had a quarrel with the chef and the chef left. Next, Claudia decided to sell her car and Karim wanted to buy it. Then, Adam, an old friend, arrived to share Karim's flat. Nathalie wanted to borrow Claudia's car. Claudia wasn't happy about the idea, but in the end she agreed.

3 🎧 Listen to the first part of this week's episode and answer the questions below.

   a What does Mario need? *A new chef.*
   b What does Nathalie need?
   c Why will Nathalie go to see Mario later?

4 🎧 Listen to the second part of this week's episode and answer the questions below.

   a Where are Karim and Adam? *In Karim's flat.*
   b What does Karim show Adam?
   c What did Adam see yesterday?

5 🎧 Listen to the rest of this week's episode. Check these facts. Write *true* or *false*, then compare your answers with another student.

   a Karim is going to pay Claudia next week. *false*
   b Claudia believes her car is in good condition.
   c Claudia thinks Mario will offer Nathalie a job as a waitress.
   d Nathalie is a good cook.
   e Nathalie knows Adam well.
   f Adam knows something about Nathalie.

Language focus

17.3

1 Look back at the ideas you wrote down in Exercise 17.2, question 2. Were your predictions right? Are you usually good at guessing what will happen when you watch soap operas?

2 🎧 Listen to the whole episode again if you need to. Say what you think will happen in the next episode. Discuss these questions.

   a Why does Nathalie need money?
   b Will Mario find out about Nathalie's cooking?
   c Will Claudia find out about her car?
   d What will happen at the beginning of the next episode?

17.4

1 Complete the following sentences about the future. Use *will*.

   a Next month, the weather
      will be colder.

   b Next year, some of my friends
      ....

   c In the next century, the weather
      ....

   d Next week, our teacher
      ....

   e In 2010, I ....

2 Look at the sentences in Exercise 1 again. Now use your own ideas to make sentences using *won't*.

   a Next month, *we won't have lunch in the garden.*
   b Next year, ...
   c In the next century, ...
   d Next week, ...
   e In 2010, ...

17.5

Nathalie said *I'm going to be the new chef. She'll be really surprised when I tell her.* She uses *going to* for a definite plan, *will* for a prediction and the present tense after *when*.

1 Complete these sentences in the same way.

   a I *'m going to buy* (buy) some flowers for my mum. She *'ll be* (be) very happy when I ......*give*...... (give) them to her.
   b My brother .... (leave) college. My dad .... (get) very angry when he .... (hear) the news.
   c I .... (not join) my friends' demonstration. They .... (be) disappointed when I .... (tell) them.
   d Our teacher .... (give) us a test. We .... (not enjoy) it when she .... (give) it to us but it .... (help) us to check our progress.

2 Now write similar sentences using your own ideas.

17.6

1 Look back at the photograph of the people in *Café Europe* and answer these questions.

   a Who is looking at the camera?
   b Who is wearing a hat?
   c Is anyone wearing a tie?

2 Write some sentences about the people in your classroom.

Everyone is writing.
No one is shouting.
There isn't anyone who enjoys homework.

17.7 **ACTIVITY**

1 Look at the pictures. What are these things?

2 Work in a group. Which of these things does everyone have in their bedroom? Which does no one have?

17.8

Claudia has her car washed regularly. What other things does Claudia have done?

Claudia has a sister, Carmen, who is a famous model. What does she have done? Talk about her house, her meals, her hair, her fingernails, her clothes and her dog. What do you and your family do yourselves? What do you have done?

Carmen

17.9 **ACTIVITY**

When Mario bought *Café Europe* he had some changes made. Work with a partner. Your teacher will give one of you a picture of the café before the changes and one of you a picture of the café after the changes. Describe your picture to your partner without showing it. Ask and answer questions. There are six changes.

EXAMPLE: *Did Mario have the walls painted? Yes he did.*

17.10 **PRONUNCIATION**

1 🎧 Look at these three sentences and listen to the recording. Each sentence has two words with the same vowel sound. Underline the words. Say the sounds, then the words, then the sentences.

  a She's got a large car.
  b My toes were all sore.
  c Take the third turning.

2 Work with a partner. Look at these sentences and underline any words containing one of the three sounds. Then copy the words into the table below.

  a My head <u>hurts</u> when I <u>talk</u> too much.
  b I saw the shirt this morning.
  c I need to earn more money.
  d I <u>can't</u> see in the dark.
  e These doors aren't dirty.
  f You must learn to work harder.
  g I only heard half the story.

/ɑː/	/ɔː/	/ɜː/
can't	talk	hurts

3 🎧 Listen to the recording and check your answers. Repeat the sentences.

17.11 **ACTIVITY**

Work in a group.

  a Decide on a story for next week's episode of *Café Europe*. Act out your story for the rest of the class.
  b Write a summary of one of the episodes your class acted.

17.12 **ACTIVITY**

  a On a piece of paper, write four sentences about what someone in the class will and won't do in the future. Don't say who you are writing about.
  b Read out your sentences and see if the class can guess who you have written about.

---

will future

I/you/he/she/it/we/they	will won't /will not	go.
Will	I, you, he, she, it, we, they	go?

everyone/everybody, no one/nobody, someone/somebody, anyone/anybody
Everyone/everybody wears trainers.
No one/nobody wears hats.
There isn't **anyone/anybody** in the room.
There is **someone/somebody** in the room.

to have something done
I **have/had** my hair **cut** by a very good hairdresser.
I **don't/didn't have** my meals **cooked**.
Do/Did you have your meals **cooked**?

Vocabulary

accident   blind   character   coastal area   episode   fee
flatmate   flood   hair dryer   headlight   lipstick   pill
population   prediction   progress   quarrel   rain(fall)
sculpture   sea level   soap opera   storm   value

to boil   to borrow   to find out   to increase   to melt
to provide   to rise   to smash   to warn

positive   (im)probable   (non)sense   recent   typical

a long way away

Exam folder 17

Reading Part 4

> In this part of the exam, you read a text and answer five questions about it by choosing A, B, C or D.

1 On the opposite page, there is a text and some questions. Don't look at the text yet. Here is question 1. What can you learn from it about the text?

> **1** Why has Alan written this letter?

2 Now look at questions 2–5 below and make guesses about what you are going to read.

> **2** Why is Parson's Place particularly important, in Alan's opinion?
> **3** What will cause traffic jams?
> **4** Alan says that ordinary people who live in the town will probably soon …
> **5** Which of these posters has Alan made?

3 Now read the text. If you don't know the meaning of a word or phrase, don't stop. Read on to the end and try to understand the text as a whole.

Exam Advice

Some of the questions ask about facts and some ask about opinions.

4 Follow these instructions.

   a Look at question 1 on the opposite page. Find clues in the text which tell you who Alan is writing to. Quickly read the whole text again and answer question 1.
   b Look at question 2 on the opposite page. Find the two sentences which give Alan's opinion about Parson's Place and underline them. Now answer question 2.
   c Look at question 3 on the opposite page. Find the paragraph in the text which talks about traffic. Read this paragraph carefully and answer question 3.
   d Look at question 4 on the opposite page. Find words in the text which mean the same as *ordinary people*. Read the whole paragraph and answer question 4.
   e Look at question 5 on the opposite page. Can you answer it without reading the text again?

I have learnt of a plan to build three hundred houses on the land called Parson's Place by the football ground. Few people know about this new plan to increase the size of our town. For me, Parson's Place is special because it is a beautiful natural area where local people can relax – the small wood has many unusual trees and the stream is popular with fishermen and bird-watchers. It's very quiet because there are few houses or roads nearby. I think that losing this area will be terrible because we have no other similar facilities in the neighbourhood.

I am also against this plan because it will cause traffic problems. How will the people from the new houses travel to work? The motorway and the railway station are on the other side of town. Therefore, these people will have to drive through the town centre every time they go anywhere. The roads will always be full of traffic, there will be nowhere to park and the tourists who come to see our lovely old buildings will leave. Shops and hotels will lose business. If the town really needs more homes, the empty ground beside the railway station is a more suitable place.

No doubt the builders will make a lot of money by selling these houses. But, in my opinion, the average person will quickly be made poorer by this plan. As well as this, we will lose a very special place and our town will be much less pleasant.

I am going to the local government offices on Monday morning to protest about this plan and I hope that your readers will join me there. We must make them stop this plan before it is too late.

- Read the text and questions below.
- For each question, mark the letter next to the correct answer – A, B, C or D.

1 Why has Alan written this letter?
  A to persuade the government to build new houses
  B to protest about a new motorway near the town
  C to encourage more people in the town to use Parson's Place
  D to inform other people about the builders' plans

2 Why is Parson's Place particularly important, in Alan's opinion?
  A because it is near the football ground
  B because lots of people live near it
  C because it is a place near the town where people can enjoy nature
  D because local people can get there easily by car from the town centre

3 What will cause traffic jams?
  A building on Parson's Place
  B building near the railway station
  C tourists in the narrow streets
  D people going to the shops and hotels

4 Alan says that ordinary people who live in the town will probably soon
  A open new shops and hotels.
  B choose to live near the station.
  C be able to buy new homes.
  D have less money.

5 Which of these posters has Alan made?

  A
  SAVE OUR
  SPORTS GROUND

  B
  SAY NO TO HOUSES
  ON PARSON'S PLACE

  C
  WE NEED HOMES
  NOT HOTELS

  D
  USE THE TRAIN
  NOT THE ROAD

Exam folder vocabulary
government   nature   neighbourhood   size   stream
to cause   to encourage   to inform   to protest
ordinary   pleasant   suitable

UNIT 18 Shooting a film

a → ....

Introduction

18.1

1 Work in a group. Look at these scenes from famous films. Can you give each film its correct title? If nobody knows the answer, have a guess.

b → ....

c → ....

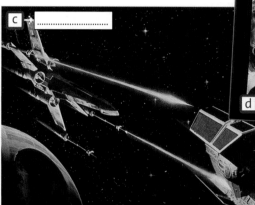

John TRAVOLTA
Olivia NEWTON-JOHN

d → ....

e → ....

f → ....

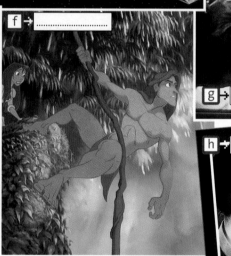

g → ....

h → ....

2 What kind of film is each one?

3 Work in a group. Tell the other students the story of a film you saw recently. Can they tell you the name of the film? Use the words in the box to help you.

> At the beginning   At first   Suddenly   Then   Next   At the end

4 What kind of film did you talk about?

5 Tell the other students what kinds of films you like best. Who is your favourite film star?

i → ....

Reading

18.2

1 Before a day's filming begins, what do the actors have to do? What do the film crew have to do?

2 Quickly read this newspaper article. How much of the film did they shoot during one day?

A Day's Work at the Seaside

Do you know how many hours' preparation are needed to make a very short piece of film? Our reporter went down to the beach to find out.

Five o'clock was very early in the morning for me but I wanted to get there to see all the preparations. The beach looked a bit different from usual and not just because the tourists were all missing at that time in the morning.

But there were plenty of people around. I noticed several caravans in the car park with men and women going in and out of them. I soon realised that one caravan was the make-up room. The actors went in as one person and came out looking like someone else. In fact they looked completely different when they came out – some older, some younger, some more handsome. One actress spent a whole hour with the make-up artist. When she went in she was 25 and when she came out she was 65! Another caravan was the dressing room and the actors went in dressed in ordinary jeans and T-shirts and came out in the clothes of the 1920s. They all looked very relaxed, sitting on picnic chairs on the beach, chatting and drinking coffee – they were obviously well-prepared.

The cameramen and women were very busy – they were moving the cameras into the right positions. The rest of the film crew were arranging the lights and microphones. I had a chat with a man called Ted – he was very keen to tell me about his job which was to clear all the rubbish from the beach. The beach needed to be completely clean and tidy and he had to make sure there was nothing modern in sight because the film is about the 1920s. He even had to carry away some surfing equipment.

The director told everyone what to do. I looked for the star of the film, Alexia Harris, but I couldn't see her anywhere. She arrived at about 10 o'clock and looked rather annoyed because she had to wait for a technician to check the microphones.

I got the answer to my question – how long does it take to shoot a film? They shot only ten minutes of film in one whole day and the film crew were there for ten hours. I think I prefer my job – at least I don't usually have to get up at 5 am! But it was fun to be a visitor for a day.

3 Read the article again. Which of the things in the picture did the film company do? What didn't they do?

4 Without reading the text again, say if these sentences are true or false.

   a It was too early for holidaymakers. *true*
   b The actors slept in the caravans.
   c In her make-up, one of the actresses looked older than she really was.
   d The actors wore their normal clothes in the film.
   e The star of the film was angry because other people were late.

5 Would you like to work for a film company? What job would you like to have? Which job is the most popular?

Language focus

18.3

Work with a partner. Look back at the article in Exercise 18.2 and complete these sentences.

When Alexia arrived,

a the actors *had changed their clothes* .... (change / clothes)

b the actors *had all visited the make-up artist.* ...... (visit / make-up artist)

c the cameramen .... (move / cameras)

d the rest of the film crew .... (arrange / lights)

e a man called Ted .... (clear / rubbish)

f the director .... (tell / everyone what to do)

g the technician .... (not / check / microphones)

When the reporter left,

h they .... (shoot / ten minutes of the film)

i the film crew .... (be / ten hours)

18.4

1 Write down the age you first did these things. Guess if you can't remember. Put ✗ if you haven't done something.

   travel abroad
   fly in an aeroplane
   learn to read
   learn to swim
   move house or flat
   start school
   see a film at the cinema
   play a computer game

2 Make sentences like these.
   By the time I was six, I'd started school but I hadn't learnt to read.

3 Ask a partner questions like these.
   By the time you were seven, had you travelled abroad?

18.5

1 What is the difference in meaning between these two sentences?

   When Alexia arrived, the cameramen had arranged the lights.
   When Alexia arrived, the cameramen arranged the lights.

2 Put the past simple or the past perfect in these sentences.

   a When the actress came out of the make-up room, she ...*waved*... (wave) to me.
   b When they stopped filming, they all .... (have) a drink.
   c When Alexia arrived, they .... (not finish) checking the microphones.
   d When I got there, the director .... (welcome) me.
   e When I arrived at the beach, the film crew .... (be) there for hours.
   f When Alexia arrived, she .... (be) annoyed.
   g When the actor came out of the dressing room, he .... (change) his clothes.
   h When I saw the film star, I .... (not recognise) her.

18.6

This is part of the story of the film which the film company were shooting on the beach. Put each verb into the correct tense – past simple or past perfect.

| decide   live   be   take   remind   not know   cover |
| not see   put   write   find   start   write   be   meet |
| dig   read   ~~return~~ |

In 1921, a woman (**a**) ...*returned*... to the town where she (**b**) .... as a teenager. She was walking along the beach when she (**c**) .... a friend who she (**d**) .... for ten years. He (**e**) .... her that one day when they were seventeen, they (**f**) .... a hole in the sand, they (**g**) .... a bottle in it with some poems inside that they (**h**) .... to each other and then they (**i**) .... it up. They (**j**) .... to find the bottle. After an hour, they (**k**) .... the place and they (**l**) .... to dig. The bottle (**m**) .... still there. They (**n**) .... it out of the hole and (**o**) .... the letters they (**p**) .... to each other ten years before. They (**q**) .... very embarrassed and (**r**) .... what to say.

1 Most of these words have the same vowel sound in the last syllable. What is it? Which two words have a different sound?

woman	important	holiday	camera	letter
appointment	newspaper	horror	preparation	telephone
actor	answer			

2 🎧 Listen and repeat the words after the recording. Were you right?

3 Here are some definitions of words. What are these words? Write them in the correct columns below.

  a They pretend to be other people in a play or film.
  b The opposite of *non-fiction*.
  c The opposite of *same*.
  d A v................ is someone who comes to your house for a short time.
  e Someone aged between 13 and 19.
  f You get them in the post.
  g An adventure film has lots of ac..... .
  h A shop .... helps you buy something.
  i You ask this before you get an answer.
  j He or she tells everyone what to do in a film.
  k A violin is a musical ....
  l He or she teaches you.

ending in *er(s)*	ending in *or(s)*	ending in *tion*	ending in *ant* or *ent*
	actors		

4 🎧 Listen and repeat the words.

18.8 **ACTIVITY**

1 Your teacher will give you a card which shows a scene from a film. Four other people in your class have other scenes from the same film. Find the people with the other scenes from your film.

2 Now work together in your group and invent an ending for your film.

18.9 **ACTIVITY**

Your teacher will give you a quiz about films. In teams, try to answer the quiz questions. Which team gets the most answers correct?

Past perfect

They	had ('d) had not (hadn't)	**moved** the cameras.
Had	they	**moved** the cameras?

When / By the time Alexia **arrived** at the beach,
= *POINT OF TIME IN THE PAST*
↓
←—←—←—←—←
they **had moved** the cameras.
the technician **hadn't checked** the microphones.

When Alexia arrived, the director had told the actors what to do.
(= *he told them before she arrived*)
When Alexia arrived, the director told the actors what to do.
(= *he told them immediately she arrived*)

Vocabulary
action film actor actress bottle cameraman/woman caravan
cartoon comedy director dressing room film crew
film star hole make-up microphone preparation movie
scene technician western

to carry away to chat to dig to remind
to shoot a film to wave

embarrassed handsome well-prepared

in sight

LANGUAGE SUMMARY

Exam folder 18

Listening Part 3

> In this part of the exam, you listen to a recorded announcement or someone speaking about a particular subject. You fill in the words which are missing from some notes. You hear the recording twice.

1 Look at this advertisement outside the Victoria Cinema and complete the spaces with the correct words.

performances   discounts   a programme
box office   screens

VICTORIA CINEMA

Ask inside for (**a**) .... of films showing this week.

(**b**) .... open from 10.30 every day.

Four (**c**) .... every day.

Two (**d**) ....

(**e**) .... for students and children.

---

2 Here are some sentences about a cinema. Complete the spaces with any suitable words.

  a The film begins at ....
  b There is a late performance on ....
  c The cinema is next to the ....
  d The film won a prize for the best ....
  e The film is in .... with subtitles.
  f The film is suitable for ....
  g The tickets cost ....
  h Phone .... for more information.

Exam Advice

You can guess what kind of words you need to listen for.

3 Look at these notes about the Victoria Cinema. Some information is missing. What kind of words will you listen for?

VICTORIA CINEMA
films showing from 7 July

One Summer Night – normally three performances but only one at 7.30 pm on (**1**) ....

Talk by the (**2**) .... of *The Violinist* on Wednesday.

Late-night film *Dead Men's Shoes* has won a prize for the (**3**) ....

On Saturday at 5 pm you can see the film *A Dangerous Game* in (**4**) .... with subtitles.

Children's film club:
at 10 am *The Young* (**5**) ....
at 11.30 am *The Mad Professor*

You can book tickets by phone between 10.30 am and (**6**) .... with a credit card.

---

4 🎧 Do this exam task.

- You will hear a recorded message giving you information about films.
- For each question, fill in the missing information in the numbered space.

5 🎧 Listen again and look at the recording script to check your answers.

Exam folder vocabulary
box office   credit card   programme   screen   subtitles

Writing folder

Writing Part 2

1 Complete each of these three sentences with words from the box.
How do you decide?

this weekend	tomorrow afternoon	last night

a I'm arriving at the station at 3.15 ....
b I've done lots of shopping ....
c I had a great time at the concert ....

2 Read the three questions below, then discuss what verbs/tenses you
will use in your answers. How do you decide?

1 You are spending the weekend at a friend's house. Write a
postcard to your brother or sister. In your postcard, you should

- say what the house is like
- say what you have done this morning
- tell him/her your plans for the rest of the weekend

2 You are spending next weekend with some friends who live in the
country. Write a postcard to them. In your postcard, you should

- say how you plan to get there
- ask about what you will all do
- tell them what time you will arrive

3 You spent last weekend at a friend's house. Write a postcard
to your friend. In your postcard, you should

- say what you enjoyed most
- tell him/her about your journey home
- tell him/her your plans for next weekend

Exam Advice

Read the question very carefully to find out what tenses you
need to use.

3 Work in a group. On a piece of paper, write an answer for one
of the questions in Exercise 2. Write 35–45 words.

4 Pass your answer to another group. Look at the piece of paper
your group is given. Which question does it answer? Has the
group used the right tenses?

Speaking

1 Work with a partner. Look at these sentences. Say if each sentence is true for you and give your partner some extra information.

a I spend lots of money on clothes because I want to look really fashionable.
Yes, that's true. I go shopping every week and I buy lots of clothes. My favourite designers are … OR *No, that's not true. I prefer comfortable, old clothes. I usually wear …*

b There aren't enough clubs for young people in this town.

c I used to live in the country.

d I'd never been to another country until last year.

e It'll probably rain tomorrow.

f Everyone in this class likes frightening rides at funfairs.

g In this country, you can get married when you are fifteen.

h The weather in this part of the world has changed since 1900.

i We have to take an exam at the end of this course.

j I'm going to watch a soap on TV this evening.

Vocabulary

2 Use one word from the box to complete each space.

adventure coast entrance from in instructions
on rope square tower tunnel

I saw an (a) *adventure* film last week. The story wasn't very easy to believe but it was quite exciting. It was about a man and a woman who were locked in a high (b) .... on a mountain and they had to reach the (c) .... where they had left a boat. So they made a (d) .... out of a shirt and climbed down from the window. They decided to walk through a (e) .... to the other side of the mountain. They didn't know where it went but (f) .... the way they found a coin from their country on the ground. Then they suddenly came out in a market (g) .... There was nobody (h) .... sight apart (i) .... one old man who was sitting in the (j) .... to a museum. He gave them (k) .... about how to reach their boat and in the end they were safe.

3 There are fifteen more words spelt wrongly in this email. Correct them.

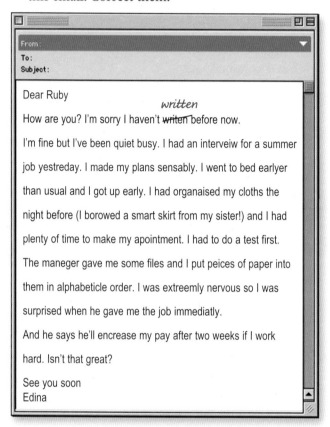

Dear Ruby

written
How are you? I'm sorry I haven't ~~writen~~ before now.

I'm fine but I've been quiet busy. I had an interveiw for a summer job yestreday. I made my plans sensably. I went to bed earlyer than usual and I got up early. I had organaised my cloths the night before (I borowed a smart skirt from my sister!) and I had plenty of time to make my apointment. I had to do a test first. The maneger gave me some files and I put peices of paper into them in alphabeticle order. I was extreemly nervous so I was surprised when he gave me the job immediatly.

And he says he'll encrease my pay after two weeks if I work hard. Isn't that great?

See you soon
Edina

4 Think about the meaning of these words. Mark the odd one out in each of these lists.

a leather (pattern) plastic silk
b chimney sofa stairs wall
c belt collar curtain sleeve
d amazing awful dull horrible
e boots gloves socks trainers
f melt predict suggest warn
g anxious nervous proud worried
h basin corridor shower toilet
i break damage save smash

Grammar

5 In each group of three sentences, only one is correct. Tick the correct sentence and put a cross by the incorrect ones.

1 A This is too big house for our family. ✗
  B This house is too big for our family. ✓
  C This house is too much big for our family. ✗

2 A I couldn't give my friend a lift because my brother had borrowed my car.
  B I mustn't give my friend a lift because my brother had borrowed my car.
  C I shouldn't give my friend a lift because my brother had borrowed my car.

3 A When the food had been ready, we ate it.
  B When the food was ready, we ate it.
  C When the food was ready, we had eaten it.

4 A My grandmother has had her dining room painted bright green.
  B My grandmother has made her dining room painted bright green.
  C My grandmother has done her dining room painted bright green.

5 A Will you come to my house after you'll finish your homework?
  B Will you come to my house after you finished your homework?
  C Will you come to my house after you finish your homework?

6 A Excuse me, what time opens this shop?
  B Excuse me, what time does open this shop?
  C Excuse me, what time does this shop open?

7 A Do you have to getting up early on Sundays?
  B Do you have to get up early on Sundays?
  C Do you have get up early on Sundays?

8 A She has a beautiful big red car.
  B She has a red beautiful big car.
  C She has a big beautiful red car.

9 A That needn't be my handbag because I haven't got one.
  B That mustn't be my handbag because I haven't got one.
  C That can't be my handbag because I haven't got one.

10 A I used to like cartoons, but now I think they're boring.
   B I use to like cartoons, but now I think they're boring.
   C I used to liking cartoons, but now I think they're boring.

11 A Are you going to wait here until the rain stopped?
   B Are you going to wait here until the rain stops?
   C Are you going to wait here until the rain will stop?

12 A The film begins at fifteen to seven.
   B The film begins at twenty-five past six.
   C The film begins at nine and a half.

6 Look at the pairs of sentences below. Use one word from the box to fill each space so that the second sentence means the same as the first.
Some words fit more than one space.

> can can't could don't have to
> has to have to might mustn't
> need used to

a It's OK to park here if you work at the hotel.
  Hotel employees _can_ park here.

b I'm not sure if that's my brother's CD player.
  That CD .... belong to my brother.

c Do not bring ice creams into this shop.
  You .... bring ice creams into this shop.

d I've never learnt Portuguese.
  I .... speak Portuguese.

e I can finish this work without your help.
  You .... help me finish this work.

f In the past, people walked more than they do now.
  People .... walk more than they do now.

g Everyone helps tidy the club after parties. It's a rule.
  Everyone .... help tidy the club after parties.

h The weather is hot so a coat is not necessary.
  It's quite hot, so you .... bring a coat.

i In England all motorcyclists wear helmets because that's the law.
  You .... wear a helmet on a motorcycle in England.

j Perhaps that's the letter about my new job.
  That .... be the letter about my new job.

k If you want to visit Japan, it's necessary to get a visa.
  You .... a visa if you want to visit Japan.

UNIT 19 Happy families

Introduction

19.1

Look at Daniel's family tree. Read what he has written about his family below and then complete the spaces using some of the words in the box.

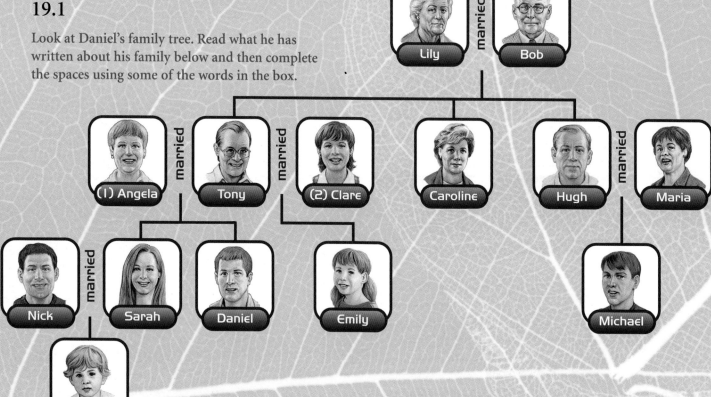

I've moved away from the town where I grew up. When I go back it's quite easy for me to visit all my relations because most of them live in the same part of town. In fact my (**a**) _grandmother_, Lily, lives next door to her (**b**) .... Caroline. And my (**c**) .... Hugh lives in the next street. My father lives about ten minutes away so my grandmother has all her children near her. That's good because her (**d**) .... , Bob, died a few years ago so she's alone now in the house. My parents divorced about ten years ago and my father remarried. My (**e**) .... Sarah and I weren't sure about our new (**f**) .... at first but now we like her a lot. She and my father have one child so I have a (**g**) .... She's called Emily. Emily is only six and I have a (**h**) .... , Anna, who is three years younger. I get on really well with my (**i**) .... Nick. Sarah, Nick and Anna live in Scotland and I often visit them. I have one (**j**) .... called Michael. We used to play together a lot when we were small.

brother-in-law	daughter
sister	cousin
~~grandmother~~	stepmother
husband	niece
uncle	half-sister
aunt	son

19.2

Work with a partner. Tell your partner about your family or another family. Your partner draws the family tree for you. Now do the same for your partner's family.

19.3

Read these descriptions. Which one are you?

Oldest children

★ expect to do well
★ are good at looking after other people
★ need to keep everything tidy
★ like keeping rules

Youngest children

★ love taking risks
★ have a good sense of humour
★ often refuse to do what other people tell them
★ are interested in studying artistic subjects

Middle children

★ are good at solving arguments
★ enjoy being with other people
★ are good managers and leaders
★ don't mind changing their plans

Only children

★ prefer being with adults
★ are quite serious
★ are afraid of failing
★ are hard-working

Listening

19.4

🎧 Listen to four people speaking. What position are they in their families? What disadvantage does each person talk about?

Speaker	Position in family	Disadvantage
Rebecca		
George		
Charlotte		
Peter		

19.5

1 🎧 Listen again and look at the descriptions in Exercise 19.3. For each person, put a tick (✓) next to the things they do or did.

2 Are any of the families in Exercise 19.4 like yours? What is the best position to be in, do you think?

3 Find other people in the class who are in the same position as you in their family.

4 Discuss how you feel about your position in your family. Do you agree with what the descriptions say? Use language like this to help you.

I agree that …
I don't agree that …
It's true that …
It's not true that …

5 Are there any other things your group wants to add to the list? Use language like this to help you.

We think …
In our opinion, …

6 Tell the rest of the class about what you discussed.

Language focus

19.6

1 The words in the box are from the descriptions in Exercise 19.3. Are they followed by *to* or *-ing*? Put them into the correct column below.

~~expect~~	~~be good at~~	need
like	enjoy	don't mind
love	refuse	be interested in
prefer	be afraid of	

followed by *to*	followed by *-ing*
expect	be good at

2 Do the same with these words from the recording. Some words go in both columns. Your teacher will give you the scripts.

look forward to		be fed up with
would like	begin	continue
start	stop	continue	try
seem	arrange	want	learn
prefer	begin	start

3 Which words are in both columns?

Grammar spot

Learn these words in a sentence. This will help you to remember if they are followed by *to* or *-ing*.

19.7

1 Look at these two sentences. What do you notice about *make* and *let*?

Rebecca says *My parents didn't make me look after my little brother.*

George says *They never let you grow up.*

2 Write down one thing your parents let you do when you were five years old and one thing they made you do. What about when you were ten?

3 Compare with other people.

19.8 PRONUNCIATION

1 🎧 Listen and repeat these words. Which two are the odd ones out?

this   the   think   there   then   mother   thing   father   other

2 🎧 Now listen to these words. For each word, decide if *th* is pronounced /ð/ as in *their* or as /θ/ in *thirsty* and write it in the correct column. Listen, repeat and check your answers.

their	thirsty	thank	that	both
birthday	thirty	they	bath	although
teeth	Thursday	weather	mouth	thousand

/ð/	/θ/
their	*thirsty*

3 🎧 Listen to these sentences and repeat them.

a They're both thirsty on Thursdays.
b I think his birthday is on the fourth Thursday of the month.
c The weather is better in the north these days.
d This thing is worth one thousand and thirteen pounds.
e Their mother had healthy teeth then.

4 Work with a partner. Try saying the sentences as fast as you can.

19.9

Read these letters on a problem page in a magazine. Write the correct form of the verb in brackets. Use either *to* or *-ing*.

Do you have a problem? Write to Tina and she'll help you find an answer.

Dear Tina,
I'm 17 and my sister is 14 and she's really annoying. When my friends come round to my house and we want (a) *to go* (go) to my room and be on our own, she expects (b) .... (be) with us and she refuses (c) .... (go) away when I ask her. She always promises (d) .... (sit) quietly but she loves (e) .... (be) the centre of attention. She always spoils everything. Why doesn't she understand that I prefer (f) .... (be) with my friends without her?
David

Dear Tina,
I have two children aged 14 and 16 and I work full-time. When I get home from work I need (g) .... (sit) down and relax for half an hour. I'm interested in (h) .... (hear) about their day and I don't mind (i) .... (help) them with their homework, but as soon as I come through the door I have to start (j) .... (cook). Then I do the ironing and tidy up the mess. They

really must learn (k) .... (help) and look after themselves but I don't like (l) .... (get) angry with them all the time. I do love them both but I'm fed up with (m) .... (do) everything for them. How can I tell them so they understand?
Joanna

Dear Tina,
My brother and I are twins. We always got on very well until we left school last year. We enjoyed (n) .... (do) the same kinds of things – music, sport, and we had the same friends. But my brother's now at university and lives in a hall of residence and I have continued (o) .... (live) at home. I really look forward to (p) .... (see) him at weekends when we arrange (q) .... (meet). But he often decides (r) .... (do) something different with his new friends and isn't interested in (s) .... (see) me. What shall I do? I'm not very good at (t) .... (say) how I feel about things so he probably doesn't know.
Martin

19.10

1 Read the magazine's answer to one of the problems. Do you agree with it?

2 Work in a group. Write the answer to one of the other problems. Read your answer to the class. Do other students agree with you?

> Dear Martin,
> You should try to have a group of friends of your own so you are busy sometimes too. Why don't you join a sports club and make some new friends or ask some of your old friends to go out with you? You ought to tell your brother how you feel and explain that he shouldn't cancel an arrangement he has made with you. I'm sure he wants to see you too but he is busier than you are. You'd better learn to do things without your brother because you both have your own separate lives now.
> Good luck.
> *Tina*

19.11 ACTIVITY

Look at this family tree. All the names are missing. You are a member of the family. Your teacher will give you a card telling you who you are. Ask other students who they are and write the names in the correct place on the family tree. Fill in these names on the family tree.

Female: Julia   Francesca   Alexandra   Sophie
Male: Simon   Tom   Sam   Robert   John   Ben   Paul   Jack

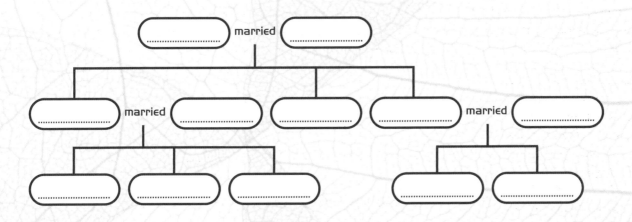

Verbs followed by *to*
to agree, to arrange, to decide, to expect, to hope, to learn, to need, to offer, to plan, to promise, to refuse, to seem, to try, to want, would like

Verbs and other words followed by *-ing*
to enjoy, to finish, to like, to look forward to, to love, to prefer, to stop, not mind

to be afraid of, to be fed up with, to be good at, to be interested in

Verbs followed by *to* or *-ing*
to begin, to continue, to start

make and let
They **made** me go to bed at 9 pm.
They **let** me ride my bicycle in the street.

Agreeing and disagreeing
We agree that ...
We don't agree that ...
It's true that ...
It's not true that ...

Giving your opinion
We think ...
In our opinion, ...

Giving advice
You **ought to** make some friends.

Vocabulary
attention brother-in-law disadvantage family tree half-sister hall of residence   leader   nephew   niece   sense of humour stepmother   uncle

artistic   clever   divorced   hard-working   jealous   next door remarried   separate   spoilt

to cancel   to do the ironing   to expect   to fail   to grow up to keep a rule   to look after   to solve an argument

LANGUAGE SUMMARY

Exam folder 19

Reading Part 5

> In this part of the exam, you have to choose the correct word to go in each space in a text.

CHECK!

a What will you do before you look at the questions?
b Which is the example?
c Before you choose your answer, what will you do?
d If you don't know the answer, what will you do?
e Where will you mark your answers?

1 Here are some words which are often tested in this part of the exam.
Choose the correct answer, A, B, C or D.

1 Only a .... people were able to come to the concert.

   A few   **B** couple   **C** lot   **D** several

2 We .... that our house had once been a hotel.

   A reported   **B** invented   **C** discovered   **D** reminded

3 The journey to Bristol .... two hours longer than usual.

   A spent   **B** took   **C** passed   **D** made

4 This desk is narrower .... my old one and the computer doesn't fit very well on it.

   A as   **B** than   **C** from   **D** to

5 She .... to wear glasses – she really can't see well enough to drive.

   A should   **B** can   **C** must   **D** ought

6 They .... off two hours earlier than usual to drive to Manchester because of the fog.

   A got   **B** took   **C** set   **D** put

7 While her brother was .... school Sarah used his computer.

   A to   **B** by   **C** on   **D** at

8 I .... walking when the weather is fine.

   A agree   **B** love   **C** want   **D** decide

2 Look at this photograph and the title of the text opposite.
What are you going to read about?

3 Do the exam task.

- Read the text and choose the correct word for each space.
- For each question, circle the letter next to the correct word – A, B, C or D.

FATHERS AND SONS

Harry Redknapp and Frank Lampard played football together for West Ham football club **(0)** ....*A*............ the 1960s. They **(1)** .... best friends and married two sisters so their sons, Frank Lampard junior and Jamie Redknapp, are **(2)** .... The boys' fathers used to take them to the football field after school and make them **(3)** .... All the hard work meant that both boys became very good **(4)** .... playing football and both have played for England like their fathers. Harry and Frank **(5)** .... playing football for West Ham in the 1980s. However, they didn't leave the club. Later, Harry became the manager of West Ham and Frank senior became assistant manager. Frank junior **(6)** .... them and played for West Ham **(7)** .... Jamie went to the other side of the country and played for Liverpool. Jamie and Frank are friends just like their fathers and **(8)** .... spending time together when they can. But they aren't married to two sisters. Jamie's wife is **(9)** .... pop star who hasn't got **(10)** .... sisters.

0	**A** during	**B** on	**C** by	**D** for
1	**A** had	**B** did	**C** were	**D** went
2	**A** cousins	**B** nephews	**C** brothers-in-law	**D** uncles
3	**A** trained	**B** train	**C** training	**D** trains
4	**A** at	**B** to	**C** with	**D** on
5	**A** continued	**B** stopped	**C** began	**D** missed
6	**A** attended	**B** added	**C** shared	**D** joined
7	**A** so	**B** but	**C** because	**D** also
8	**A** enjoy	**B** want	**C** decide	**D** agree
9	**A** the	**B** one	**C** a	**D** that
10	**A** some	**B** no	**C** few	**D** any

Exam folder vocabulary
to discover   to fit   to invent   to put off   to take off
assistant

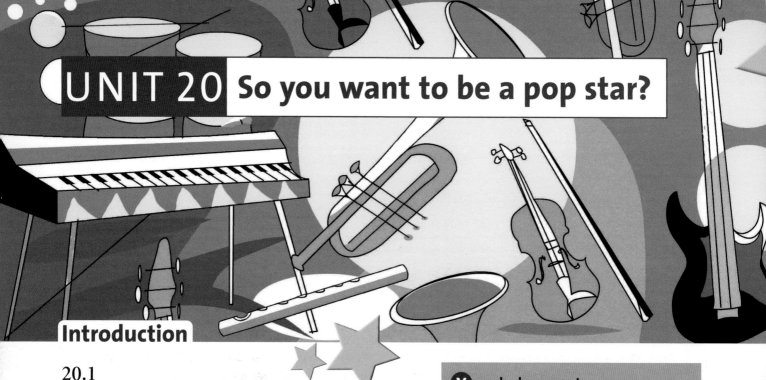

UNIT 20 So you want to be a pop star?

Introduction

20.1

1 🎧 Listen to six different musical instruments and say what they are. Use the pictures above to help you.

a ....   b ....   c ....
d ....   e ....   f ....

2 Do you play an instrument? What instrument would you like to play? Do you sing?

3 🎧 Listen to the different musical instruments again and compare them. You can use the following words:

fast/slow   loud/quiet
happy/sad/cheerful   beautiful
boring/dull/exciting/crazy   modern/traditional

EXAMPLE: *The trumpet was the loudest.*
The violin sounded sadder than the drums.

4 Which instruments might you hear in a classical concert, a jazz concert and a rock concert?

5 What kind of music do you like listening to?

20.2

The person who plays a guitar is a guitarist. What do we call people who play the piano, the violin, the drums and the trumpet? Add *er, or, r* or *ist* to these words to make the names of jobs.

act *actor*	employ	photograph
art	farm	report
dance	journal	teach
direct	manage	
dive	novel	

Vocabulary spot

We often add *er, or* or *r* to nouns or verbs to make a word which is a job. Sometimes we add *ist*. Keep a list of the different jobs you learn. Add these to the jobs you learnt in Unit 3.

Reading

20.3

1 A TV station has had a competition to find a new pop band. The judges had to choose one of the bands below to go into the final. Look at the notes they made when they were watching the bands. Quickly read what they said. Match the band to their picture.

2 Which bands do you think came first, second, third and fourth? You will find out later.

Texas Team

Mara, the singer, sang more confidently than the other singers but she wasn't always in tune. The dancing was OK. They danced less professionally than the other bands but they made a lot of effort so it was exciting to watch. The violinist didn't play as loudly as the other musicians so we couldn't tell how good he was – the drums and the guitar were very loud but quite good.

Third Avenue

The guitarist, Jason, played extremely well – he played much better than the guitarists in the other bands. In fact, he's the best young guitarist I've heard for a long time. They didn't dance as well as the other bands and the drummer needs a lot of practice. The singer didn't look very happy. That was a shame because he's got a good voice. The keyboard player was quite good.

Eastside

They are excellent dancers, especially Shane. Every step was perfect but their music wasn't as good as their dancing. The lead guitarist played everything too loudly and they didn't have a bass guitar or any drums. The main singer was quite good but she didn't sing as well as the others we heard. We couldn't hear the keyboard player.

The Storm

They enjoyed performing. The singer sang beautifully. The songs were much more traditional than the ones the other bands sang but they performed them perfectly. The two guitarists sounded very good. Their dancing was quite good too. The drummer played much more quietly than the drummers in the other bands but she did well.

Language focus

20.4

1 Read the judges' notes again and answer these questions, choosing one of the bands.

    a Which drummer played loudly?
      Texas Team
    b Which drummer played badly?
    c Which violinist played more quietly than the others in the band?
    d Which band sang the most beautifully?
    e Which band danced the best?
    f Which band danced the worst?
    g Which band played better than all the others?

2 Now look at the judges' notes about Texas Team. Underline in the text the answers to these questions.

    a How did Mara sing?
    b How did Texas Team dance?
    c How did the violinist in Texas Team play?

3 Copy the sentences you have underlined and then write them in two different ways.

    a Mara sang more confidently ....*than the other singers.*
      The other singers sang less ....
      The other singers didn't sing ....
    b Texas Team danced less professionally ....
      Texas Team didn't ....
      The other bands danced ....
    c The violinist in Texas Team didn't play ....
      The ....
      The ....

4 Now write sentences to compare these people.

    a The Storm's drummer with the other drummers.
    b Jason and the other guitarists.
    c The Eastside singer with the other singers.

20.5

1 🎧 The judges announce the winner to go through to the final. Listen to their decision. Who came first, second, third and fourth? Did you guess correctly?

2 🎧 Listen again to the judge's speech and complete the spaces in these sentences.

    a The violinist played ....*so quietly*.... that we couldn't hear him.
    b They are .... they should enter for a dance competition.
    c The singer looked .... we thought maybe he didn't want to win!
    d The singer had .... that we had to give them first place.

3 Make six sentences from this table. Write them down.

a They danced so	excited	(that)	they were jumping up and down.
b The fans were so	well		I wanted to watch them for ever.
c The concert was in such	good seats		we couldn't hear the band.
d The seats were so	a small room		there wasn't space for everyone.
e The fans made such	expensive		we could see very well.
f We had such	a terrible noise		we couldn't afford to go.

    EXAMPLE: *They danced so well (that) I wanted to watch them for ever.*

4 Look at the recording script. What does the judge say to the people who won and to the people who didn't win? Underline the expressions he uses.

20.6

🎧 The winner goes through to the final with two other bands.
Listen to the bands who play in the final. You have to make a decision on who comes first, second and third. Write some notes.

20.7 **PRONUNCIATION**

1 🎧 Listen to some words and write them down. If you can think of more than one way to spell the word, write them both down.

2 Write the words you heard in these pairs of sentences.

    a The best band ....*won*.... the competition.
        Only ....*one*.... group can win.
    b .... do the winning band come from?
        What shall I .... tonight?
    c Come ....
        I can't .... the violinist.
    d I really like .... music.
        The winning band is over ....

    e I swam in the ....
        Can you .... that boat over there?
    f They .... like to win.
        My desk is made of ....
    g Their .... is called Harry.
        The .... is shining.
    h .... mother is 50 tomorrow.
        The bus comes once an ....

20.8

1 Here is an interview with the band which won. Read it through quickly. Then complete the spaces with the words in the box below.

| although | as | as soon as | because | but | either | or | ~~so~~ | so |

How did you feel when you knew you'd won?

Mark: We were really surprised. We'd heard all the groups (a) .... we knew they were brilliant.

Michelle: I cried. I'd really hoped to win (b) .... I still couldn't believe it.

Do you all get on well?

Anika: Yes (c) .... we have arguments like any band, we like doing the same things and we care about each other. We've been together for two years now (d) .... we know each other really well.

Tanya: I hope we'll be together forever.

Michelle: Yes, we go out together in the evenings (e) .... we like doing the same things.

What are you all going to do now?

Jamie: Well, (f) .... we've won the whole competition, we're going to appear on the *Pop in the Park* programme on Saturday.

Anika: And then we're going to record a CD (g) .... we can.

Mark: After this interview, I'm (h) .... going to go out dancing (i) .... lie on the sofa. I can't decide.

2 The band were asked another question. Join their sentences together using the words in the box. Use each word once only.

| because | ~~but~~ | although | or | so |

> **What do you do in your spare time?**

Jamie: I play football a lot. I won't have much time to do that in future.

I play football a lot but I won't have much time to do that in future.

Michelle: I try to go to the gym three times a week. I like to keep fit.

Anika: I go shopping. I go swimming.

Mark: I go racing on my motorbike. I'm not very good at it.

Tanya: I used to go ice-skating every week until I hurt my back. I can't do that any more.

20.9 ACTIVITY

1 Write five questions about pop music (or another kind of music) and give them to your teacher with the answers.

2 Work in teams and answer as many questions as you can.

Comparison of adverbs

loudly	more loudly	(the) most loudly
well	better	(the) best
badly	worse	(the) worst

Mara sang **more** confidently **than** the others.
The others did**n't** sing **as** confidently **as** Mara.
The others sang **less** confidently **than** Mara.
Mara sang (the) most confidently.

So and such

So + adjective or adverb

The singer's voice was **so beautiful** (that) .... (*adjective*)

The singer sang **so beautifully** (that) .... (*adverb*)

Such + noun (with or without adjective)

The fans made **such a noise** (that) .... (*singular noun*)

The singer had **such a beautiful voice** (that) .... (*adjective + singular noun*)
The singers had **such beautiful voices** (that) .... (*adjective + plural noun*)

Connectives

because, as, so, either ... or, or, although

Vocabulary

argument drum drummer effort employer farmer the final flute ice-skating instrument judge
lead/bass guitar keyboard musician novelist piano pianist shame voice violin violinist

to announce excellent professional(ly) spare (time) in tune well done bad luck never mind better luck next time

Exam folder 20

Listening Part 1

In this part of the exam, you listen to seven short recordings and decide which of three pictures answers the question. You hear the recording twice.

CHECK!

a What will you look at before you listen?
b What will you think about before you listen?
c What will you do if you can't answer a question the first time?
d What will you do if you can't answer a question the second time?
e How many times will you hear the recording?

🎧 Do the exam task.

- For each question, there are three pictures and a short recording.
- Choose the correct picture and put a tick (✓) in the box below it.

1 Where will they meet?

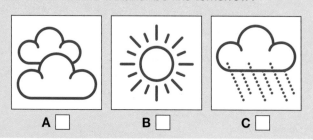

A ☐   B ☐   C ☐

2 What time will the boy catch the bus?

A ☐   B ☐   C ☐

3 Which band does Robert play in?

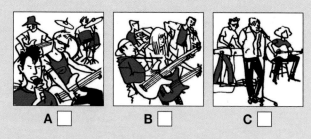

A ☐   B ☐   C ☐

4 Which is Lisa's new T-shirt?

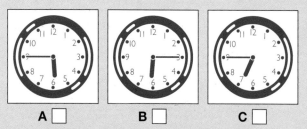

A ☐   B ☐   C ☐

5 What will the weather be like tomorrow?

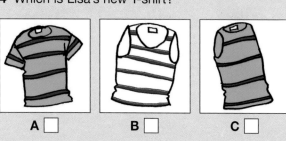

A ☐   B ☐   C ☐

Exam Advice

Sometimes you need to listen for a lot of information, sometimes only one small detail.

Writing folder

Writing Part 3

1 Read the exam question below and discuss what different kinds of stories you could write. For example, could it be a story about

a visit?
a crime?
a journey?
a party?
a ghost?
a spy?

- Your English teacher has asked you to write a story.
- Your story must begin with this sentence:

  It was dark when I entered the house.

- Write your **story** in about 100 words.

2 Work in a group. Think about one kind of story from Exercise 1. Talk about what will happen in your story.

3 Write down five words which you need to tell your story. Are there any important words which you need that you don't know? Can you change the story to use words you know? Tell other people what you decide.

4 How can you make a story more interesting? Look at this paragraph.

I went into town to buy a CD. There was a man outside the shop. He was worried. He had a piece of paper. He asked my name. I told him. He smiled. He gave me a prize.

5 Now look at the paragraph below.

Yesterday, I went into town to buy a CD. A tall man with a long white beard was standing outside the shop. He seemed rather worried and he was looking nervously at a piece of paper. When he saw me, he asked, 'What's your name?' Although I didn't know him, I told him. Suddenly he smiled. 'You've won a prize!' he announced, and gave me a large brown envelope with my name on it.

a What adjectives has the writer added? Mark them in a colour.
b What adverbs has the writer added? Mark them in a different colour.
c The writer has added the words which the man said. Mark them in a different colour.
d Underline the other changes the writer has made.

Exam Advice

- Don't tell a story which doesn't fit the sentence you are given.
- Don't plan to write a story which needs words you don't know.
- Do think about the words you will use.
- Do try to make your story interesting by using different kinds of words.

6 Choose one of the sentences below to begin a story. Don't write the story, but write some notes, including some useful words.

When I reached the station, the train had left.

I found the book on my way home from school.

We took the wrong turning off the main road.

When we arrived at the hotel, the owner looked very worried.

7 Work with a partner. Tell your story to your partner.

8 Write your story in about 100 words.

Writing folder vocabulary
ghost   main

Introduction

21.1

1 What is it like to be a millionaire? Do you know any? Perhaps you're one! What is different about the everyday life of very rich people?

2 Work in a group and read the section of this magazine article your teacher tells you to look at. Work together to make sure you understand it.

TEEN millionaires

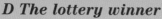

From time to time, we all dream about being very, very rich. But is it really great? Is the millionaire's life really one big party? We asked some real teen millionaires about their lives and came up with some surprising answers.

A The tennis star

Anna Kournikova was a millionaire in her mid-teens. By the age of 18 she'd been a professional tennis player for four years. She'd competed against top players all over the world. She'd also earned hundreds of thousands of dollars from advertising all sorts of things, including bras! But she didn't just spend her time playing tennis and looking pretty. A professional tennis player spends many hours a day keeping fit and working on her skills. She can't go out clubbing every night. She also spends weeks and sometimes months living away from home, in hotels or rented flats.

B The movie star

Have you seen the film *ET*? Remember that sweet little six-year-old, Drew Barrymore? She made a lot of money from that film. But did she enjoy being a film star? By her mid-teens, Drew had already made a lot of mistakes. She had serious problems and couldn't work. Luckily, she managed to get her life straight again, and now she's a grown-up film star. She's one of the most highly paid stars in Hollywood, but she doesn't let it spoil her life. She's learnt how to stay in control.

C The heiress

Athena Roussel is the granddaughter of the famous Greek shipping billionaire Aristotle Onassis. Most of us can't begin to imagine that amount of money. There is probably nothing we can think of that she can't afford. But can we imagine growing up like Athena? Her mum died when she was six. People have tried to kidnap her several times. She can never go anywhere without her bodyguard. Can you imagine it?

D The lottery winner

In the United Kingdom, you can buy tickets for the national lottery when you're 16. That's what Greg Stevens did. And he won £8,800,000! When you have that amount of money, there isn't much you can't buy. And Greg certainly enjoyed spending his money on all kinds of things. But there was one thing he couldn't buy. And that was the thing he wanted most. Can you guess what it was? (Answer at the bottom of the page.)

3 Tell other students about the person you read about. Listen to what they tell you about the other people. Which of them will have happy lives, do you think? Why?

He wanted to buy a season ticket for Manchester United football club, but although there are 35,000 season tickets, they are all sold years in advance.

Listening

21.2

1 🎧 You are going to hear four telephone conversations. Listen and decide which conversations are between friends and which are business conversations.

2 🎧 Listen again and put the conversations in the correct order.

1 .... 2 .... 3 .... 4 ....

21.3

🎧 Now listen to the first three conversations again in the correct order. Here are some of the things the people talk about. Write down the words they use.

Conversation 1

a Say who you are when you make a phone call.
 This is Ivan.
b Tell someone the reason why you are phoning.
c Ask for another person's phone number.
d Ask a friend to wait.

Conversation 2

a Ask to speak to someone.
b Tell a caller that the person they want cannot speak to them.
c Ask a caller to phone again at another time.

Conversation 3

a Ask for a caller's name.
b Ask a caller to wait.
c Ask a caller what he/she wants.

21.4 **PRONUNCIATION**

1 🎧 Listen to the end of Conversation 1 again. What is Mrs Lee's telephone number? How does Helen say it?

2 Say these telephone numbers, then write them in words.

a 357798   *three five double seven nine eight*
b 01223 277203
c 020 7584 3304
d 44 1273 509672

3 🎧 Listen and check your answers.

21.5

Complete the spaces in these telephone conversations with the expressions from the box.

| a friend   a friend of   ask for   I'm ringing |
| to ring you   may I speak   give me the number |
| hang on   one moment   how can I |
| how about   ~~this is~~   told me   meeting you |
| very kind of   would you like to   let me know |

1

Joe: Hello?
Sheila: Hello, Joe. (a) *This is* .... Sheila.
Joe: Oh, hi, Sheila. How are you?
Sheila: Fine, thanks. (b) .... to ask for your advice.
Joe: Oh, really?
Sheila: You told me (c) .... when I decide to buy a car.
Joe: Oh, of course.
Sheila: Well, can you (d) .... of that garage you use?
Joe: Oh, yes. I've got it here somewhere. (e) .... a minute. Here it is. It's 474747. (f) .... Barry Greenway. And say you're (g) .... of Joe's.
Sheila: OK. Thanks very much.
Joe: That's OK. (h) .... how you get on.

2

Secretary: Sunny Motors.
Sheila: (i) .... to Barry Greenway, please?
Secretary: May I have your name?
Sheila: Oh, yes. It's Sheila White. I'm (j) .... Joe's.
Secretary: (k) .... please.
Barry: Hello, Sheila? (l) .... help you?
Sheila: I need to buy a car. Joe (m) .... to contact you.
Barry: Oh, right. (n) .... come and see me? (o) .... this afternoon at half past four?
Sheila: Oh, thanks very much. It's (p) .... you to help me.
Barry: Not at all. I look forward to (q) ....

21.6

Practise these telephone conversations. Work in groups of four.

1 **Student A**
You want to buy a motorbike. Your friend knows a good motorbike shop.
Phone him/her and ask for the phone number.

Student B
You know someone who sells motorbikes. This is his business card.

STEVE ELLIS MOTORBIKES
new and second-hand

Phone 503498
for excellent service
and good prices

2 **Student A**
Phone the motorbike shop. Ask to speak to Steve Ellis. When you speak to him, explain why you are phoning him.

Student C
You are Steve's assistant. Answer the phone and pass the call to Steve.

Student D
You are Steve. Suggest a time to meet.

Language focus

21.7

1 You're a millionaire. Give orders to your butler for him to tell the other servants.

a chef *Tell the chef to make a chocolate cake.*
b maid ....
c accountant ....
d gardener ....
e secretary ....
f driver ....

2 Helen told Ivan to ring her. Look at the words she said. Now write the words these people said.

> You told me to ring you.

> Ring me.

a Ivan asked Mrs Lee to advise him.
   Please advise me.
b She asked the man to open the boot of his car.
c I asked the children to get out of the car.
d She told Tom not to eat all the cheese.
e I asked the students to work quietly.
f We told our friends not to wait for us.

Ⓥocabulary spot

Remember that *please* is an important word in English. People use it very often in everyday situations.

3 Report these requests and commands.

a Please help me, Julie. She asked Julie *to help her* ....
b Can you close the window please, Sara. She ....
c Don't forget your wallet, Michael. He told ....
d Phone your dad from the airport, Angela. Angela's mum ....
e Don't sit there, Maggie. He told ....
f Please don't use my shampoo, Mandy. She ....
g Phone the doctor immediately, Ronnie! He ....

21.8

1 Complete this table.

Subject	I	you		she			
Object			him		it	us	
Adjective							their
Pronoun	mine						

2 Ivan said to Helen: *A friend of yours is an accountant.*
This is another way of saying *One of your friends is an accountant.*
Rewrite these sentences using *a ..... of ..... .*

a One of my classmates is a dentist.
A classmate of mine is a dentist.

b One of Clara's aunts works in this office.
An aunt of Clara's works in this office.

c One of your classmates said you were ill.

d She saw one of her friends on television last week.

e Kamran's lucky because one of his cousins owns a hotel in London.

f One of Pedro's colleagues lives in our road.

g I didn't realise that one of their friends played football for England.

h I heard that one of my students met the Prime Minister last week.

i I believe one of our neighbours has won the lottery.

21.9 ACTIVITY

1 Group A: You are journalists. You are going to interview some teenage millionaires and write articles about them later. Discuss the questions you will ask.

Group B: You are teenage millionaires. Your teacher will give you each a different card which shows how you got your money. Think about your life. What do you do every day? What's good about your life and what's bad about it?

2 Work with students from the other group. The journalists now interview the millionaires and make notes.

3 Now work with another student, swapping roles.

4 Look at page 136. Write a short article about the millionaire you interviewed. Say how he/she got his/her money and describe some of the advantages and disadvantages of his/her life.

21.10

🎧 Helen has a message on her answering machine which plays when she is out. Listen to it again and write it down. Do you have a message like this on your phone? Write one for your phone in English.

Asking about language
What does X mean?
I don't quite understand Y.
Can you explain Z?

Telephone language
This is Ivan.
I'm ringing/calling/telephoning to …
Can you give me her (phone) number?
Hang on a minute.
I can't speak to you just now.
I'll call you back when I'm free.

May I have your name?
I'm afraid she isn't available this afternoon.
Can you call back tomorrow?

May I speak to Mrs Lee, please?
One moment, please.
How can I help you?

Possessive adjectives and pronouns
one of my friends   a friend of mine
one of Helen's friends   a friend of Helen's

Reporting requests and commands

Requests and commands	*Reported requests and commands*
Please help me (Helen).	He asked Helen/her to help him.
Can you wait in the car, please.	He asked me to wait in the car.
Please don't move the box (Ivan).	She asked Ivan/him not to move the box.
Phone me tonight, Lenny.	He told Lenny to phone him tonight.
Don't touch my desk.	She told me not to touch her desk.

Vocabulary

accountant   amount   billionaire   bodyguard   bra   gardener   maid   millionaire
season ticket   secretary   servants   service   skill

to call   to call back   to earn   to hang on   to kidnap   to make a phone call   to ring

by the age of   in advance   in control   second-hand

Exam folder 21

> In this part of the exam, you read a text and decide if ten sentences are correct or incorrect.

1 You have to decide if the words in the question mean the same as the words in the text. Complete the words in the expressions on the right so they match the expressions on the left.

a	our busiest day	the m _ _ _ people
b	reduced	pay l _ _ _
c	up to six	m _ _ _ _ _ _ of six
d	forbidden	not a _ _ _ _ _ _
e	beyond the park	out _ _ _ _ the park

2 The text opposite is about a shopping and leisure centre. Look at the sentences (1–10) in Exercise 4. What will you read about in the text?

3 Read the text quickly. As you read, underline the parts of the text which contain the answers to the questions.

Exam Advice

The questions are in the same order as the information in the text. Some parts of the text are not tested.

4 Read the question and the part of the text carefully.
Is each sentence correct or incorrect?
If it is correct, write A.
If it is not correct, write B.

1 The park stays open later than the shops every day in summer.
2 There are the most people at the centre on Fridays.
3 There is an information centre on the same floor as the cinema.
4 The nightclubs are next to the swimming pool.
5 Students pay less for afternoon performances at the cinema than evening performances.
6 The centre has its own hotel.
7 The maximum number of people in a boat is six.
8 It is forbidden to ride hired bicycles outside the park.
9 Each level of a car park has different coloured signs.
10 The bus journey from the railway station takes 15 minutes.

THE WESTGATE CENTRE

The Westgate Centre offers 200 shops, a swimming pool, restaurants, a bowling alley and two nightclubs as well as 30 acres of parkland with three lakes.

Opening hours

Shops	Mon–Fri	10 am–9 pm
	Sat	9 am–8 pm
	Sun	10 am–5 pm

Park	9 am–4.30 pm in winter
	9 am–7 pm in summer

We have thousands of visitors every day, our busiest day of the week being Friday. To avoid the crowds, come on a Monday or Tuesday.

Inside the centre

When you arrive, go to one of our information offices to get a map. There is one by the main bus stop and another at the bottom of the escalator which goes up to the cinema.

The shops are all on the ground floor and you will find everything from specialised furniture stores to clothes shops and department stores as well as restaurants, a bowling alley and a swimming pool. On the first floor above the pool you will find a 12-screen cinema and two nightclubs. If you wish, you can buy entrance tickets for any of these facilities except the nightclubs from the information centres. Before 5 pm entrance tickets to all facilities are reduced for students and the over-sixties.

If you wish to stay overnight, the information centre can give you a list of accommodation in the area, ranging from grand hotels to Bed and Breakfast accommodation.

Outside the centre

Make time to visit the 30 acres of parkland which surround the centre. Boats for up to six people can be hired and taken out onto one of the lakes for £12 an hour.

Bicycles can be hired every day for £6 an hour. There are 4 kms of paths but you are not allowed to take hired bicycles beyond the park.

Travel

The centre is located one mile from the M49. Just follow the signs from Junction 13. There is free parking for 10,000 cars and there are six car parks. Car parking spaces are never more than five minutes' walk away from an entrance. Remember where your car is parked by looking at the coloured signs – no car park uses the same colour and each level in the car parks is numbered.

It is just as easy to visit the centre by train. There is a rail service every 15 minutes from Central London. When you reach Barnwell station, jump on a number 19 bus to the centre. It's a five-minute journey and there's a bus every 15 minutes.

Exam folder vocabulary
bowling alley   department store   escalator
forbidden   leisure   maximum   reduced
to allow

UNIT 22 Strange but true?

Introduction

22.1

1 Look at the photographs on this page. Discuss what you think they could be. Which ones show real things? Which ones show tricks, in your opinion?

Use words like these:
It could be …
It might be …
It can't be …
It must be …
I think someone made it.
I don't think it's real.
It's a trick photograph/computer picture.

2 Have you ever seen something you couldn't explain, or do you know anyone who has? Tell the other students about it. Why do you think science fiction stories are so popular?

Reading

22.2

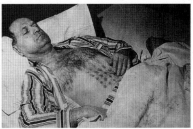

1 Look at the photographs. What do they show?

2 Read the reports in the magazine. Which ones match the photographs?

What did they say?!?

1 Mac Brazel had a farm in New Mexico, USA. One day in 1947, he found some strange silvery pieces of material in a field. Not far away a man called Grady Barnett found a large disc-shaped object which had crashed to the ground. They also found some bodies. Barnett and Brazel said that the bodies looked like humans but they were not humans.

The US army has a base at Roswell near Brazel's farm. Soldiers arrived at the farm. They ordered everyone to go away. They collected everything the people had seen. Later they announced that a weather balloon had crashed there. They showed journalists some material. They said it was part of a weather balloon.

Mac Brazel said that he had seen a different kind of material. He told the journalists that he did not believe the soldiers.

2 In early 1958, the Brazilian ship *Almirante Saldhana* was in the South Atlantic near Trinidade Island. Many of the crew said that on 16th January they had seen a strange UFO above the island. They said that it had had a ring around it like the planet Saturn. Although it moved away very quickly, a photographer on the ship had time to take a picture of it.

3 Canadian Stephen Michalak described what happened to him in 1967. He said he had gone to search for gold in a lake. Suddenly he saw two UFOs in the sky. He told people one of them had landed near him and he explained that he had approached it. Although it was very hot, he touched it. His shirt caught fire. For three weeks he was ill, with strange burns on his chest and stomach.

4 On 27th October, 1974, John and Elaine Avis and their children saw a UFO in Essex, in England. They said that they had been on their way home in foggy weather and their journey had taken much longer than usual. Later, John Avis said that he remembered entering the UFO. He reported that the aliens inside it had been two metres tall. He said that they had examined him like doctors.

5 Franck Fontaine told a lot of people that aliens had kidnapped him. Two of his friends said that on 6th November 1979, at Cergy-Pontoise in France, they had seen a light all round Franck's car and then Franck had disappeared. Franck said aliens had taken him to their spacecraft and he had woken up a week later in the middle of a field. He said that he had arranged a meeting with the aliens in August 1980. Two hundred people said they believed him and went to meet the aliens but they did not arrive.

3 Discuss the stories. Do you believe them? Can you explain any of them? Look at page 145 for some explanations.

Language focus

22.3

1 Look at the sentences in the direct speech column. Who said them?

Who?	Direct speech	Indirect speech
a *Barnett and Brazel*	The bodies look like humans.	*They said that* the bodies ....*looked*....... like humans.
b	A weather balloon crashed here.	*Later they announced* that a weather balloon *had crashed there*.
c	It's part of a weather balloon.	They said it .... part of a weather balloon.
d	I saw a different kind of material.	Mac Brazel said that he .... a different kind of material.
e	I don't believe the soldiers.	He told the journalists that he ....
f	On 16th January we saw a strange UFO.	Many of the crew said that on 16th January ....
g	It had a ring around it like the planet Saturn.	They said that it ....
h	I went to search for gold in a lake.	He said ....
i	One of them landed near me.	He told people ....
j	I approached it.	He explained that ....

2 Work with a partner. Look at the sentences in the direct speech column on page 143 again. Find the parts of the magazine article which report them and underline them. Copy the missing words into the spaces in the indirect speech column.

3 Now underline anything in the indirect speech column which is different from the direct speech column.

EXAMPLE: *The bodies look like humans.*
They said that the bodies looked like humans.

4 Look back at reports 4 and 5 in the magazine article. Write the sentences which report what people said on the right and the words they actually said on the left.

Direct speech	Indirect speech
We were on our way home.	They said that they had been on their way home.

5 Now underline the words which change.

22.4

1 Work with a partner. Tell each other what these people said. Use the present simple or the past simple. Write your answers in the spaces when you finish.

a He said he knew Robbie Williams.

> I know Robbie Williams.

b She said she worked in London.

> ....

c They told us they lived in New York.

> ....

d We explained that we didn't have any money.

> ....

e He told me he had visited Paris last year.

> ....

f She said she hadn't played volleyball last weekend.

> ....

2 Work with a partner.
Tell each other what these people said. Use the present simple or the present perfect. Write your answers in the spaces when you finish.

a I explained that I'd already had lunch.

> *I've already had lunch.*

b They told her they had lost the keys and didn't know what to do.

> ....

c He said he hadn't seen a UFO yet but he hoped to see one soon.

> ....

d She told me she had already met some aliens and that they spoke excellent English.

> ....

e I told him I'd never eaten Martian food before.

> ....

3 Report what these people said. Write your answers.

a
> I enjoy films about space travel.

He said *he enjoyed films about space travel.*

b
> I don't enjoy westerns.

She said ....

c
> We're both fans of Manchester United.

They said ....

d
> I haven't seen my brother for three weeks.

She said ....

e
> My mum made me a great birthday cake.

He said ....

f
> My friend didn't invite me to her party.

She said ....

22.5 PRONUNCIATION

1 Cross out the consonants which are silent in these words. Practise saying the words.

comb when honest

2 Work with a partner. How many words can you find in each sentence with a silent consonant? Mark the word. Who finishes first?

a Do you (know) (what) the (answer) is? *Three*
b The knives might be in the high cupboard.
c I've broken my wrist, my thumb, my knee and my foot.
d That foreigner could be a scientist.
e You need a bright light to write the receipt.
f Let's meet in half an hour.

3 Look at the words you found in Exercise 2. Are the silent consonants at the beginning, middle or end of the words? Write the words in the correct part of the table below. Cross out the silent letters. Are any letters always silent?

Beginning	Middle	End
know	what	high

4 🎧 Listen and repeat the sentences.

	Did you believe them? (see page 143)
1	Many years later Major Marcel, one of the soldiers, told journalists that the army had deceived people. Some people now say that the army was testing secret materials for spy planes.
2	There has been no explanation. Perhaps it was a trick of the light. Perhaps it was an alien spacecraft.
3	We do not know what really happened. Perhaps he was telling the truth!
4	Perhaps they got lost on the foggy roads. Some psychologists think that people remember dreams about UFOs and think they are real.
5	Later, Franck's friend said that it had been a joke.

22.6 ACTIVITY

1 Work with a partner.
Find out what other people think about UFOs. Ask as many people as possible about the statements in the Public Opinion Survey on page 201.

2 When you have finished, write a report. Use numbers (or percentages, if you like).

EXAMPLE:
We spoke to twenty people.
Five people said they believed in UFOs.
Eleven people said they weren't sure about UFOs.
OR
25% said they believed in UFOs.
55% said they weren't sure about UFOs.

22.7 ACTIVITY

Work in a group. Your teacher is a famous person. The first group to guess who he/she is wins the game.

a Your group sends one person to ask the teacher for a clue.
b That person goes back to the group and reports what the teacher said.

EXAMPLE: *She said she lived in the USA.*

c Then the group sends a different student for another clue.
d If your group thinks you know who the famous person is, you can write the name on a piece of paper and show it to the teacher. If you are wrong, your group must miss a turn of hearing the clues.

Reported speech

What people say ⟶	*Reporting what people said*
Present simple	*Past simple*
I see aliens quite often.	She said **she saw** aliens quite often.
I don't believe you.	He said **he didn't believe her.**
Present perfect	*Past perfect*
I've seen lots of aliens **here.**	She said **she'd (had) seen** lots of aliens **there.**
You haven't really seen them.	He said **she hadn't really** seen them.
Past simple	*Past perfect*
I saw some aliens last week.	She said **she'd (had) seen** some aliens last week.
We didn't see any.	They said **they hadn't seen** any.

Vocabulary

alien army base balloon button circle cloud crop object percentage possibility psychologist spacecraft survey trick UFO (Unidentified Flying Object)

to approach to believe (in) to catch fire to collect to deceive to examine to land to search

foggy round strange

Exam folder 22

Listening Part 4

In this part of the exam, you listen to a conversation between two people and decide whether six sentences are correct or incorrect. You hear the recording twice.

1 In this part of the exam, the speakers usually express opinions, beliefs and feelings. Look at the words in the box. Can you fit them into the sentences below?

> anxious astonished ~~certain~~
> cheerful cross embarrassed
> grateful unsure

a Are you absolutely _certain_ where Rebecca lives? You've never visited her before.

b We're rather .... about our cat. We haven't seen him for two days.

c Lennox was .... when he saw me at school. He thought I was away on holiday.

d They wanted to give her a present, but were .... what to buy.

e How do you stay so .... when everyone else is sad?

f Giles was .... when he met his boss at the football match. He had told her he was ill.

g I'm very .... for all your help. You've been very kind.

h I'm very .... with my brother because he borrowed my new CD without asking.

2 Can you match each statement on the left with the one on the right which means the same?

a I approve of that.
b I respect you.
c I disagree with you.
d I doubt whether that will happen.
e I expect something to happen.
f I dislike that.
g I intend to do that.
h I prefer one thing to another.

1 I'm not sure that something will happen.
2 I have a good opinion of you.
3 I like this better than that.
4 I don't like that.
5 That's a good idea.
6 I don't agree with your idea.
7 I think something will probably happen.
8 I plan to do that.

3 Before you listen, look at the instructions for the exam task. What do you learn about the people and their conversation?

- You will hear a conversation between a girl, Dina, and a boy, Jason, about Dina's sister, Jessica.

Exam Advice

Listen carefully to what both speakers say. They will give their opinions and agree or disagree with each other.

4 🎧 Now do this exam task.

- Look at the six sentences for this part.
- You will hear a conversation between a girl, Dina, and a boy, Jason, about Dina's sister, Jessica.
- Decide if each sentence is correct or incorrect.
- If it is correct, put a tick (✓) in the box under A for YES. If it is not correct, put a tick (✓) in the box under B for NO.

		A YES	B NO
1	Jason is surprised to see Dina near his work.	☐	☐
2	Dina is going on holiday soon.	☐	☐
3	Jason respects Jessica's attitude to work.	☐	☐
4	Dina feels sorry for Jessica.	☐	☐
5	Dina believes Jessica saw a ghost.	☐	☐
6	Jason intends to visit Jessica soon.	☐	☐

Writing folder

Writing Part 1

- Here are some sentences about going to a cinema.
- For each question, complete the second sentence so that it means the same as the first, **using no more than three words**.

1 The Regent Cinema is near my house.
The Regent Cinema is not _far from_ my house.

2 The cinema has seven screens.
There _____ seven screens in the cinema.

3 I go there every Saturday with my friend.
I go there _____ Saturdays with my friend.

4 We pay £5 each for the tickets.
The tickets _____ £5 each.

5 Last week my brother said he wanted to come with us.
Last week my brother said, 'I _____ to come with you.'

6 My sister is too young to come with us.
My sister isn't _____ to come with us.

7 The film was so long that I fell asleep.
It was such _____ that I fell asleep.

8 I found the film boring.
I was _____ by the film.

9 The title of the film was *The Last Man*.
The film was _____ *The Last Man*.

10 My brother said it was the worst film he'd ever seen.
My brother said, '_____ the worst film I've ever seen.'

Exam folder vocabulary
attitude
to approve   to disappear   to doubt   to intend   to respect
anxious   grateful

Exam Advice

The sentences are all about one topic.

UNIT 23 Best friends?

Introduction

23.1

1 We can't choose our family but we can choose our friends.
   Look at the following list. Which of these are important to you?
   Mark this list 1–10 (1 is the most important, 10 is the least important).

   A best friend should:
   - be honest.
   - be fun to be with.
   - like the same music as me.
   - like my other friends.
   - live near me.
   - have lots of money.
   - share my sense of humour.
   - be kind when I'm unhappy.
   - support the same football team as me.
   - like doing the same things as me.

2 Work in a group. Compare your answers.
   What did most people put first, second
   and third? What wasn't important?

3 Can your group think of other things
   you would like to add to the list?

4 Look at the photographs of people on
   this page. Which person would you like
   to make friends with? Think about why.

5 Which person in the photographs is
   the most popular? Why?

Ⓥocabulary spot

Write expressions with the same word together.

```
                    to be friends
                         ↑
to make friends ← [ friend ] → best friends
                         ↓
                    friendship
```

Listening

23.2

1 🎧 Listen to three conversations between people who have just met. Look at these questions and choose pair 1, pair 2 or pair 3. Put a tick (✓) in the correct box.

Which pair do you think:	1	2	3
will probably become friends?			
might become friends?			
won't get on with each other?			

2 🎧 Listen again. Decide if these statements are true or false.

Pair 1 (Monica and Alex)

a Alex has been to parties at the college before. *true*

b Monica and Alex agree about the music at the party.

c Alex apologises for what he says about the people at the party.

d In the end, Monica gets tired of talking to Alex.

Pair 2 (Francis and Neil)

e Francis finds the work in the restaurant easier than on the building site.

f Francis and Neil have similar interests to the other waiters.

g Francis and Neil support the same football team.

h Francis and Neil arrange to go to the match together.

Pair 3 (Carla and Kate)

i Peter told Carla about Kate's flat.

j There will be three people living in the flat.

k Carla plays more than one musical instrument.

l Kate and Carla agree that they are both untidy.

Language focus

23.3

1 Look at these pairs of sentences. Join each pair using *who* or *which* to make one new sentence.

a He's got a friend. He sometimes gets free tickets.
He's got a friend who sometimes gets free tickets.

b There's a match on Wednesday evening. It'll be really good.
There's a match on Wednesday evening which will be really good.

c There are some customers over there. They're waiting for a table.

d There's one other person. He's studying biology.

e I play an electric guitar. It has a volume control.

f I saw a flat. It's very near the university.

2 Now choose *who* or *which* for each of these sentences.

a They usually play the kind of music **who/which** I hate.
They usually play the kind of music which I hate.

b What about that girl **who/which** I saw you with just now?

c I'll introduce you to some people **who/which** you'll like.

d I'm just a bit nervous of people **who/which** I don't know.

e It's very different from the job **who/which** I had last summer.

3 Answer these questions.

a Can you put *that* instead of *who/which* in the sentences in Exercise 1? What about in the sentences in Exercise 2?

b In which sentences can you leave out *who* and *which*?

4 When do we use *where* and *whose* to join two sentences? Put *where* or *whose* in these spaces.

EXAMPLE: *Let's go over there. It's less crowded.*
Let's go over there where it's less crowded.
I have a friend. Her hobby is rock climbing.
I have a friend whose hobby is rock climbing.

a I want to find a place *where* I can have parties.

b I know a café .... you can get really good ice cream.

c I work in a restaurant .... owner is Italian.

d That's the disco .... I lost my wallet.

e I met a girl .... mother used to be my teacher.

23.4

1 Read this poem which was on a friendship website. It was written by a girl. Do you think she was writing about another girl or a boy?

2 What is the poem about? What has happened? Has this ever happened to you?

3 Other people wrote to the website to give their opinions about the poem. Complete the spaces with *who*, *which* or *whose*.

   a I had a friend ...*who*... did this to me but I forgave him.

   b I often say things .... I think are a joke but my friend doesn't.

   c I have a friend .... jokes always upset me.

   d I don't think before I speak so I often say things .... upset my friends.

   e This poem was written by someone .... friend is angry.

   f I have a friend .... I can't trust any more.

   g This poem reminded me of something .... happened to me.

   h I had a friend .... was very bossy and I got tired of him.

4 In which sentences can you put *that*? Which sentences need nothing in the space?

5 Now write some sentences using *who*, *which*, *whose* or *where*.

   I have a friend ...
   I like music ...
   I enjoy watching films ...
   I live in a town ...

Grammar spot

Try to learn each adjective with its preposition(s). Write them in your notebook.

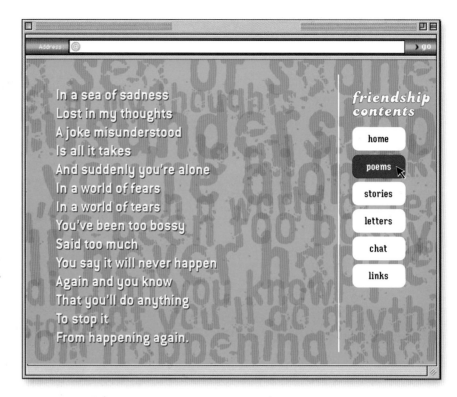

In a sea of sadness
Lost in my thoughts
A joke misunderstood
Is all it takes
And suddenly you're alone
In a world of fears
In a world of tears
You've been too bossy
Said too much
You say it will never happen
Again and you know
That you'll do anything
To stop it
From happening again.

friendship contents

home
poems
stories
letters
chat
links

23.5 ACTIVITY

Work in a group. Your teacher will give your group a list of nouns which all begin with the same letter. Write a definition for each of the nouns and then pass them to another group. Do not write the nouns. The other group will guess the nouns and decide which letter they all begin with.

EXAMPLE: *[artist] someone who paints pictures*
              [airport] a place where you catch a plane
              [apple] something which is red or green and grows on trees

23.6

Match the beginnings and endings of these sentences from the conversations. Which preposition (e.g. *of*, *from*, *about*) follows which word?

EXAMPLE: *It's kind of Samantha to ask me.*

a It's kind	**of** interesting people.
b I'll never get tired	**from** the job I had last summer.
c I'm not very keen	**of** people I don't know.
d This room is full	**of** listening to it.
e I'm nervous	**about** the match.
f It's very different	**of** Samantha to ask me.
g They aren't really interested	**at** it.
h I'm quite excited	**for** inviting me to live with you.
i I'm quite good	**with** me.
j My parents are always getting angry	**on** the music.
k Thank you	**in** the same kind of things as students.

23.7 PRONUNCIATION

1 Look at the expressions below. When do we join a word to the word which follows when we speak?

kind_of you
full_of people
nervous_of people
tired_of school
good_at football
bad_at history
fed_up with school
keen_on music
interested_in people

2 🎧 Listen and repeat.

3 Now look at these sentences. Mark all the words which you will join when you say the sentences.

a It's kind_of Samantha.
b This room is full of interesting people.
c I'm quite good at it.
d She's bad at playing the guitar.
e I'm not very keen on this kind of music.
f I'll never get tired of this song.
g I'm not interested in talking.

4 🎧 Listen and repeat.

23.8

Write some sentences. Use the words in the table below.

EXAMPLE: *I'm not keen on going to classical concerts.*
My mum gets tired of tidying everyone's rooms.

I My best friend My parents Some of my classmates Young children Men Women My teacher My mum	am/is/are get(s)	(not)	keen tired nervous bad excited good angry afraid interested fed up	on of at about in with	....

23.9

1 Read these quotations from a website. Do you agree with them?

2 Write your own quotation.

A real friend is someone who ...

The Friendship Page

'Everyone is a friend until they prove they aren't.'

'A true friend is someone who you can trust with your secrets.'

'The secret to friendship is being good at listening.'

'Best friends of the same sex are better than best friends of the opposite sex.'

'One true friend is better than 100 relatives.'

'A real friend is someone who will tell you when you have spinach stuck in your teeth.'

Subject relative clauses
I saw a **flat**. **It** is very near the university.
I saw a flat **which/that** is very near the university. (**which** = a thing)
There are some **customers**. **They** are waiting.
There are some customers **who/that** are waiting. (**who** = person)

Object relative clauses
I saw a **flat**. I liked **it**.
I saw a flat **which/that** I liked. OR I saw a flat I liked. (NOT a flat which I liked it)
We met a **girl**. We knew **her**.
We met a girl **who/that** we knew. OR We met a girl we knew. (NOT a girl who we knew her)

Relative clauses with where and whose
I want to find a place **where** I can have parties.
Kate is the person **whose** flat I share.

Adjectives followed by prepositions
kind **of** you   full **of** people   angry **with** my friend

Adjectives followed by prepositions (and -ing)
good/bad **at** (playing) tennis
nervous **of** (talking to) people
different **from** (doing) the last job
keen **on** (playing) football
tired **of** (playing) the guitar
sorry **for/about** (hurting) my friend
interested **in** (visiting) Japan
pleased/angry/happy/sad/nervous/excited **about** (hearing) the news
fed up **with** (living with) my parents
Also: thank you **for** (giving me) this present

Introducing people
Alex, I'd like you to meet Monica./Alex, meet Monica.
Monica, this is Alex. Alex, this is Monica.
Pleased to meet you. / Hi.

Vocabulary
building site   friendship   quotation   supporter   type   volume
volume control
to chat   to support (a football team)   to trust   to prove   to upset
bossy   honest

Exam folder 23

Reading Part 1

In this part of the exam, you look at five short texts. There are three possible explanations – A, B or C. You have to decide which one says the same as the text.

CHECK!

a What kind of texts will you read?
b What kinds of words are sometimes missing from signs?
c What should you do if you don't know the answer?

Exam Advice

Check that the answer you choose means exactly the same as the text.

- Look at the text in each question.
- What does it say?
- Mark the letter next to the correct explanation – A, B or C.

1

> Dear Mariana,
> The hotel is wonderful – just as you described it. Thank you for recommending it. We've already booked for next year! Karin

A Mariana has visited the hotel Karin is staying in.
B Karin has stayed in the hotel before.
C Karin and Mariana are going to the hotel together next year.

2

> ## BUY TWO FILMS AND GET ONE FREE

A Films are only sold in packs of three.
B You get a discount when you buy two films.
C You get three films for the price of two.

3

> Jan
> If Peter rings, tell him I have posted the book to him because I didn't have time to go to his house. Michael

A Jan should tell Peter to bring the book back.
B Michael has gone to Peter's house.
C Peter will receive the book in the post.

4

> Carlos
> We have to be at college by 9 tomorrow instead of 9.15. I'll pick you up by the crossroads as usual, but at 8.30. Jack

Jack is asking Carlos to
A meet him earlier than usual.
B take him to college by car.
C see him in a different place from usual.

5

> MAKE SURE THIS DOOR IS SHUT WHEN YOU LEAVE THE BUILDING

A Use another exit when this door is shut.
B Do not leave this door open when you go out.
C This door is the only exit from this building.

Speaking Part 2

In this part of the exam, you are given some pictures. You work in pairs and try to arrive at a decision together about a situation which the examiner describes to you.

1 You are going to spend the day in the city centre with another student. You will travel there by bus. Look at these pictures. They show the things you want to do.

2 Think about these questions.

    a What do you want to buy?
    b Which shops will you visit?
    c Are any of the things you need to buy heavy?
    d When will you go to the bank?
    e When will you go to the café?

3 Write down different ways of:

    a making suggestions
    b agreeing and disagreeing
    c giving your opinion

4 Work with a partner and talk about where you need to go and in which order. You have three minutes to agree.

Exam Advice

Try to agree with your partner but don't worry if you don't.

UNIT 24 I've got an idea

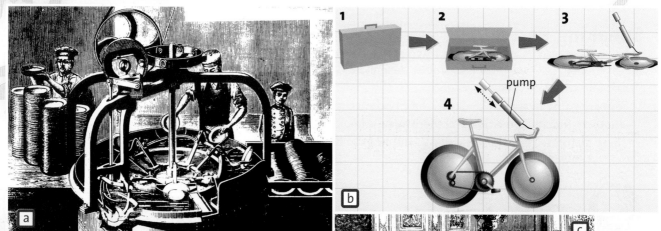

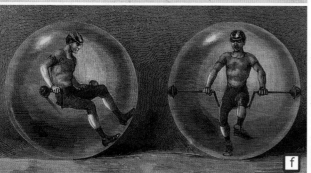

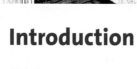

Introduction

24.1

1 Look at the pictures of inventions. Can you guess what they are used for?

2 🎧 Listen to someone talking about two of the inventions. Which ones are they? What are they used for? Were you right?

3 Work with a partner to write a description of one of the inventions (or another one you can think of) and read it out to the class. Use the language in the box to help you. Can other students guess what it is?

It's round/square.	It's a kind of ...	It's like a ...
It's used for ...-ing.	It's made of ...	It must be ...
It can't be ...	It might be ...	It could be ...

4 Which of these inventions have been successful?

5 What recent inventions have you heard or read about? Which invention from the last hundred years is the most important in your life?

Reading

24.2

1 Here are three paragraphs which begin three
different texts about inventions. Read the
first text opposite. What is it about?

2 Now read the other two texts.
Which inventions are they about?

Charles D. Seeberger's invention

Moving chains were used by people in
ancient Egypt to transport water in and
out of the fields. But it wasn't until the 1890s
that moving stairs were invented by Charles D.
Seeberger. His stairs could transport people.

3 Can you find some verbs in the past passive
in the texts above? Underline them.

24.3

1 Each text has three more paragraphs but they are mixed
up. Work in a group: Ben and Jerry, Charles D. Seeberger
or Hubert Cecil Booth. Find the three paragraphs which
finish your text. Then put them in the correct order.

a The station hired a man who had a wooden leg to
demonstrate how easy it was to use the escalator. Some
people went up and down several times before going to catch
their train just because they enjoyed the experience. After
that, escalators were put in shops and other public buildings.

b Because of this, local restaurants and shops asked them to
make ice cream and deliver it. A year after the parlour
opened, a 'free ice cream cone' day was held as a thank you
to customers.

c People complained about the number of stairs they had to
climb up and down so the first escalator was opened in
London in an underground station on 4 October 1911. Notices
were displayed at the top and bottom of the escalator: 'Please
do not sit on the moving stairs. Step off with the left foot first.'

d He had a better idea. He was in a restaurant one day and he
decided to demonstrate. He placed a handkerchief over the
back of his seat, put his lips to it and the dirt was sucked
into the handkerchief. A ring of black spots appeared on the
handkerchief.

e Now a worldwide business, the company produces new
flavours all the time. Each flavour is tested for at least six
months before it is sold in shops. Sometimes the company
holds competitions and asks for suggestions. About 275,000
tourists visit the factory each year.

Ben and Jerry's invention

Ben and Jerry's famous products are sold in a range of
delicious flavours with unusual names such as Rainforest
Crunch and Peanut Butter Cup. Two childhood friends, Ben
Cohen and Jerry Greenfield, started the company. They had
the idea of working together when they were at school and
The Homemade Ice Cream Parlour was opened by Ben and Jerry
in May 1978.

Hubert Cecil Booth's invention

One day Hubert Cecil Booth went to see an inventor
demonstrate his new dust-removing machine at a London
railway station. A huge air blower was placed over the open
door of a train. The idea was to blow dirt into a bag which was
put over another door. A lot of dust was pushed up into the air
but then came down again inside the train instead of inside the
bag. Booth didn't think it was a very good idea.

f It was so noisy that it frightened horses in the streets. After
a while, rich people had their houses cleaned by the machine
and the King and Queen invited Booth to Buckingham Palace
to demonstrate it.

g They made the ice cream themselves and each flavour was
given a crazy name. People could listen to live music while
they ate ice cream and the parlour became very popular.

h He was convinced this was the answer so a machine was
built. The first model was named 'The Puffing Billy' and a
whole team of men was needed to operate it. One man
worked the machine while another man guided a long hose
inside offices or houses to clean them.

i The first escalators were built in shops and railway stations in
the USA at the end of the nineteenth century. More and more
people were using the underground trains in Britain especially
after clean electric trains replaced dirty steam trains in 1906.

2 Change groups so there is someone who has
read each text in your group. Ask the other
people in your group what their text is about.

EXAMPLE: *What was your invention? How did the
idea start? What happened next? Was it successful?*

They tell you the order they chose. Read their
texts to check if they were right. Underline any
vocabulary you don't know and ask for their
help when you have finished.

3 Find some verbs in the past passive in your text.
Underline them.

24.4

Put the words below under the correct heading.

dust   a flavour   a public building
to transport   to clean   a cone   a machine
a factory   moving stairs   dirt   a spot
a handkerchief   an underground station
a customer   to step on/off   a product

Ice cream	Escalator	Vacuum cleaner

Vocabulary spot

Learn words from a reading text in groups. It will help you remember them.

Language focus

24.5

Rewrite these sentences so they have the same meaning. Change the verbs from passive to active.

a   The aeroplane was flown to Miami.
The pilot *flew the aeroplane* to Miami.

b   The passengers were shown the emergency exits by the steward.
The steward .... the emergency exits.

c   Lunch was served during the journey.
The stewards .... during the journey.

d   The passengers weren't told where to wait for their luggage.
The airport staff .... where to wait for their luggage.

e   My passport wasn't stamped.
The immigration officer .... my passport.

f   When the luggage arrived, one man was ordered to open his suitcase by the customs officer.
When the luggage arrived, the customs officer .... his suitcase.

24.6

Grammar spot

Revise irregular past participles, e.g. *give → given, tell → told*, because you need them to make the passive.

Here are some sentences about the inventions in the texts. Write each sentence in the passive.

a   About 275,000 tourists visit the factory each year.
The factory *is visited by about 275,000 tourists each year.*

b   Ben and Jerry don't make the ice cream themselves now.
The ice cream *isn't made by Ben and Jerry themselves now.*

c   The station manager hired a man with a wooden leg.
A man with a wooden leg ....

d   The company holds competitions.
Competitions ....

e   'The Puffing Billy' frightened horses.
Horses ....

f   The British didn't build the first escalators.
The first escalators ....

g   The King and Queen invited Booth to Buckingham Palace.
Booth ....

h   Clean electric trains replaced dirty steam trains.
Dirty steam trains ....

i   The company produces new flavours all the time.
New flavours ....

24.7 **ACTIVITY**

1   You are in Group A or B. Your teacher will give you a list of inventions.
Decide when they were invented and where. You need to make some guesses.

2   When you have finished, you have a chance to ask the other group six questions. They have the answers. Choose the things you are most unsure of so you can make as many true sentences as possible.

24.8

What do you think will be invented in the next fifty years? Can you think of something which will make life easier at home or at work or for travel? Who will it be used by? What will it be made of? How will it work? Write a few sentences about it.

EXAMPLE: *A car will be invented which doesn't need a driver. It will be made of plastic. It will be driven by a computer. It will be programmed to take the correct road.*

24.9 PRONUNCIATION

1 Look at these sentences. Find words ending in *r* or *re*. If they are followed by a word beginning with a vowel, join them together.

   a Sugar‿and salt are‿added.
   b Shops asked them to deliver ice cream.
   c The mixture is frozen.
   d There are four escalators in the station near my house.
   e He had a better idea.
   f Where is Ben and Jerry's ice cream sold?

2 🎧 Listen and repeat.

3 Look at these sentences. Which words will you join when you say them?

   a Television was‿invented‿in the 1920s.
   b Where are escalators used?
   c Ben and Jerry's ice cream is sold in many places.
   d Many shops have escalators.
   e Some inventions aren't successful.
   f I met him at four o'clock.
   g Some people went up and down all day.
   h I've lost your address.

4 🎧 Now listen and repeat. Were you right?

24.10 ACTIVITY

1 Read these descriptions of everyday things. What are they?

They are used all over the world, in both hot and cold countries. Today they are made of material and metal. They can be used instead of a coat to keep you dry. They can be folded up and put in a bag or pocket when they are not needed.

They are made of wood and a black stone. The black stone is in the centre and the wood is around the edge. One end is sharpened. They are long and thin. They are very cheap. They are used mainly for drawing.

2 Work in a group. Write a description of an everyday object to read to the class. Try to answer these questions in your description:

Where is it used?
What is it made of?
What is it used for?
What does it look like?

3 Read your description. Other students may interrupt if they can guess what it is. Can you get to the end of your description before they guess?

Describing objects
It's made of ...
It's round/square.
It's a kind of ...
It's used for ...-*ing*.
It might be ...
It could be ...
It must be ...
It can't be ...
It's like a ...

Passive (past simple)
Moving chains **were used** by people in ancient Egypt.

People in ancient Egypt **used** moving chains.

The escalator **was invented** by Charles D. Seeberger.

Charles D. Seeberger **invented** the escalator.

Steam trains **weren't used** underground after 1906.
Was the bicycle **invented** in 1869?

Passive (future)
A new kind of bicycle **will be invented**.
It **won't be made** of metal.
Will it **be made** of plastic?

Dates
1834 (eighteen thirty-four); 1908 (nineteen oh eight);
2010 (two thousand and ten)

Vocabulary
chain childhood company (ice cream) cone dirt dust electric electric battery emergency exit flavour handkerchief invention inventor match microwave oven model printing spot

to clean to demonstrate to operate to step off to suck

convinced worldwide

Exam folder 24

Listening Part 3

In this part of the exam, you listen to a recorded announcement or someone speaking about a particular subject. You fill in the words which are missing from some notes. You hear the recording twice.

CHECK!
a What do the instructions tell you?
b What should you do before you listen?
c Are the words you write down the same as the ones you hear?
d How many times do you hear the recording?

1 Look at the instructions in the task below. What is the man going to talk about?

2 Look at the exam task and answer questions a and b.

   a What is the name of the museum?
   b What kinds of words will you listen for?

- You will hear a man talking on the radio about a museum.
- For each question, fill in the missing information in the numbered space.

The Weston Museum of Science

First opened: in the year (**1**) .... in the Market Square.

Museum opening hours: every day from 9 am–5 pm except (**2**) .... from 9 am–9 pm

Exhibition in new gallery: learn about the (**3**) ....

Children's activity this week: (**4**) ....

Café: open all day on the (**5**) .... floor.

Until 24 July: the (**6**) .... is closed.

3 🎧 Listen to the recording and fill in the missing information.

Exam Advice

You usually have to write one word but sometimes you have to write two.

4 🎧 Listen again and check your answers.

5 🎧 Look at the script and listen again.

6 Mark the answers on your script and check them.

Writing folder

Writing Part 3

1 Can you match the halves of these sentences? Underline the words which help you.

a I really like that band
b I was listening to music
c While I was watching the band
d Although I like music
e The music was so loud
f I used to like folk music
g I enjoy listening to music
h You can have this CD

1 I don't own many CDs.
2 but I don't play an instrument.
3 when I fell asleep.
4 because I don't like it.
5 but now I prefer rock music.
6 that we couldn't talk.
7 my mobile was stolen.
8 so get me a ticket too.

2 Read the beginning of a letter which Alessia wrote to her English friend, Sophie. Can you join any of the sentences? Use some of the words you underlined in Exercise 1.

> Dear Sophie,
>
> I went to a concert last week. My friend bought the tickets. She couldn't go. She was ill. My brother came instead. The band was good. I didn't want the music to stop. My brother doesn't like listening to their CDs. He enjoyed the concert. The concert finished at 11 o'clock. We went backstage to meet the band.

3 Look at the words in the box and put each one under the most suitable heading.

awful enjoyable
enormous excellent
exciting extraordinary
fantastic great hopeless
large strange terrible
tiny unexpected useless
well-known wonderful

good	bad	big	small	unusual	famous

4 Read the next part of Alessia's letter. Use some of the words from Exercise 3 to replace the words which are underlined.

5 Imagine you went to a concert last week. Write a letter to an English friend and tell him/her who you went with, who was playing and what you thought of the concert. Write about 100 words.

> It took a long time to get out of the hall because there was such a <u>big</u> crowd. We saw a <u>famous</u> actor and his girlfriend. She was wearing <u>unusual</u> clothes. She looks <u>good</u>, but my brother says she's a <u>bad</u> actress. We had a <u>good</u> evening. See you soon.
>
> Love, Alessia

Exam Advice

Remember to join some of your sentences to make your writing more interesting.

Writing folder vocabulary
backstage
extraordinary hopeless tiny useless well-known

UNITS 19–24 Revision

Speaking

1 Work with a partner. Look at these sentences.
Say if you agree with them and why.
Find out your partner's opinion.

a It's good to have lots of brothers and sisters.
Yes, I agree. You can play with them when you are younger. What do you think?
OR *No, I don't agree. In my opinion that's not true because …*

b Most children are spoilt by their grandparents.

c It isn't good to be famous when you are a teenager.

d Most pop singers have an easy life.

e Everyone should learn a musical instrument.

f It's a good idea to make friends with people who have different interests from you.

g Cars are the worst things that were ever invented.

Vocabulary

2 Complete these phone conversations.
Use the sentences in the box.

> This is John.
> Hang on a minute.
> I'll call you back later.
> May I have your name?
> I can't speak to you just now.
> I'm afraid he's not available this morning.
> ~~I'm ringing to find out about a CD I ordered.~~
> Can you call back after lunch?
> Can you give me his number?

Shop assistant: The Music Shop.
    Regina: Oh, yes, hello. **(a)** *I'm ringing to find out about a CD I ordered.*
Shop assistant: **(b)** ....
    Regina: Regina Hopper.
Shop assistant: Oh, yes. You can collect it today.
    Regina: Great, I'll come in later. Thanks.

Receptionist: Emsworth and Company.
    Regina: May I speak to John Evans, please?
Receptionist: **(c)** ....
    Regina: Oh. I need to speak to him today.
Receptionist: **(d)** ....
    Regina: OK, thanks.

    Regina: Hello, John? This is Regina.
      John: **(e)** ....
        We're very busy.
    Regina: But I need to talk to you.
      John: **(f)** ....
    Regina: Well, don't forget.
      John: No, I won't.

    Regina: 272501.
      John: Regina? **(g)** ....
    Regina: Oh, good. I've got that CD you wanted for your dad.
      John: Great. Why don't you phone him?
    Regina: **(h)** ....
      John: Have you got a pen?
    Regina: **(i)** .... Yes, OK.
      John: It's 632665.
    Regina: Right. I'll call him now.

3 Put these words into groups: adjectives, verbs, people or things.

battery bodyguard bossy button cancel
chain deceive drummer earn escalator fail
honest inventor jealous judge keyboard
nephew nervous pianist search sensitive
spoilt trust vacuum cleaner

Adjectives:

Verbs:

People:

Things:

Grammar

4 In each group of three sentences, only one is correct. Tick the correct sentence and put a cross by the incorrect ones.

1 A He agreed meeting me at the bus station. ✗
  B He agreed to meet me at the bus station. ✓
  C He agreed meet me at the bus station. ✗

2 A Our team prepared more carefully than the others.
  B Our team prepared the most carefully than the others.
  C Our team prepared less carefully as the others.

3 A You really ought try this new shampoo.
  B You really ought to try this new shampoo.
  C You really ought trying this new shampoo.

4 A I don't mind waiting while you get ready.
  B I don't mind wait while you get ready.
  C I don't mind to wait while you get ready.

5 A Can you explain me this sentence?
  B Can you explain this sentence to me?
  C Can you explain this sentence mean?

6 A We're very excited about winning the match.
  B We're very excited for winning the match.
  C We're very excited of winning the match.

7 A What the spaceship looks like?
  B What does the spaceship looks like?
  C What does the spaceship look like?

8 A I've read the magazine you recommended.
  B I've read the magazine that you recommended it.
  C I've read the magazine you recommended it.

9 A The team captain made them to practise on Saturday afternoon.
  B The team captain made them practising on Saturday afternoon.
  C The team captain made them practise on Saturday afternoon.

5 Choose one of the words in the box to fill each space in this newspaper article. If no word is necessary mark –.

> who   which   where   whose

THIEVES MAKE A MISTAKE

The car of the pop star Saskia Labelle, (a) ....*who*.... arrived in town yesterday, was damaged by two young men (b) .... broke a window and took a jacket (c) .... was on the back seat. Saskia's secretary, (d) .... jacket it was, said the thieves probably believed it was Saskia's.
The men, (e) .... were both tall with fair hair, were described by a security guard (f) .... had seen them in the hotel (g) .... Saskia was staying.
The concert (h) .... Saskia is giving tonight will start at nine o'clock at the City Hall. She will sing songs from her new CD (i) .... is called *Girltalk*.

6 Look at the pairs of sentences below. Complete the second sentence in each pair so that it means the same as the first.

a He told her to leave the room.
  '*Leave the room*,' he said.

b These machines were invented many centuries ago.
  People .... many centuries ago.

c Jill asked Ali to phone her after his exam.
  'Please .... after your exam,' said Jill.

d The building will be opened by the president.
  The president .... the building.

e Mary told her grandson not to play football in the sitting room.
  .... in the sitting room,' said Mary to her grandson.

f My brothers are given more money than me.
  My parents .... more money than me.

g My boyfriend said he'd rung me but I hadn't answered the phone.
  My boyfriend said 'I .... the phone.'

h The police examined the strange vehicle very carefully.
  The strange vehicle .... very carefully by the police.

i Our neighbours feed our dog when we're away.
  Our dog .... when we're away.

j 'I've won the lottery!' shouted Annie.
  Annie shouted that .... the lottery.

k My best friend will give me a lift home.
  I .... home by my best friend.

UNIT 25 Shop till you drop

Introduction

25.1

1 Look at the photographs. What do they show?

2 Work with a partner. Look at one of the photographs. Make a list of all the advantages and disadvantages of shopping that way.

3 Compare your list with the rest of the class.

4 Discuss which ways of shopping are most suitable for the following people and give reasons why.

   a busy parents
   b teenagers
   c people who live a long way from a city
   d old people

5 What's your shopping style? Do this quiz to find out.

Find out how you spend your money!

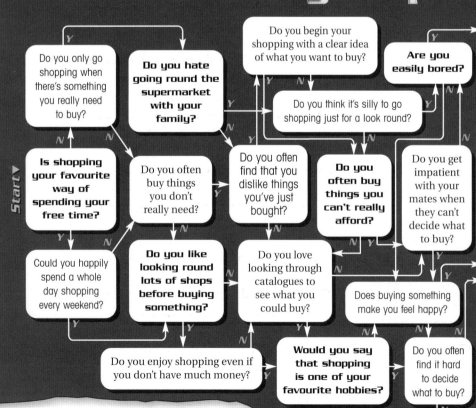

Start ▼

Do you only go shopping when there's something you really need to buy?

Do you hate going round the supermarket with your family?

Do you begin your shopping with a clear idea of what you want to buy?

Are you easily bored?

Do you think it's silly to go shopping just for a look round?

Is shopping your favourite way of spending your free time?

Do you often buy things you don't really need?

Do you often find that you dislike things you've just bought?

Do you often buy things you can't really afford?

Do you get impatient with your mates when they can't decide what to buy?

Could you happily spend a whole day shopping every weekend?

Do you like looking round lots of shops before buying something?

Do you love looking through catalogues to see what you could buy?

Does buying something make you feel happy?

Do you enjoy shopping even if you don't have much money?

Would you say that shopping is one of your favourite hobbies?

Do you often find it hard to decide what to buy?

You're a cool customer!
You're really well organised. You know just what you want to buy and usually have a good idea where you'll find it. You don't spend a lot of time shopping – you go straight to the right place and buy what you need. As soon as you've paid for what you've bought, you want to go home. That's fine – but you should have a look round the shops sometimes … you might find a brilliant bargain!

You're a wild shopper!
You're just the craziest shopper ever! You may plan to buy something sensible like a new notebook – and then you come home with something quite different and completely unnecessary, but much more fun! When you see something you love, you want it and you want it right now – you don't want to wait and you certainly don't want to save up until you can afford it. That's OK, but make sure you don't end up with no money for essentials – sometimes you just have to save up for a week or two for what you really want!

You're a brilliant browser!
Shopping is one of your main hobbies and you love walking round lots of different shops and looking for bargains. You're really good at finding bargains because you're very patient and you rarely pay the full price for anything. And if you've been browsing for hours and then have to go back to the first shop for the best bargain, you really don't mind!

6 Do you agree with the result?

Listening

25.2

🎧 Listen to Andy phoning his older brother Darren and decide whether these statements are true or false.

a Andy wants Darren to collect him from the city centre. *true*
b Darren complains that Andy spends too much money on clothes.
c Andy saw some shirts he liked in the market.
d A woman spoke to Andy when he was leaving a store called *Tempo*.
e The manager thought that Andy had stolen a pullover.
f Andy was questioned by a police officer.
g The shop assistant agreed with Andy's story.
h Andy apologised to the manager for the trouble he had caused.

Language focus

25.3

1 Write these statements as you heard them in the conversation in Exercise 25.2.

a 'They're selling some quite cool ones in the market.'
A friend told me *they were selling some quite cool ones in the market.*
b 'I've sold them all already.'
The man who runs the stall said ....
c 'I want to try them on.'
I said to the assistant ....
d 'That's OK.'
He said ....
e 'They don't fit.'
I told the assistant ....
f 'Yes, I am.'
I said ....

> **G**rammar spot
>
> Remember that tenses change when we report speech in the past – see Unit 22.

2 Look at these statements from the conversation. Write down the exact words the people said.

a I said I had.
Andy said, ...*'Yes, I have.'*......
b She said she was the store detective.
She said, ' .... '
c I agreed, although I added that I wasn't very happy about it.
I said, ' .... '
d I told him I'd bought a pullover at about 9.30.
I told him, ' .... '
e I tried to explain I'd thrown away the *Tempo* bag and had put the pullover in the shoe shop bag.
I tried to explain, ' .... '
f I said I didn't remember who had served me.
I said, ' .... '
g He said he was sorry for troubling me and he told me I was welcome to use his phone.
He said, ' .... '

25.4

Write down the exact questions the people asked. What changes do you need to make?

a She asked me if I was leaving the shop.
......*'Are you leaving the shop?'*......
b She asked me if I'd paid for everything in my bag.
' .... '
c She asked me if I would come to the manager's office with her.
' .... '
d The manager asked me how long I'd been in the shop and how many things I had bought.
' .... '
e I asked what was going on.
' .... '
f He asked me whether I had a receipt for the pullover.
' .... '
g They asked which assistant had served me.
' .... '
h Then the store detective asked the manager if he wanted her to call the police.
' .... '
i I asked her if she remembered me.
' .... '

25.5 ACTIVITY

Where are these people?
What are they saying? Your teacher will give you some cards. Match the two parts of the conversations.

25.6

1 Rhiannon wants to get a job in a shop. The manager interviews her and asks her some questions. After the interview, Rhiannon tells her friend Frederika what she was asked. Complete the spaces.

She wanted to know (a) *how old I was* . Next she asked if (b) .... any foreign languages and whether (c) .... in a shop before and (d) .... Then she wanted to know (e) .... to work every morning. And then she asked if (f) .... immediately!

2 Would you like to work in a shop? Why?/Why not?

25.7

Complete this email with the reported forms of the questions below.

Dear Christopher
Would you like to come for a day out with me? I want to celebrate some good luck. Here's what happened.
Last month on my way to school I found a wallet lying on the pavement. It had a lot of money in it, but no cards. I took it to the police station. The police officer asked me a lot of questions. He wanted to know (a) *where I had found it* .
Then he asked (b) ...., and
(c) .... Then he got out a book and asked
(d) .... and wrote it down. He also wanted to know (e) .... and (f) ....
I didn't understand why he was asking so many questions.
Then he asked (g) .... When I asked him why, he said that if no one claimed the wallet, it would be mine. So then I didn't mind all the questions!
And guess what – no one has claimed the wallet.
Where shall we go to celebrate?
Robin

a Where did you find it?
b What time did you find it?
c Were you alone?
d Where do you live?
e How long have you lived there?
f Will you be at that address for the next month?
g Do you have an email address?

25.8

Andy said:
*There are **too many** people at the bus stop.*
*I haven't got **enough** money for a taxi.*

Complete these sentences with *enough*, *too much* or *too many*.

a I don't like this burger, it's got *too much* cheese in it.
b Have we got .... food for everyone?
c Be careful, there's .... juice in that jug. It's going to spill.
d There are .... CDs on this shelf, they're going to fall off.
e We haven't got .... time for a drink before we go out.
f I don't like rooms with .... furniture in them.
g There are .... customers in this shop. We haven't got .... assistants to help them all.

25.9 ACTIVITY

You are going to play the Whispering Game.
Follow your teacher's instructions.

25.10 PRONUNCIATION

1 🎧 Listen to the recording. Underline the stressed word in each answer.

1 A Did you say ten o'clock?
  B No, I said <u>two</u> o'clock.
2 A Did you say there were five guests?
  B No, I said there were nine guests.
3 A Did you say we had a spelling test?
  B No, I said we had a reading test.
4 A Did you say you came by air?
  B No, I said I came by car.
5 A Did you say she was a doctor?
  B No, I said she was a teacher.
6 A Did you say you came from France?
  B No, I said I came from Greece.

2 🎧 Listen again and repeat.

3 Work with a partner. Take turns to ask questions and give answers like the ones in Exercise 1. Use the words below. Be careful of the stress in the answers.

a Did you say / live / Bonn? (Rome)
  Did you say you lived in Bonn? No, I said I lived in Rome.
b Did you say there / be / fifteen students? (sixteen)
c Did you say we / want / ham sandwiches? (jam)
d Did you say she / be / model? (actress)
e Did you say it / be / quarter to eleven? (quarter to seven)

25.11

Andy said:
Dad gave me some money.
The store detective showed the manager the pullover.
We can say this in a different way:
*Dad gave some money **to** me.*
*The store detective showed the pullover **to** the manager.*

1 Rewrite each of these sentences without *to*, so that it means the same as the one before.

a The passengers gave their tickets to the driver when they got on the bus.
  The passengers gave *the driver their tickets when they got on the bus.*
b I sent a postcard to my parents from London.
  I sent ....
c Will you send the bill to my boss?
  Will you send ....
d He wrote a long letter to me when he arrived in India.
  He wrote ....
e On my birthday the children brought my breakfast to me in bed.
  The children brought ....
f Can you bring some more bread to us, please?
  Can you bring ....

2 Rewrite these sentences, adding *to*.

a Take the headteacher this note, please.
  Take ....
b Show the immigration officer your passport.
  Show ....
c We took our classmate some fruit when he was ill.
  We took ....

25.12 ACTIVITY

Play the card game with the cards your teacher gives you.

Reported questions
Yes/no questions + if or whether
Do you remember me?   I asked her **if she remembered** me.

Do you have a receipt for the pullover?
He asked me **whether I had** a receipt for the pullover.

Will you come to the manager's office with me?
She asked me **if I would come** to the manager's office with her.

Wh- questions
What's going on?
I asked **what was going on**.

Which assistant served you?
They asked **which assistant had served me**.

Verbs with two objects

give + **person** + object	= give + object **+ to person**
Darren gave **Andy** a lift.	= Darren gave a lift to **Andy**.
Dad gave **me** some money.	= Dad gave some money **to me**.

There are **too many** people at the bus stop.
There's **too much** juice in that jug.
I haven't got **enough** money for a taxi.

Vocabulary
bargain catalogue fitting room hypermarket pullover receipt
refund stall wallet

to bring back   to browse   to try on

wild   in stock   in town

Exam folder 25

In this part of the exam, you read a text and decide if ten sentences are correct or incorrect.

CHECK!

Read these sentences about Reading Part 3.
If a sentence is correct, write A. If it is incorrect, write B.

a The instructions tell you what the text is about.
b The sentences are in the same order as the information in the text.
c You need to understand every word in the text to answer the questions.

- Look at the sentences below about a supermarket called Sainsbury's.
- Read the text on the opposite page to decide if each sentence is correct or incorrect.
- If it is correct, write A.
- If it is incorrect, write B.

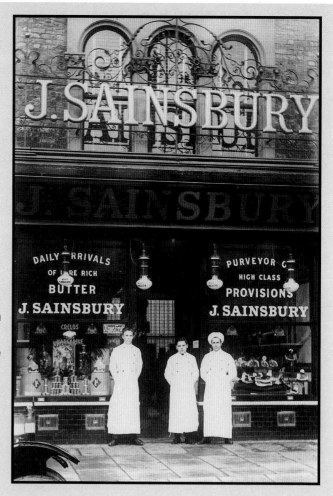

1 When the first Sainsbury's shop opened, it sold meat as well as milk, butter and eggs.

2 Shoppers paid more at Sainsbury's shop because of the quality of the food.

3 Sainsbury's second shop was in central London.

4 In the nineteenth century, some Sainsbury's shops were open until 2 am.

5 After 1900, some of the food sold came from other countries.

6 In 1900, people spent more of their income on food than they do now.

7 In the 1920s, Sainsbury's gave shoppers more choice than other shops.

8 It was possible to have your food delivered by Sainsbury's in the 1970s.

9 English people enjoyed self-service shopping when it was first introduced.

10 It took more than 30 years for every Sainsbury's shop to become self-service.

Exam Advice

Don't spend too long reading the text. Read it quickly and find the parts of the text which answer the questions.

SAINSBURY'S SUPERMARKETS

One of the most successful supermarkets in Britain is Sainsbury's. The first shop was opened nearly 150 years ago. In 1869, John James Sainsbury and his wife, Mary Ann, opened a small shop selling fresh milk, butter and eggs in Drury Lane, London. Other products like meat and vegetables weren't introduced until later. The shop became well known because, in spite of the food being of higher quality than at other shops, the prices were not higher. The business was so successful that by 1882, John James Sainsbury had opened three more shops in London, followed by a shop just outside London in Croydon.

Working conditions in nineteenth-century shops would seem hard to us but Sainsbury's workers were well looked after. In return, they had to work long hours. In fact, Saturday evening was often the busiest time. After closing, the shop had to be cleaned and tidied and it could be after 2 am before the workers were able to leave.

By 1900, Sainsbury's was importing food from abroad. People have always complained about how much they have to pay for their food, but it is worth noticing that food is much cheaper now, compared to average wages, than it was in 1900.

By the 1920s, the design of many of the shops had changed and a typical Sainsbury's shop had six departments offering a much wider range of products than other food shops. Each shop offered home delivery throughout the surrounding area, an important service in the days before most people had cars. This service came to an end during the 1960s as people had their own transport but has come into fashion again with the twenty-first century since people started ordering their food on the internet and having it delivered.

By 1939, there were 244 shops around the country and everything sold was stored in London before being delivered to each shop around the country. This system didn't change until the 1960s.

The first self-service shop opened in June 1950 in Croydon. The long counters, long queues and chairs for customers were replaced with checkouts. It was expected that people would miss what they were used to but there was no need to worry because people welcomed the change. However, it was nearly thirty years before all Sainsbury's traditional shops had been replaced with modern supermarkets.

In 1974, Sainsbury's first out-of-town supermarket opened on the edge of Cambridge and today most towns in Britain have a Sainsbury's nearby, some having one just outside the town and one in the town centre.

Exam folder vocabulary

counter   checkout   delivery   income   self-service   wages

to deliver   to import

however

UNIT 26 Persuading people

Introduction

26.1

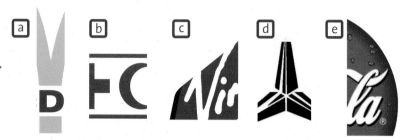

1 Here are parts of some famous logos. Do you recognise them?

2 Look around the room.
How many logos can you see?
How important are logos to you?

3 Look at these adverts. What are they advertising? Which advert is the most successful? Which advert is the least successful?

4 How important are adverts in your life? Do you take any notice of them?

Reading

26.2

Read the photo story and think about the answers to these questions.

a What does Robert say he wants to do on his birthday?
b When is he planning to celebrate his birthday?
c What are the boys planning?
d Do they all think the plan is a good idea?
e How does Carolina know about the party?
f Does she think Robert will enjoy it?
g What does she think will happen if a lot of people are invited?
h What does she decide to do? Do you agree with her decision?

26.3

1 Read these questions. Look at the underlined verbs. What do they mean? Can you guess?

2 Now answer the questions.

    1 What does Robert's mother do?
        A <u>persuade</u> him to spend his birthday with someone else
        B <u>explain</u> to Robert why she has to go to the meeting
        C <u>complain</u> about how much time he spends on the computer
        D <u>promise</u> to celebrate with him

    2 What do the boys want to do?
        A <u>organise</u> a party at Robert's house
        B <u>spoil</u> Robert's birthday plans
        C <u>influence</u> the way Robert spends his free time
        D <u>find out</u> what Robert's parents are really like

    3 What does Carolina want to do?
        A <u>suggest</u> the boys tell Robert about the party
        B <u>apologise</u> to the boys for listening to their conversation
        C <u>inform</u> Robert's parents about the party
        D <u>warn</u> Robert about the party

    4 What does Danielle do?
        A <u>encourage</u> Carolina to tell Robert's parents
        B <u>recommend</u> that Carolina tells Robert
        C <u>persuade</u> Carolina not to do anything
        D <u>prevent</u> Carolina from going to the party

V ocabulary spot

Verbs like *suggest, inform, warn*, etc. are often used in multiple-choice questions, especially in PET Reading Part 4. Make sure you know what the verbs in this exercise mean.

26.4

Put the correct verb from the box into each space. Use the correct form of the verb.

a We ......*explained*...... our problems to the receptionist.
b Our volleyball captain .... the team to practise every day.
c Do advertisements .... your decisions about where to shop?
d My doctor .... that I should try a new skin cream.
e The tour guide .... the tourists that they might miss their flight.
f The police .... the crowd from entering the square.
g Did the girls .... for making such a mess?

apologise	encourage
~~explain~~	influence
prevent	recommend
warn	

Language focus

26.5

Look at the tenses in this sentence, then complete the sentences below.

*If only a few people **go** to the party, **it won't** be a problem.*
***He'll have** a really good time **if** the boys **organise** a party for him.*

a The boys will know Carolina was listening to their conversation if she ......*tells*...... (tell) them what she thinks.
b If lots of people go to the party, the house .... (be) a mess.
c If the house is a mess, Robert's parents .... (get) angry.
d If Robert goes to his granny's house, the party .... (not happen).
e If the meeting is cancelled, Robert's parents .... (stay) at home.
f Robert will go to his granny's house if he .... (feel) lonely.
g If Carolina tells Robert about the party, Robert .... (not/have) a surprise.
h If Robert gets some computer games for his birthday, he .... (be) happy.

26.6

1 Rewrite these sentences using *unless*.

a If Robert doesn't go to his granny's house, he will be at home.
   Unless Robert goes to his granny's house, he will be at home.
b If the meeting isn't cancelled, Robert's parents will be away.
c If Carolina doesn't tell Robert about the party, it will be a surprise.
d Robert will enjoy the party if the boys don't ask too many people.
e If the boys don't organise a party for Robert, he won't have one.
f Robert's parents won't know about the party if Carolina doesn't tell them.

2 Now write sentences with *if* or *unless* by joining the two halves. Make any necessary changes.

EXAMPLE: *You'll miss the appointment unless you leave now.*
          You'll miss the appointment if you don't leave now.

a You'll miss the appointment		I miss the bus.
b We'll play basketball in the park		you post it by five o'clock.
c I can come shopping with you	**if**	you help me with my revision.
d I won't tell anyone		you leave now.
e I'll be home at four o'clock	**unless**	you tell me the secret.
f I won't pass my exam		you lend me some money.
g The letter will get there tomorrow		it's raining.

26.7

1 Look at these two sentences. What is the difference in meaning between *When Robert's parents come home* and *If Robert's parents are at home*?

When Robert's parents come home, they'll take him out for a meal.
If Robert's parents are at home, there won't be a party.

2 Sometimes you can use either *if* or *when* in the same sentence but the meaning changes. Look at these two sentences. What is the difference in meaning?

If Robert answers the door, he'll be surprised.
When Robert answers the door, he'll be surprised.

3 Choose *if* or *when*. In two of the sentences you can use either. What is the difference in meaning?

a Everyone will be hungry *if/when* we arrive late, so we'd better hurry!
b I'll eat that sandwich *if/when* you don't want it.
c I'll go to university *if/when* I pass this exam.
d *If/When* those shoes are still in the shop, I'll buy them.
e *If/When* we get to the town centre, we'll ask for directions to the theatre.
f I'll video the football match for you *if/when* I get home in time.
g I'll learn to drive *if/when* I'm seventeen.
h *If/When* I buy a new computer, I'll give you my old one.
i I'll be very disappointed *if/when* there are no tickets left.

26.11 ACTIVITY

1 Do you believe in superstitions? Look at these pictures. Do these things mean bad luck, good luck or nothing in your country? Write some sentences.

EXAMPLE: *If you open an umbrella indoors, you will have bad luck.*

2 Work in a group and compare your answers. Add some more superstitions.

26.8 ACTIVITY

Work in a group. What happened next in the photo story in Exercise 26.2? Write a fourth conversation and act it out.

26.9 PRONUNCIATION

1 🎧 Listen to this conversation and underline the words (or parts of words) which are stressed.

Joanna:	<u>What's</u> the <u>time</u>?
Michael:	Five to nine.
Joanna:	Oh, dear.
Michael:	What's the problem?
Joanna:	It doesn't matter.
Michael:	Tell me.
Joanna:	I'm late for college. Can you give me a lift?
Michael:	Of course I can.
Joanna:	Thank you.
Michael:	You're welcome.

2 🎧 Listen again and then practise the conversation.

26.10

Look at these adverts. Write some slogans.
Use *if*, *when* and *unless*.

First conditional
If + present simple, will-future
If the boys **organise** a party, Robert **will have** a good time.
Robert **will have** a good time **if** the boys **organise** a party. (*no comma*)
Unless Robert **goes** to his granny's house, he **will be** at home.
(= **If** Robert **doesn't go** to his granny's house, he **will be** at home.)
If Robert answers the door, he'll be surprised. (= we don't know if he'll answer the door)
When Robert answers the door, he'll be surprised. (= we know he'll answer the door)

Vocabulary
logo slogan superstition
to influence to persuade to prevent
to recommend
lonely strict
none of your business

Exam folder 26

Speaking Part 1

In this part of the exam, the examiner talks to each student and asks a few questions. The students say a number and also spell a word for the examiner.

CHECK!

a How many people are in the room for the speaking test?

In Part 1:

b Who do you speak to?

c What subjects will the examiner probably ask you about?

d What can you say if you don't understand?

e How long does this part last?

1 Say the number your teacher points to.

2 Spell the word your teacher says.

3 Think of as many things as you can to say about your school and learning English. Tell the class.

4 Work with a partner. One of you writes down questions to ask about someone's family. The other one writes down questions to ask about someone's hobbies or interests.

5 Ask your partner your questions and answer his/her questions. Exchange questions and ask and answer again.

Exam Advice

Don't answer the examiner's questions with just *yes* or *no*.

Speaking Part 2

In this part of the exam, you are given some pictures. You work in pairs and try to arrive at a decision together about a situation which the examiner describes to you.

CHECK!

a What will the examiner give you?

b Who will you talk to?

c What can you say if you don't understand?

d How long do you and your partner need to talk?

e What will happen if you can't think of anything to say?

Exam Advice

Learn ways of making suggestions, giving your opinion, agreeing and disagreeing.

1 You and your partner are planning a holiday together. Look at the pictures on page 203. Think about the differences between the places.

2 Can you think of other advantages/disadvantages of each holiday? Which one would you like to go on?

3 Work with a partner. You are going on holiday together to one of the places in the pictures for one week. Talk about the following questions and try to come to a decision together.

Where will you go? How will you travel?
Where will you stay? How will you spend your time?

Writing folder

Writing Part 3

1   Here is part of a story. Can you use these four words to complete the spaces?

| after | when | while | next |

> I went into my hotel room and **(a)** .... I had locked the door, I opened the envelope from my bank. There was a letter and some money in it. First, I counted the money. **(b)** .... , I looked at the letter. **(c)** .... I was reading it, I heard a sound in the bathroom. I put the letter in my pocket and went to the bathroom door. Somebody was having a shower – in my bathroom! What should I do? I was still trying to decide **(d)** .... I heard the shower stop.

2   Work with a partner. Put these sentences in the correct order to tell the rest of the story. Which words help you to understand the order in which things happened?

   a 'What are you doing here?' we said at the same time.
   b In the evening, the hotel gave us a free meal.
   c Then he looked at the key which was still in my hand.
   d When he saw me he looked angry.
   e A man came out wearing a towel.
   f After he had put his clothes on, we went to see the receptionist.
   g Suddenly the bathroom door opened.
   h She apologised and gave him a different room.
   i We've been friends ever since.
   j 'I suppose they've given one of us the wrong key,' he said and began to laugh.

3   Write a story called *The surprise*. Write about 100 words. How many of the words in the box below can you use in your story?

| after | already | ever since | in the morning | next | still | when | while |

Exam Advice

A story can be about an everyday event.

Writing folder vocabulary
to count   to lock

UNIT 27 Travellers' tales

Introduction

27.1

1 🎧 Listen to a song and say which of the photographs you think it fits best.

2 Look at the words of the song below. Some of them are missing. Can you guess what sort of word (noun, adjective, verb, preposition) you need for any of the spaces?

3 🎧 Listen to the song again and write down the missing words.

*Somewhere the sun is (**a**) ....*
*somewhere the (**b**) .... is blue*
*somewhere the (**c**) .... lining is (**d**) .... for me and you.*

*And I know that the (**e**) .... is a (**f**) .... one to travel on*
*over (**g**) .... mountains and by the sea strand*
*(**h**) .... of the valley the sun (**i**) .... shines upon*
*to the (**j**) .... glades of that sweet promised (**k**) ....*

4 Why is the singer travelling, do you think?

🅖rammar spot

We can talk about reasons for travelling using nouns or verbs:
on holiday, *on* business but *for pleasure*
travelling *to meet* new people, travelling *to see* the world

5 Look again at the photographs. Why are the people in them travelling?
Can you think of other reasons why people travel?

6 What is the best way to travel, in your opinion?

Listening

27.2

1 If you don't know the meaning of a word, think about the answers to these questions.

    a Does it look like a word in your own language?
    b Can you say whether the word is a person or a thing?
    c Is it made of other words you already know?
    d Can you guess the meaning of the word from the words around it?

2 Look at these words and think about their meanings.

    a accordion   **b** nanny   **c** volunteer   **d** boardwalk
    e archaeologist   **f** campfire   **g** basement

3 🎧 Listen to a radio programme and write down what you think the words in Exercise 2 mean.

4 Say how you guessed each word.

27.3

1 🎧 Listen to the radio programme again and complete these notes using between one and three words in each space.

    a Joe helped to look after ....*cows*........ on a farm.
    b The farmer's wife made excellent ....
    c Natasha was paid £ .... a week.
    d A friend helped Natasha to write ....
    e Owen worked on an island in ....
    f The weather was often ....
    g Jennifer's hands and .... hurt while she was working in the desert.
    h She liked the desert because it was beautiful and ....
    i Martin was introduced to the old man by ....
    j The old man's .... asked Martin to paint her basement.

2 Would you like to do any of the work described in the programme? Why? Which work would you definitely not want to do? Why not?

Language focus

27.4

1 Look at these sentences from the radio programme. Can you remember which adverb was at the beginning of each sentence?

    a *Luckily/Surprisingly/Actually*, a Finnish friend helped me to write a little notice.
    b *Obviously/In fact/Unfortunately*, I liked helping to save the forest.
    c *Unluckily/Surprisingly/Of course*, the sun was really hot during the day, but it was very cold at night.
    d *In fact/Luckily/Unfortunately*, digging is very hard work.
    e *Fortunately/Actually/Obviously*, we needed to be quite fit.
    f *Of course/Surprisingly/Luckily*, his landlady was so satisfied with the job I did that she asked me to paint her basement.
    g *Unfortunately/Obviously/In fact*, I had a letter from someone last week offering me work there next summer.

2 Which of the adverbs in Exercise 1 have the same meaning?

3 Now complete these sentences using your own ideas.

    a I went to bed very late last night. Surprisingly, *I wasn't tired this morning.*
    b Some people say that English weather is always bad. Actually, ...
    c My sister bought a lottery ticket last week. Unfortunately, ...
    d The film star said he hadn't got any money. Of course, ...
    e This jacket looks really expensive. In fact, ...
    f My friend suggested we should have a party the night before my exam. Obviously, ...

4 Choose two adverbs from Exercise 1 and write sentences with each one like the sentences in Exercise 3.

27.5

1 Look at these sentences from the radio programme.

> **Every** evening the old farmer played his accordion.
> It rained nearly **every** day.
> **Each of** the workers had a small tent.
> **Each** person told their friends about me.
> I looked after the little one **all** day.
> I liked **all** the people there.

   a Which of these expressions (*every, each of, each, all*) can be followed by a plural noun?

   b What is the difference between *every day* and *all day*?

2 Use *each, every* or *all* to complete these sentences. There are two possible answers for some sentences.

   a *All* the travellers were hungry.
   b .... of the buses goes to a different city.
   c .... suitcase was opened by the customs officer.
   d Don't keep .... your money in the same place.
   e We phoned .... the hotels in the city.
   f .... of the cities we visited has a good variety of shops.
   g .... tourist was given a map of the town.
   h Our flight was late so we spent .... afternoon in the airport.
   i I've looked in .... bag twice, but I still haven't found my passport.

27.6

1 Look at these sentences from the radio programme. Then complete the sentences using the verb and *myself, yourself,* etc.

> You obviously **enjoyed yourself** there.
> We needed to know how **to look after ourselves**.
> She helped me to write a little notice about **myself**.

   a Does your brother need a babysitter when your parents go out? No, he *looks after himself.* (look after)
   b Were you listening to the radio in your room or were you .... (talk to)
   c Susan mustn't carry that heavy box. She might .... (hurt)
   d Hello, everyone! Please .... (help) to drinks.
   e It rained every day when we went camping so we .... (not enjoy)
   f Sometimes I .... (ask) why I work so hard.
   g Don't worry about them. They can .... (look after)

2 Choose some verbs from the sentences in Exercise 1 and write three sentences.

   EXAMPLE: *I don't like people who help themselves to my things without asking me.*

Grammar spot

Check that you understand the difference between these sentences.

They're looking at each other.   They're looking at themselves.

27.7 **ACTIVITY**

Play word-building snap with one or two other students. Your teacher will give you the cards.

27.8 **PRONUNCIATION**

1 Practise the sounds /eə/ and /ɪə/. Can you find them in this sentence?

Here's your chair.

2 🎧 Listen and repeat these sentences, then mark the words with the sounds /eə/ or /ɪə/ in different colours. When you have checked your answers, put the words into the columns below.

   a He rarely feels fear.
   b He's got fair hair and a beard.
   c Take care on the stairs, dear.
   d There's a box of pears near the door.
   e Where did they appear from?
   f The volunteers worked in pairs.
   g The engineer steered the old car carefully.
   h She was wearing a pair of gold earrings.
   i On a clear day you can see the sea from their garden.

/eə/	/ɪə/
rarely	fear

3 Work with a partner. Take turns to repeat the sentences again. Listen to each other's pronunciation.

27.9

1 Look at these sentences from the radio programme, then rewrite the sentences below with an active verb.

Some students **are helped by** *their parents* (passive).
Some parents **help** *students* (active).
I **was given** *a room* (passive).
The farmer **gave** *me a room* (active).

a I was employed as a nanny.
A Finnish family ....*employed me as a nanny.*......

b I wasn't paid.
No one ....

c The buildings were buried for hundreds of years.
Sand ....

d I was employed by lots of people.
Lots of people ....

e Our listeners will be encouraged by those stories.
Those stories ....

2 Look at this email which a volunteer sent to a friend. What does Chris feel about his summer job?

Hi Eddy
You said you wanted to hear what I did this summer.
Actually, I was working as a volunteer on our local beach.
It looks a real mess sometimes. When I was a child, people didn't drop their rubbish on the beach but they do now and tourists start fires sometimes. So this summer volunteers cleaned the beach every evening. They collected thousands of empty bottles. Next year the government will employ someone to organise the volunteers. Pollution damages lots of beaches but I hope it won't spoil this one.
So, you see I was doing something useful for once.
I'll probably do it again next year. What about you?
Chris

3 Chris also wrote a short report about his work for the local paper. Rewrite the sentences from the email using passive verbs. Decide whether you want to use *by* in each sentence.

Young volunteers clean up town beach
By Chris Appleton

This summer I joined other volunteers to help clean up the local beach. In the past, rubbish (a) *wasn't dropped on the beach* but nowadays you see it everywhere and sometimes fires (b) .... But this summer the beach (c) .... every evening and thousands of empty bottles (d) .... Next year someone (e) .... to organise the volunteers. Every year lots of beaches (f) .... but I hope our local beach (g) ....
  I will probably work on our beach again next year and I hope some of my friends will volunteer with me.

27.10 ACTIVITY

1 Read the questionnaire on page 204 and discuss the questions it asks.

2 Use the questionnaire to find out who is the most earth-friendly person in your class (or your school, or your family). Score the answers using the key. What advice would you give to someone who gets a low score?

3 Write three sentences describing:

a earth-friendly people who would get a high score.
b people who would get an average score.
c people who don't worry about the earth and who would get a low score.

All/Every/Each

All the visitors **want** to see the castle.
They go into **every/each** room in the building.

Each student **takes** a turn in this game.
Each of the students **takes** a turn.
Each of them **takes** a turn.

We went to the beach **every day** last week.
We stayed on the beach **all day** yesterday.

Reflexive pronouns

I looked after **myself** when my parents were away.
If **you** talk to **yourself**, people may think you're mad.
Did **you** hurt **yourself** when you fell off your bicycle?
Did **you** hurt **yourselves** when you fell off your bicycles?
She didn't enjoy **herself** on holiday.
He asked **himself** why he had been so silly.
We helped **ourselves** to drinks.
They helped **themselves** to sandwiches.

Vocabulary

accordion air-conditioning archaeologist basement boardwalk environment forest human being
individual mealtime mist mushrooms nanny playgroup repair responsibility society volunteer

to destroy to heat to produce to reward to shine to turn up (heating)

definitely (un)fortunately home-made in fact obviously
of course out of this world satisfied surprisingly tasty

Exam folder 27

In this part of the exam, you read five descriptions of people. For each one, you choose one text to match it.

CHECK!

a How many questions are there?
b How many texts are there?
c How many texts are not used?
d Can the same text be the answer to two questions?
e What should you do after you have read the questions?
f What should you check before you choose an answer?

- The people below all want to travel in Europe.
- On the opposite page there are eight advertisements.
- Decide which advertisement (**letters A–H**) would be the most suitable for each person (**numbers 1–5**).
- For each of the numbers write the correct letter.

1 Cassie spent some time last summer travelling around Europe by bus and train. Next month she wants to visit a friend she met in Italy but she can't afford the fare.

2 Andy wants to travel alone around Europe for two months in the summer making his own decisions about how long he spends in each place.

3 Rachel wants to travel in Europe but she has very little money. She is free for nine months before she goes to university.

4 The Roberts family want to see as much as possible in Europe but have only two weeks. They want someone else to make all the hotel and travel arrangements for them.

5 The Graham family want to spend their holiday in the countryside, away from crowds and traffic. They would like to get some exercise while they are away.

Exam Advice

When you think you have found the answer, read the text carefully. There may be one or two details which make it wrong.

A

SPECIAL OFFER on rail tickets.
Unlimited travel through ten European countries
during June, July and August for only £450.
Family discounts. No minimum stop between journeys.
Apply at least one month before travelling.

B

Express coaches London to Switzerland or Italy.
Special discounts this month on one-way tickets.
Air-conditioned coach with toilet. Two stops for meals.
Sandwiches and drinks on sale during the journey.
Phone now for details of departure times and
unbelievable prices.

C

*Do you have experience of travelling
around Europe? Do you want to visit Italy?*
Responsible young adult required to look after six
teenagers travelling from London to Rome by train.
Ticket and meals paid during journey.
Depart in two weeks.

D

**Take the worry out of your holiday in France, Italy
or Spain and save money on hotels and petrol.**
On our ten-day holidays, you cycle on paths between
campsites. When you arrive, everything is ready for you:
tent, barbecue and swimming pool! You can organise dates
to suit your family. And you'll get fit in beautiful countryside.

E

Would you like to spend six months travelling
in southern Europe?
American family requires nanny to help with their children.
We will pay for all meals, travel costs and give you £30
pocket money a week. The right attitude is more important
than qualifications or experience. Interviews next week.
Phone for further information.

F

Our business is your pleasure.
See the best of southern Europe in a fortnight.
Air-conditioned coach tours visit the most beautiful and
historic cities in Spain, Southern France and Italy. Spend
each night in a comfortable hotel with a swimming pool
and enjoy the local food in a carefully chosen restaurant.
Special prices for families and single travellers.

G

Leave everything to us. If you are a business traveller
and frequently need to travel to France or Italy but
don't have time to spend booking tickets, call Quick-
ticket now. We store all your details on our computer,
how you prefer to travel, usual destinations, etc.
All you do is call or email one day before your journey.

H

Planning to travel in Europe this summer?
We are three students looking for a fourth to share
costs travelling by car and camping for about six weeks.
We have planned our route through five countries but would
be prepared to make some changes.

Exam folder vocabulary
decision pleasure qualification
historic (un)limited minimum

UNIT 28 What would you do?

Introduction

28.1

1 Do you recognise any of the people in the photographs? Why are they famous?

2 Match the adults to the photographs of them when they were children. Use the words in the box to help you.

I think that ...	I agree that ...	I don't agree that ...
It might be ...	It could be ...	I think it's ...
A used to ...	A still has ...	A has the same ...

3 Compare your answers with other students and talk about how you made your choice.

4 Choose one of the children and imagine what he/she was thinking.

		grow up		be ...
When	I	become famous	I	work ...
If		earn lots of money		live ...
		become a ...		have ...

Reading

28.2

1 Here are six texts about jobs you can have working with celebrities. Look at the jobs in the box and match them with the correct paragraph. If you don't know what all the jobs are, try to guess while you are reading. Don't worry about any words you don't understand.

personal trainer	fashion designer
bodyguard	celebrity chef
personal assistant	stylist

www.mychat.com

Do you fancy being a star but know you never will be? Then working for a star could be the job for you. With plenty of cash and no journalists looking through your rubbish bins, it could be perfect.

A Stars take a lot of interest in what they eat so what do they do when they feel hungry but don't want to get their hands dirty? Employ me, of course. I have to be very good at my job because I'm responsible for preparing meals not just for my boss but for all his famous friends. Would you like my job? Yes? In that case you should get good qualifications and then work in one of the best restaurants for at least a couple of years. And of course your own TV show will help too.

B Who do you think makes those stars look 100% perfect? It doesn't just happen by accident. It's my job to make sure my celebrity looks wonderful at all times. Imagine if you had someone to shop and choose clothes for you! You too would look like a star, all the time. The best thing about my job is that I go everywhere with my boss because famous people can't afford to make any mistakes in public, can they? I'm with her nearly all the time whether she's at home or on holiday.

C My job is to make sure the boss is never in danger and I need to be strong, both physically and mentally, to do that. I have to see problems in advance before they happen and, if there is any trouble, I have to be there at once. I'm closer to the star than anyone. And I have to do what she does and keep her in sight all the time. So don't forget that if the boss wants to spend every night dancing in a nightclub, I'll be there too. In fact I sometimes spend 24 hours at work without a break.

D I get the chance to experience the life of the rich and famous without actually being famous myself. I take phone calls and look at all the fan mail, plan parties and do all the jobs the star doesn't want to do. I travel first class with the star, make sure she arrives everywhere on time and meet lots of famous people. I have to stay very calm and not mind being shouted at even when I've done nothing wrong. In my job you can earn lots of money like a star but I'm never on the front page of the newspaper just because I've got a new boyfriend.

E I'm essential to a star who wants to look good. I'm the only person who tells a celebrity what to do and they listen to me. I watch and shout instructions while they cycle, run and lift weights. There's also a chance of someone famous falling in love with me – it has happened before.

F At present I have celebrities knocking at my door because they like my clothes. And if I'm lucky they invite me to events where everyone can see the clothes I've designed. I have to keep my ideas up-to-date because no star wants to be seen in something that looks old-fashioned. Of course, in the end if they decide they don't like my clothes any more, I'll be famous one day and unknown the next.

2 Work in a group. Read the texts again and think about the answers to these questions. Underline any words you don't know and talk about them in your group.

Text A
1 What is meant by *to get their hands dirty*?
2 What does *I'm responsible for* mean?

Text B
3 What does a stylist do?
4 Why is he/she so important?

Text C
5 Why does a bodyguard have to be strong both physically and mentally?
6 What might be a disadvantage of the job?

Text D
7 What kind of jobs does a personal assistant do?
8 Why might he/she get shouted at?

Text E
9 Why can a personal trainer tell a star what to do?
10 What might happen?

Text F
11 What does *knocking at my door* mean in the text?
12 What does *up-to-date* mean?
13 What might happen?

Ⓥocabulary spot

Sometimes the words in an expression do not mean exactly what they say, e.g. *they are knocking at my door, to get their hands dirty.*

3 Think of four advantages and four disadvantages of being famous. Would you like to be famous? Why?/Why not?

Language focus

28.3

1 Look at these sentences. Which speaker (a or b) is talking about something which will probably happen?

   a If I work in the restaurant every evening, I'll save enough money for a holiday.

   b If I worked for a pop star, I'd go to exciting places.

2 You read about some celebrity jobs in Exercise 28.2. Can you think of any others? Would you like a celebrity job? Choose one. Who would you like to work for? Make some sentences.

   EXAMPLE: *If I was/were X's bodyguard, I'd …*

28.4

Put the verbs in brackets into the correct tense. Use the second conditional.

a If we ___lived___ (live) near the sea, we 'd go (go) to the beach every weekend.

b If I .... (not have) so much homework to do, I .... (go) out with my friends.

c I .... (buy) a new computer if I .... (have) plenty of money.

d If I .... (own) a plane, I .... (fly) in it every day.

e If Andrea .... (get up) earlier, she .... (not be) late every day.

f If my neighbours .... (be) friendly, I .... (invite) them to my party.

g If Suzi .... (be) old enough, she .... (learn) to drive.

h My brother .... (teach) you the guitar if he .... (have) time.

28.5

Complete these sentences using your own ideas.

a If I was a pop star, *I'd write amazing songs.*

b If you lose your purse, *I'll lend you some money.*

c If I had a helicopter, ...

d If you spoke perfect English, ...

e If I go to bed late tonight, ...

f If you don't help me with this work, ...

g If you were a beautiful model, ...

h If I didn't do any homework, ...

28.6

Read these sentences from the texts. Fill in the missing prepositions without looking back at the texts.

at	by	in	on

a You should work in one of the best restaurants for ___at___ least a couple of years.

b It doesn't just happen .... accident.

c Famous people can't afford to make any mistakes .... public.

d I'm with her nearly all the time whether she's .... home or .... holiday.

e My job is to make sure the boss is never .... danger.

f I have to see problems .... advance before they happen.

g If there is any trouble I have to be there .... once.

h I have to keep her .... sight all the time.

i I sometimes spend 24 hours .... work without a break.

j I make sure she arrives everywhere .... time.

k There's also a chance of someone famous falling .... love with me.

l .... present I have celebrities knocking at my door.

m Of course, ... the end if they decide they don't like my clothes any more, I'll be famous one day and unknown the next.

Vocabulary spot

Learn these expressions as they are very common. People may not understand you if you use the wrong preposition, e.g. *The train arrived **on** time* (at the correct time) or *I got to the cinema **in** time* (just before the film started).

28.7 PRONUNCIATION

1 Decide what is missing from these sentences. Use the box to help you. Write the whole word at the end of each line.

's	've	'll	'd	're

a If I had a car, I ___'d___ lend it to you. *would*

b Wait for me – I .... almost finished watching this programme.

c They .... be late if they don't hurry.

d They .... already arrived when I got there.

e If she lived near her friends, she .... be happier.

f You .... not listening to me, are you?

g This is the first time he .... played the trumpet in public.

h We .... ring you if we go swimming next weekend.

i She .... coming home late tonight.

2 🎧 Listen to the sentences and check your answers.

3 🎧 Listen and repeat.

4 🎧 Look at these sentences and listen to the recording. If what you hear is exactly the same as what you see, mark ✓. If it is different, circle the letters which are different and write what you heard.

a They'(ve) already left. *They'd*
b He'd help you.
c The pop star's leaving.
d It'd be too dark to see anything.
e I've seen the programme before.
f She'd got plenty of money.

28.8

1 Look at what some people said they would take to a desert island.

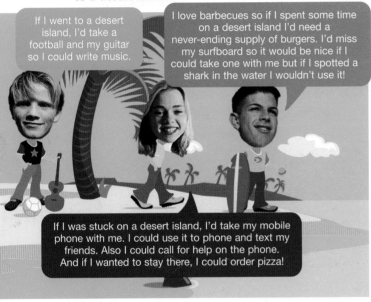

If I went to a desert island, I'd take a football and my guitar so I could write music.

I love barbecues so if I spent some time on a desert island I'd need a never-ending supply of burgers. I'd miss my surfboard so it would be nice if I could take one with me but if I spotted a shark in the water I wouldn't use it!

If I was stuck on a desert island, I'd take my mobile phone with me. I could use it to phone and text my friends. Also I could call for help on the phone. And if I wanted to stay there, I could order pizza!

2 Think of two things you would take to a desert island and why. Think of two things you would miss. Write the sentences on a piece of paper without your name on it and give it to your teacher.

3 Work in a group. Your teacher will give you some pieces of paper. Decide who wrote them.

4 Think about one of your favourite stars and imagine how they would answer.

1 Do this quiz.

1 **What would you do if a hotel receptionist was rude to you but then forgot to add your phone calls to your bill?**
Would you:
a) go back and tell her?
b) run away as fast as possible?
c) go home, then feel bad and phone the hotel?

2 **What would you do if you saw an old lady stealing food from the supermarket?**
Would you:
a) take no notice?
b) offer to help the old lady to carry the food to the checkout?
c) call an assistant?

3 **What would you do if you went shopping with your friend and he/she decided to buy some clothes which looked terrible?**
Would you:
a) tell him/her the truth?
b) suggest something else which suited him/her better?
c) let him/her buy them because he/she liked them?

4 **What would you do if you saw your favourite star when you were out shopping?**
Would you:
a) scream and point at him/her?
b) just walk past?
c) ask him/her for an autograph?

5 **What would you do if you found out that your best friend had two boyfriends/girlfriends at the same time?**
Would you:
a) ask your friend how he/she would feel in the same situation?
b) tell one of the boyfriends/girlfriends?
c) say nothing – it's not your problem?

6 **What would you do if your friend invited you to go on holiday with her family but you didn't like her mum?**
Would you:
a) explain how you feel about her mum and refuse the invitation?
b) say nothing and go on the holiday ?
c) invent an excuse not to go?

Solution

Score 10–14
Congratulations! You think about other people's feelings and try to do the best thing. You are a good friend.

Score 6–9
You need to be careful or you won't have many friends. You are very honest but you need to consider other people's feelings too. Remember to think before you speak.

Score 15–18
You are very kind and you think about other people's feelings. Remember to think about yourself too (and don't let other people walk all over you!).

1	a) 3	b) 1	c) 2
2	a) 3	b) 2	c) 1
3	a) 1	b) 2	c) 3
4	a) 2	b) 3	c) 1
5	a) 1	b) 3	c) 2
6	a) 1	b) 2	c) 3

2 Exchange quizzes. Look at the solution and tell your partner what kind of person he/she is.

Second conditional

If + past simple, would + verb
If I **had** a lot of money, I'**d buy** a motorbike.
If I **had** a lot of money, I **wouldn't work**.
If Elena **was/were** a bodyguard, she'**d work** for a pop star.

would + verb (no comma) + if + past simple
I'**d buy** a motorbike **if** I **had** a lot of money.

Vocabulary

autograph celebrity fan mail personal trainer shark situation stylist trouble truth to consider

calm physically mentally never-ending responsible for up-to-date

at home at least at once at present at work by accident in danger in public in time in sight on holiday on time

LANGUAGE SUMMARY

Exam folder 28

In this part of the exam, you listen to a recording of one person speaking or an interview and answer six questions by choosing A, B or C. You hear the recording twice.

CHECK!

a What do the instructions tell you?
b What do you have to do?
c What should you do before you listen?
d How can the questions help you?
e How many times will you hear the recording?
f What should you do if you don't know the answers?

Exam Advice

If you don't hear the answer to a question, don't spend time worrying about it. You will miss the answer to the next question too!

1 🎧 Do the exam task.

- You will hear a radio interview with a young actor called Paul.
- For each question, put a tick (✓) in the correct box.

1 Paul first appeared on TV in a
A ☐ soap opera.
B ☐ children's drama.
C ☐ quiz show.

2 What does Paul say about playing Frank?
A ☐ He didn't like Frank's personality.
B ☐ He wanted to have a bigger part.
C ☐ He did it for too long.

3 What problem did Paul have when he was in the soap opera?
A ☐ He couldn't trust anyone.
B ☐ He got very tired.
C ☐ He didn't like people recognising him.

4 What did Paul realise when he was in a theatre play?
A ☐ He preferred acting in theatres to TV programmes.
B ☐ He enjoyed performing to an audience.
C ☐ He didn't know how to act on stage.

5 In the future, what does Paul want to act in?
A ☐ TV programmes
B ☐ theatre plays
C ☐ films

6 How do Paul's parents feel about his choice of career?
A ☐ worried
B ☐ disappointed
C ☐ surprised

2 🎧 Look at the script and listen again. Underline the words in the script which give you the answer to each question.

3 Now use a different colour and underline the words in the script which tell you why the other options are wrong in each question.

Writing folder

Writing Part 1

- Here are some sentences about going shopping.
- For each question, complete the second sentence so that it means the same as the first, **using no more than three words**.

1 My friend and I took the bus to town last week.
My friend and I went to town ....._by bus_..... last week.

2 My friend forgot to bring her purse.
My friend didn't .... bring her purse.

3 She asked me how much money I had in my purse.
She asked me, 'How much money .... in your purse?'

4 First we went into a shop called *Stella's*.
First we went into a shop .... name was *Stella's*.

5 We couldn't afford the clothes in *Stella's*.
The clothes in *Stella's* were .... for us.

6 We bought nothing in *Stella's*.
We didn't .... in *Stella's*.

7 The shop next door is owned by my mother's friend.
My mother's friend .... the shop next door.

8 Although she showed me lots of clothes, I couldn't choose.
She showed me lots of clothes .... I couldn't choose.

9 We said, 'If we don't hurry, we'll miss the bus.'
We said, 'Unless .... , we'll miss the bus.'

10 We had such a tiring day we fell asleep on the bus.
We were so .... we fell asleep on the bus.

Exam Advice

Write one, two or three words.

Exam folder vocabulary
stage
to support
disappointed

UNIT 29 What's on the menu?

Introduction

29.1

Look at the photograph. Your teacher will give you a letter (or letters) from the alphabet. Find as many things as you can beginning with that letter.

29.2

1   Work in a group. You are going on a picnic together. Look at the food in the photograph and decide what you will take. Write a list on a piece of paper.

2   Pass your list around the class. Look at each group's list. Is anyone taking too much or too little? Decide which group has the healthiest picnic and which group has the least healthy picnic.

3   What food do people take on picnics in your country? What is different from the things you chose?

29.3

1   The words below are all names of food but the letters are in the wrong order. What are the words?

a bruger *burger*	**f** sifh	**k** iol
b cagabbe	**g** hotgdo	**l** apenut
c schip	**h** maj	**m** tals
d eefcof	**i** limk	**n** spachin
e crame	**j** roommush	**o** rugas

2   Work in a group. Divide the words into two lists.

Healthy: ....

Unhealthy: ....

3   How important do you think a healthy diet is? Is your diet healthy?

Ⓥocabulary spot

Many adjectives make their opposite with *un*, like *healthy/unhealthy*, for example, *able, grateful, happy, lucky, important, necessary, sure, true, usual.*

Listening

29.4

1 Look at the pictures. Which place would you prefer to eat in?

2 🎧 Listen to five conversations and match the speakers to the pictures.

Language focus

29.5

1 Read Conversations 1 and 2. Try to remember what the people said and complete the spaces.

Conversation 1

Alison: So, let's go and eat. I'm hungry.

Daniel: So (a) ..*am I*. . Where shall we go?

Alison: There are plenty of restaurants round here. Do you like Mexican food? Or what about Thai?

Beata: Can you tell me what Thai food tastes like? I've never tried it.

Daniel: No, nor (b) ....

Alison: Well, I love it. It's quite spicy.

Beata: Oh, is it? I'm not very keen on hot spices.

Daniel: No, neither (c) ....

Alison: OK. Er, so not Thai or Mexican. There's a good Italian restaurant further up the road.

Daniel: Oh, I love Italian food.

Beata: Really? So (d) ....

Alison: Right, let's go there then.

Conversation 2

Graham: Good evening. Table for two?

Greta: For three, please. We're meeting a friend.

Graham: Certainly. Smoking or non-smoking?

Greta: I don't smoke.

Brigitte: Neither (e) ...., so non-smoking, please.

Graham: Thank you. There's a table just there, near the window.

Brigitte: That'll be all right.

Greta: Yes, it's fine.

Graham: Would you like to order any drinks before your friend arrives?

Brigitte: Er, yes. I'm really thirsty. I can't wait.

Greta: Neither (f) ....

Brigitte: I'd like an orange juice, please.

Tina: Hi! Sorry I'm late. I got lost.

Brigitte: So (g) .... It's hard to find it, isn't it? Never mind. Come and sit down. We're just getting some drinks.

Tina: I'll have a mineral water, I think.

Greta: So (h) ....

Graham: Still or sparkling?

Tina: Still, please.

Graham: Thank you. I'll bring the menu in a moment.

Greta: Thank you.

2 🎧 Listen again and check your answers.

29.6

Agree with these statements by using
So ... or *Neither/Nor ...* .

a I've never been to this restaurant before. *Nor have I.*
b I want to come here again.
c I'm vegetarian.
d I enjoyed the main course.
e I don't like this ice cream.
f I won't finish all this.
g I'll come here again.
h I'm going to give the waiter a big tip.
i I can't eat any more.
j I've really enjoyed this evening.
k I'm not hungry now.
l I've always wanted to try Indian food.

29.7 **ACTIVITY**

Your teacher will give you a card.
Tell other people what you think about the subject on your card. Respond to what they say about theirs. If you and another student both agree with each other's statements, swap cards and talk to someone new.
Say things like these:

I love spicy food.	*So do I.* or	*Really? I don't!*
I'm not afraid of spiders.	*Nor am I.* or	*Really? I am!*
I've got a motorbike.	*So have I.* or	*Really? I haven't!*

29.8

1 🎧 **Look at these conversations and listen to them again. Underline what is different from what you hear.**

Conversation 3

Bob: Now, what are we going to have?
Carl: What do you recommend?
Bob: They do home-made soup, that's usually very nice. And there's always a hot dish.
Carl: Oh, yeah. I see. 'Today's special', it says on the board. <u>What is that?</u>
Bob: It says underneath, look. Lancashire Hotpot.
Carl: It sounds a bit funny. Has it got meat in it?
Bob: It's made of lamb with potatoes and onions, cooked for a long time. A traditional dish from the north of England. Very good on a cold day like today.
Carl: Oh, right. I'm a vegetarian so I won't have that.
Bob: OK. We'll ask for a menu. Would you like a starter?
Carl: No, thanks. I'll just have a main course. I don't want to fall asleep this afternoon.
Bob: No, neither do I. OK, now, where's the waiter?

Conversation 4

Gary: Yes?
Tammy: One burger, one milkshake, one vegeburger and one cappuccino, please.
Gary: What flavour milkshake?
Tammy: Oh, sorry. Rosie, what flavour milkshake does your friend want?
Rosie: Oh, she didn't say.
Tammy: Oh, typical.
Rosie: What flavours have you got?
Gary: Chocolate, strawberry, banana and vanilla.
Rosie: She'd like strawberry, I think.
Gary: OK. Now do you want to eat in or take away?
Tammy: Take away. Oh, and one portion of chips.
Gary: OK. That's six twenty-five.
Tammy: Here you are.
Gary: Enjoy your meal.
Rosie: Thank you.

Conversation 5

Nigel: Excuse me!
Marco: Yes? Can I help you?
Nigel: I hope so. You see, we ordered a tuna salad and a baked potato with cheese fifteen minutes ago! Is there a problem?
Marco: I'm sorry, we are very busy, as you see.
Nigel: But we said we were in a hurry and the waitress promised to be quick.
Laura: Are we going to get our food soon? We have to catch a train at one fifty-five.
Marco: OK. What did your waitress look like?
Nigel: Oh, here she comes now.
Anna: I'm ever so sorry. Someone else took your order by mistake.
Nigel: All right. Thank you. Now we can eat.
Laura: This potato isn't properly cooked. Part of it is almost raw!
Nigel: Oh, no. Well, that's it. I'm going to see the manager.

2 You want to ask a tour guide the questions below. Ask politely, using the words in the box, adding *if* when necessary. Write down your polite questions.

> Can you tell me … ?
> Can you remember … ?
> Do you know … ?
> I'd like to know … .
> Can you find out … ?

a How much does a burger cost?
Can you tell me how much a burger costs?

b Is the service included?
Do you know if the service is included?

c Where is the toilet?

d Do they serve vegetarian dishes?

e What flavour ice cream have they got?

f Can we sit outside?

g When does this café close?

h What is the name of this dish?

3 Do you go to restaurants? What kind of restaurant is your favourite? Do you prefer to sit down to a three-course meal or eat fast food?

29.9 PRONUNCIATION

1 🎧 Listen to the recording. Underline the sound /ə/. Listen again and repeat.

a cup of coffee

2 🎧 Now do the same with these sentences. Listen again and repeat.

a glass of milk and some pieces of cake
some ice cream but no burgers

3 🎧 Work with a partner. Underline the sound /ə/ in these sentences. Then listen to the recording and check what you underlined. Listen again and repeat.

It's made of eggs and sugar.
He wants a cup of tea and a sandwich.
I'd like a slice of meat and some potatoes.
You can have a bag of crisps but not a packet of biscuits.
They've got fish and chips and meat and rice but no bread and cheese.

29.10 ACTIVITY

1 Student A: You are an English person who is visiting a foreign country. You don't speak the language. Ask the waiter to explain two things on the menu for you and then order a three-course meal.

Student B: You are the waiter. You speak English.
Take the customer's order and answer his/her questions. One of the dishes he/she orders is not available. Apologise.

2 Now change roles.

So do I and Neither/nor do I

I'm hungry.	So am I.	I'm not hungry.	Neither/nor am I.
I like Italian food.	So do I.	I don't like Italian food.	Neither/nor do I.
I'm having lamb.	So am I.	I'm not having lamb.	Neither/nor am I.
I've tried it.	So have I.	I've never tried it.	Neither/nor have I.
I got lost.	So did I.	I didn't get lost.	Neither/nor did I.
I was waiting.	So was I.	I wasn't waiting.	Neither/nor was I.
I'm going to have …	So am I.	I'm not going to have …	Neither/nor am I.
I'll have …	So will I.	I won't have …	Neither/nor will I.
I can …	So can I.	I can't …	Neither/nor can I.

Direct questions

What is that?
Has it got meat in it?
What flavour milkshake does your friend want?
What flavours have you got?
What did your waitress look like?
Is there a problem?
Are we going to get our food soon?

Polite questions

Can you explain what that is?
I'd like to know if it's got meat in it.
Do you know what flavour milkshake your friend wants?
Can you tell us what flavours you've got?
Can you remember what your waitress looked like?
Can you find out if there's a problem?
Can you find out if we're going to get our food soon?

Asking for food in a restaurant

I'll have …
Can I have …
I'd like …

Apologising

I'm so sorry.
I do apologise.

Vocabulary

banana biscuit cabbage cake carrot celery cheese chicken cola cream crisps cucumber cup dessert dish fork fruit juice grape hot dog jam knife lamb lemonade lettuce loaf main course menu milkshake mineral water oil onion peanut pear pepper pizza plate portion potato(es) salad salt sausage slice spice spinach spoon starter strawberry tart tomato(es) tuna

to eat in   to get lost
to take away

baked cooked funny (= strange) non-smoking raw sparkling spicy still (drink)

Exam folder 29

Reading Part 4

> In this part of the exam, you read a text and answer five questions about it by choosing A, B, C or D.

CHECK!

a Do all the questions ask about one part of the text?

b Do you need to read all of the text carefully?

- Read the text and questions below.
- For each question, circle the letter next to the correct answer – **A**, **B**, **C** or **D**.

I've read and heard so many good reports of the Thai restaurant *The Golden Spoon* that I decided to try it myself. The menu appeared to be all in Thai but then we noticed the English translations. When the waitress realised it was our first visit, she came across as she knew it would take us a long time to choose. In the end we ordered what she recommended because we didn't know where to start – there was so much choice. Because it was early on a Monday evening (they are open from midday to midnight without a day off), it wasn't too busy but it got busier later and in fact they recommend that you book, even on Mondays.

The Golden Spoon offers a wide range of extremely tasty food, mostly quite spicy, but that was fine with me. Even the vegetarian among us had plenty of choice. Everything was cooked quickly and perfectly. The first course looked rather small, but there were six more courses to follow and we couldn't finish all of them.

The entrance to the restaurant is rather dark and the inside isn't much better. The Thai family who run it (the father and grandfather do all the cooking) have been there since 1975 and haven't really changed it since then. There are some Thai paintings on the wall which are probably rather beautiful but they are very dusty so it's difficult to tell. But none of that is important because I didn't go there to look at the walls. What I did look at was our meal being prepared in the kitchen, which is in one corner of the restaurant, and that was a wonderful sight. The meal cost more than I had expected but was worth it.

1 What is the writer trying to do?

  A suggest changes a restaurant could make

  B recommend the food in a restaurant

  C describe what he ate in a restaurant

  D complain about the service in a restaurant

2 What does the writer say about the waitress?

  A It was impossible for her to serve so many customers.

  B It was difficult to choose from the menu without her help.

  C She translated the menu from Thai for them.

  D She took a long time to take their order.

3 What did the writer think of the food?

  A It was too spicy for him.

  B There weren't enough vegetarian dishes.

  C There was too much of it.

  D It was not cooked properly.

4 What did the writer particularly like about the restaurant?

  A the paintings on the walls

  B the entrance

  C the prices

  D the position of the kitchen

5 Which of the following is an advertisement for the restaurant?

A

The Golden Spoon

Run by the same Thai family for more than 25 years.
Recommended in local guidebooks.
Booking advised. Open 12–12 every day.

C

The Golden Spoon

New chef from Bangkok Restaurant.
Meals available to eat in the restaurant every day from 12–12 or take away.

B

The Golden Spoon

Local restaurant recently improved – more space available.
Run by same Thai family since 1975.
Book early so you are not disappointed.
Open 12–12 every day.

D

The Golden Spoon

Compare our prices with other Thai restaurants and you will be pleasantly surprised.
Open every day except Monday from 12–12.

Speaking Part 3

> In this part of the exam, you and your partner are each given a photograph of a similar topic. You take turns to tell the examiner about your photograph.

1   Look at page 205. Work with a partner. Choose one photograph each.
    Before you talk to your partner, think about what you will say.

What kind of restaurant is it?
What are the people doing?
What are they wearing?
Are the people enjoying themselves?
What else can you see?

Exam Advice

Describe the people, what they are doing and the place.

2   Describe your photograph to your partner.

Speaking Part 4

> In this part of the exam, you and your partner have a discussion about the topic of the photographs in Part 3.

1   Work with a partner. Can you remember ways of giving your opinion?
    Can you remember ways of agreeing and disagreeing?

2   Discuss these questions with your partner.

Which of the restaurants in Speaking Part 3 would you like to eat in?
Do you often go to restaurants?
What kind of restaurant is your favourite?
Do you prefer to sit down to a three-course meal or eat fast food?

Exam Advice

If you have no opinions on the subject, invent some!

Exam folder vocabulary
dusty

UNIT 30 Blue for a boy, pink for a girl?

Introduction

30.1

1 Do you like doing any of these things or would you like to do them? Write them down.

I like/would like to …
I don't like/wouldn't like to …

2 What are your three favourite school subjects?

3 Do you agree with any of the following statements?

   a Men and women should earn the same salary for the same job.
   b Boys find it easier than girls to use computers.
   c Boys and girls should study the same subjects at school.
   d Boys are physically stronger than girls.
   e In a government, there should be the same number of men and women.
   f A girl can ask a boy to go out with her.
   g Mixed football teams are a good idea.
   h Girls find it easier than boys to talk about their feelings.
   i Girls study harder than boys.
   j Boys are braver than girls.

Reading and Language focus

30.2

1 Read extracts A–E from Jake's diary. Some of the verbs are in brackets. Put them into the correct form. Try to remember what you have learnt about verbs in this course.

2 Read extracts F–J from Lucy's diary. Some of the verbs are in brackets. Put them into the correct form. Try to remember what you have learnt about verbs in this course.

A Monday

I'm ordinary I suppose – nothing special. Most important of all, not special enough for Lucy. Lucy is great – really pretty and always smiling. In class I .... (sit) as close to her as I can. She never .... (speak) to me but I .... (sit) there until she .... (notice) me. This term I .... (ask) Lucy to go out with me. In my dreams, she always .... (say) 'yes', but real life .... (be) a different thing. I'm pleased I .... (choose) for the school football team. I'm looking forward .... (play) tomorrow.

B

This morning after coming out of the English class, I .... (look) for Lucy when I .... (turn) the corner and .... (see) her with Gary Smart. He was really close to her and he .... (have) his hand on her arm, so I was right. I'm sure they're going out together. I turned and .... (run) out of the building. How childish of me – no wonder Lucy isn't interested in .... (go) out with me! But why Gary?

C

What a surprise! Lucy and her mate, Sophie, ... (come) to watch tonight's game! I was so nervous. I .... (score) a goal but Lucy hardly noticed me. I think she was just there to see Gary Smart. I .... (chat) to Lucy and Sophie after the match. I still want .... (ask) her to go out with me but I'm afraid of .... (say) the wrong thing, so maybe I .... (write) her a note instead.

D

Changed my mind about writing to Lucy. I'm sure she .... (never agree) to go out with me. She's so funny and popular – I .... (see) her with her friends when I was walking to school this morning, and they all .... (laugh) when I .... (go) past. I must be one big joke to them. I heard Gary Smart talking about Lucy while we .... (change) for football training. He seems .... (like) her, and she probably .... (like) him too. Lots of girls do. I can't see why myself – unless muscles, cool clothes and a great haircut are your thing.

E

Great. She's going out with Gary Smart, but she .... (want) me to do her homework for her. I must be the class idiot. But I .... (help) her because it's a chance to spend some time with her. Perhaps if she thinks I'm clever, she .... (ask) me for help again.

F Monday

I'm fed up with boys. Honestly, when they .... (whistle) at you, they .... (think) they're really cool but they're just embarrassing. They .... (expect) you to laugh at their stupid jokes. The only nice boy in our class is Jake, but I hardly know him. He's really sweet and funny. I always .... (smile) at him when I .... (see) him but I'm worried that he .... (not like) me. Anyway, my mate, Sophie, told me that Jake .... (pick) for the school football team last week, so maybe I .... (go) and support the team when they .... (play) tomorrow.

G

I'm sorry we laughed at Jake yesterday. I decided .... (find) a way of seeing him after classes. He's so good at maths. That's the best way to get close to him – if I .... (ask) him for his help with the maths homework, I .... (have) a chance to spend more time with him. I .... (bump) into Gary Smart outside the sports hall. He .... (just have) a swim and he looked really pleased with himself. He even .... (put) his hand on my arm. He's really not my type.

H

It's very late. Sophie and I .... (watch) Jake play football tonight and he .... (score) a goal. Before going home we .... (chat) to him. He said he .... (never play) for the team before. On the way home, I told Sophie I was thinking of asking Jake to go out with me and she said she .... (think) it was a good idea. But what .... (do) if he .... (not be) interested in .... (go) out with me? I .... (be) so embarrassed.

I

Finally found the courage to ask Jake about the maths homework. He .... (not seem) too pleased but he agreed .... (help) me. We .... (meet) in the library on Monday night, so before .... (go out), I .... (ask) Sophie to do my hair and make-up. I'm really looking forward to .... (spend) some time with Jake.

J

I .... (talk) about Jake with Sophie and the others today at school when he .... (walk) past. We all started .... (laugh). I hope Jake doesn't think I'm silly.

3 Work in a group and compare your answers.

30.3

1 Work with a partner. Read Jake's first entry (A) together and then Lucy's (F). These were both written on Monday. The other entries are in the wrong order. Decide what Jake wrote on Tuesday, Wednesday, Thursday and Friday and then do the same for Lucy. Write the correct day in the spaces on page 193.

2 🎧 Listen to Jake and Lucy reading their diaries. Did you have the correct order? Did you write the correct verbs?

G **rammar spot**

Look at any of the verbs you got wrong. Make sure you know why you got these wrong and revise any of the ones you weren't sure about.

3 Answer these questions together.

 a Why did Lucy go to watch the football match?
 b Why did Jake think Lucy was at the football match?
 c Why did Jake decide to write a note?
 d Why was Lucy worried about asking Jake to go out with her?
 e What did Jake think when he heard the girls laughing?
 f What did Jake think about Lucy and Gary Smart?
 g Why did Lucy ask Jake for help with her maths?
 h What did Lucy think of Gary Smart?
 i Why do you think Jake wasn't pleased when Lucy asked him for help with her maths?

4 🎧 Now listen to what Jake and Lucy wrote next and think about the answers to these questions.

 a Why was Lucy confused at first when she met Jake in the library?
 b Why did Jake write Lucy a note instead of asking her to go out with him?
 c Where did Lucy find the note?
 d How did Lucy feel when she read the note?
 e Was the bowling trip successful?
 f Do you think this is a true story?

V **ocabulary spot**

Some words are used mainly by young people (or older people in very informal conversations). Write some down from the diaries.

30.4 **ACTIVITY**

Work in teams. Your teacher will hold up two cards – one has a letter on it, e.g. P, and the other card has an area of vocabulary, e.g. food. Your team must quickly write down as many food words as possible beginning with P. You only get a point if the words are spelled correctly. You get two points if you have a word that no other team has.

30.5

1 Look at these sentences. What does *hardly* mean?

 *I **hardly** know Jake.*   *She **hardly** noticed me.*

2 Rewrite the underlined words using *hardly*.

 a I hadn't seen Monica for ten years and <u>it was difficult for me to recognise her.</u> *I hardly recognised her.*
 b Now my friend is at university <u>I don't see her very often</u> during term time.
 c There was a noisy party next door last night so <u>I slept very little.</u>
 d My cousin has hurt her foot so <u>she only danced once or twice</u> at the disco.
 e I was only four when my family moved from Scotland so <u>I only just remember it.</u>

3 Look at these sentences.

 *We did **hardly any** maths.*   ***Hardly anybody** likes Jake.*

 Now complete the sentences below using *hardly*. Add any other words you need.

 a The weather was fine nearly every day last week – there was __hardly any__ rain.
 b .... came to my party because lots of my friends were busy that day.
 c I bought a very expensive pair of trainers yesterday so I have .... money left now.
 d .... in Britain speaks Japanese.
 e The sale was a great success – at the end there was .... left.
 f It's difficult travelling on Sundays because there are .... buses.

4 Write some sentences using *hardly*.

 a I hardly ever …
 b I have hardly any …
 c Hardly anyone I know …

30.6 PRONUNCIATION

Your teacher will give you a card with some words on it. Listen to the words your teacher reads out. Do they have the same vowel sound as any of the words on your card?

30.7

1 Read these sentences from the diaries. What do you notice about the words following *before* and *after*?

> *Before going home, we chatted to Jake.*
> *Before going out, I'll ask Sophie to do my hair.*
> *After coming out of the English class, Jake looked for Lucy.*
> *After handing back my maths book, Jake walked away.*

2 Rewrite these sentences using *before* or *after*.

a Lucy heard that Jake was playing in the match, then she went to watch it.
   After *hearing that Jake was playing in the match, Lucy went to watch it.*

b Jake played in the match, then he talked to Lucy. After ....

c Lucy asked Jake for help with her maths, then she met him in the library. Before ....

d Jake saw Lucy with Gary, then he felt sad. After ....

e Lucy asked Sophie to do her hair, then she went out with Jake. Before ....

f Jake met Lucy in the library, then he decided to write her a letter. After ....

g Lucy got a letter from Jake, then she told him she liked him. After ....

3 Write three true sentences about yourself using *before* or *after*. Use these ideas if you wish.

> go to cinema in the evening / eat dinner
> *I go to the cinema in the evening after eating dinner.*

have breakfast / clean teeth
do homework / watch TV
set alarm / get into bed
check bank account / buy new clothes

30.8 ACTIVITY

Your teacher will give you a set of cards. Use the cards to practise *before* and *after* with the past simple.

30.9

Look at the different ways of saying goodbye in the Language Summary and decide when you would use them. Match them to these situations.

a When you're not sure if you'll see someone again.
b When you'll see someone again the same day.
c When you say goodbye to someone you've only just met.
d When someone is setting off on a trip.
e When you have been someone's guest or they have helped you a lot.
f When you expect to see someone again.
g Any time!

Hardly + verb
I **hardly** know Jake.
She **hardly** noticed me.

Hardly + any + noun
We did **hardly any** maths.

Hardly + anybody/thing
Hardly anybody likes Jake.
There is **hardly anything** in my bag.

After/before + -ing
After handing back my maths book, he walked away.
Before going home, we chatted to Jake.

Vocabulary
alarm bowling guy muscles my type
the class idiot your thing whistle

to notice to spoil

childish embarrassing gorgeous hardly smart sweet

Saying goodbye
Goodbye.
See you later.
Hope to see you again.
Thank you for everything.

See you soon.
I've enjoyed meeting you.
Have a good journey.

Exam folder 30

Listening Part 4

In this part of the exam, you listen to a conversation between two people and decide whether six sentences are correct or incorrect. You hear the recording twice.

🎧 ● Look at the six sentences for this part.
● You will hear a conversation between a boy, Andy, and a girl, Sarah, about dancing.
● Decide if each sentence is correct or incorrect.
● If it is correct, put a tick (✓) in the box under **A** for **YES**. If it is not correct, put a tick (✓) in the box under **B** for **NO**.

CHECK!
a How many speakers are there?
b What should you do before you listen?

		A YES	B NO
1	Andy is doing dancing classes instead of computer classes.	□	□
2	Andy has told few people about his love of dancing.	□	□
3	Sarah thinks Andy should tell his friends about his dancing.	□	□
4	Andy's aunt persuaded him to learn to dance.	□	□
5	Andy feels happier when there are other boys in his dancing class.	□	□
6	Sarah agrees with Andy's parents about his plans for the future.	□	□

Speaking Part 3

In this part of the exam, you and your partner are each given a photograph of a similar topic. You take turns to tell the examiner about your photograph.

Look at the two photographs on page 206. Work with a partner. One of you will describe photograph A and the other will describe photograph B. Take turns to tell each other about your photograph.

CHECK!
a What will you talk about?
b What will you say if you don't know the English word for something?
c How long will you try to speak for?

Exam Advice

Don't worry if you don't know what is happening in the photograph. Just describe what you can see.

Speaking Part 4

In this part of the exam, you and your partner have a discussion about the topic of the photographs in Part 3.

Work with a partner and discuss these questions.

a Which kind of dancing would you prefer to watch?
b Do you like dancing?
c Do you think it is important to learn to dance?
d Do boys learn to dance in your country? What kind of dancing?
e Why do you think fewer boys enjoy dancing than girls?
f Do you think boys should be encouraged to learn to dance?
g What other activities do you think boys should be encouraged to do?
h What activities should girls be encouraged to do?

CHECK!
a Who will you speak to?
b What will you do if you have no opinions?
c How long will you speak for?

Exam Advice

Speak clearly so the other student can understand you.

Writing folder

Writing Part 1

> In this part of the exam, you are given a sentence. You have to complete a second sentence so that it means the same as the first.

- Here are some sentences about going to a restaurant.
- For each question, complete the second sentence so that it means the same as the first, using no more than three words.
- Write only the missing words.

Example: All the students in my class went to a restaurant together.
_____ _Everyone_ _____ in my class went to a restaurant together.

1 The restaurant is usually crowded because it's so good.
It's usually crowded because it's _____ good restaurant.

2 It's less crowded on weekdays.
It isn't _____ on weekdays.

3 Before choosing our food, we asked the waiter's advice.
We asked the waiter's advice, then _____ our food.

4 The waiter recommended a fish dish.
The waiter said, 'If I _____ you, I'd have the fish dish.'

5 The service charge wasn't included in the bill.
The bill _____ the service charge.

Writing Part 2

> In this part of the exam, you have to write a note, email, card or postcard in 35–45 words. There are three points which you have to write about.

You and some friends are planning to go to the cinema.
Write a note to an English friend called Jerry. In your note, you should

- tell him which film you are going to see
- invite him to come with you
- say when and where you are meeting your friends

Write 35–45 words.

Writing Part 3

> In this part of the exam, you have to write a letter or a story in about 100 words. There are two questions to choose from.

- This is part of a letter you receive from an English penfriend.

> So, that's me and my family. What about you?
> Can you tell me something about you and yours?

- Now you are writing a letter to this penfriend.
- Write your **letter** in about 100 words.

OR

- Your English teacher has asked you to write a story.
- Your story must begin with this sentence:

  When we set out, the sky was blue and the sun was shining.

  Write your **story** in about 100 words.

Exam folder vocabulary
to concentrate   to forgive
keen

Writing folder vocabulary
bill   service charge

Speaking

1 Work with a partner. Look at these sentences. Say if each sentence is true for you and give your partner some extra information.

   a The town where I live has good shops. *Yes, I agree. There are two shopping centres and a market.* OR *No, I don't agree. In my opinion, that's not true because most of the shops sell the same things.*
   b I find adverts on TV annoying.
   c I enjoy travelling.
   d I saw a famous person in the street once.
   e I look for bargains when I go shopping.
   f I like eating food from other countries.
   g It's important for families to eat together.
   h I use the internet for shopping.

Grammar

3 A journalist interviewed the president's bodyguard. Later, the journalist met her friend and told her about the interview. Report what she said to her friend.

   a What do you like best about your job?
   I asked him *what he liked best about his job.*
   b Did you always want to be a bodyguard?
   I wanted to know *if he had always wanted to be a bodyguard.*
   c When did you decide to be a bodyguard?
   I wanted to know ....
   d What other jobs have you done?
   I asked him ....
   e Will you always work as a bodyguard?
   I asked him ....
   f Which countries have you visited?
   I wanted to know ....
   g Do you work hard?
   I asked him ....
   h How much money do you earn?
   I wanted to know ....
   i Do you have any hobbies?
   I asked him ....
   j What will happen to your job after the election?
   I asked him ....

Vocabulary

2 Think about the meaning of these words. Mark the odd one out in each of these lists.

   a chicken (tuna) sausage lamb beef
   b cucumber peanut lettuce tomato celery
   c fork dessert knife plate cup
   d biscuit cake chocolate jam egg
   e pepper pear strawberry grape banana
   f lemonade juice glass cola water
   g cream bread cheese milk butter
   h cabbage spinach onion orange carrot

4 Here are the bodyguard's answers. Use the words in the box to complete the spaces.

   | all enough every hardly if if ~~too many~~ too many too much when unless |

   a There are *too many* things to tell you.
   b No, but .... my brothers are teachers and I wanted to do something different.
   c I was working in an office and I was spending .... time sitting at a desk.
   d I've done .... jobs to tell you about them all.
   e .... I'm 50, I'll look for a quieter job.
   f There are .... any countries that I haven't visited.
   g I work .... day of the week.
   h Well, I'll never be a millionaire .... I win the lottery.
   i I don't have .... time for hobbies.
   j .... the president wins the election, I'll continue working for him. .... he doesn't win, I'll work for the new president.

Grammar

5 Read this email and put the verbs in brackets into the correct tense.

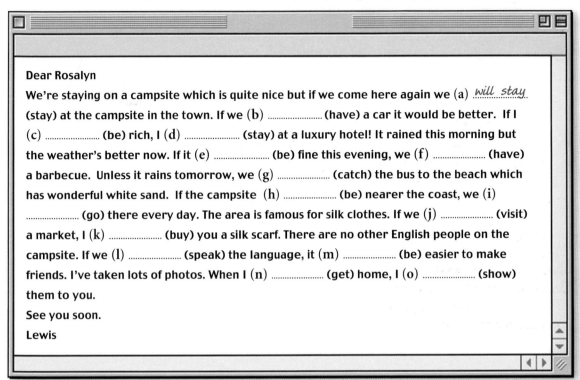

Dear Rosalyn

We're staying on a campsite which is quite nice but if we come here again we (a) _will stay_ (stay) at the campsite in the town. If we (b) .... (have) a car it would be better. If I (c) .... (be) rich, I (d) .... (stay) at a luxury hotel! It rained this morning but the weather's better now. If it (e) .... (be) fine this evening, we (f) .... (have) a barbecue. Unless it rains tomorrow, we (g) .... (catch) the bus to the beach which has wonderful white sand. If the campsite (h) .... (be) nearer the coast, we (i) .... (go) there every day. The area is famous for silk clothes. If we (j) .... (visit) a market, I (k) .... (buy) you a silk scarf. There are no other English people on the campsite. If we (l) .... (speak) the language, it (m) .... (be) easier to make friends. I've taken lots of photos. When I (n) .... (get) home, I (o) .... (show) them to you.

See you soon.

Lewis

Vocabulary

6 Read these conversations and use the words in the box to complete the spaces.

afford bring change fit fitting ~~help~~ matches receipt refund size stock store try

Assistant 1: Can I (a) _help_ you?

Boy: Oh, yes please. Where are the T-shirts?

Assistant 1: Over there.

Boy: I can't (b) .... those. Have you got any cheaper ones?

Assistant 1: Most of the cheaper ones are in our other (c) .... in the city centre but we have a few here. What (d) .... are you?

Boy: I'm not sure. Can I (e) .... these on?

Assistant 1: Certainly. The (f) .... room is over there.

Boy: Thanks.

Boy: This blue one (g) .... my trousers but it doesn't (h) .... Have you got a bigger one?

Assistant 2: Sorry. We only have a few of those in (i) ....

Boy: Oh, well, I'll take the white one. Can I (j) .... it back if I (k) .... my mind?

Assistant 2: Of course. You can have a (l) .... if you keep the (m) ....

Visual materials

Exercise 4.9
Student A

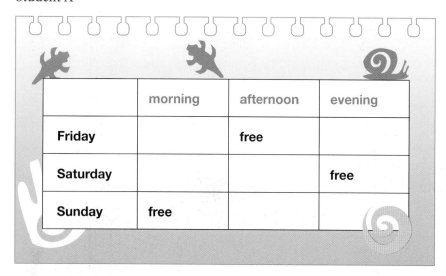

	morning	afternoon	evening
Friday		free	
Saturday			free
Sunday	free		

Exercise 14.9

Exercise 22.6

Public Opinion Survey

Which of these statements is true for you?

1 I believe in UFOs. ☐
I'm not sure about UFOs. ☐
I don't believe in UFOs. ☐

2 I believe there's life on other planets. ☐
I think life on other planets is a possibility. ☐
I'm sure that there is no life on other planets. ☐

3 I enjoy science fiction films. ☐
I like reading science fiction novels. ☐
I don't like science fiction. ☐

4 I've seen a UFO. ☐
I've never seen a UFO. ☐

5 I've met an alien. ☐
I've never met an alien. ☐

6 I know someone who has seen a UFO. ☐
I don't know anyone who has seen a UFO. ☐

7 I know someone who has met an alien. ☐
I don't know anyone who has met an alien. ☐

Exercise 4.9
Student B

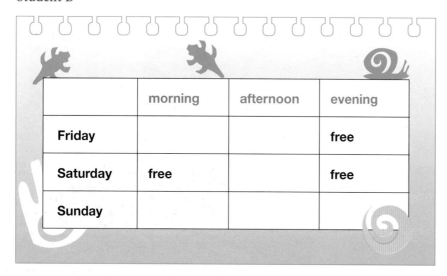

	morning	afternoon	evening
Friday			free
Saturday	free		free
Sunday			

Exercise 14.9

How earth-friendly are you?

1 When you travel to school or work, you

A are driven there by someone else who then returns home. ○

B drive yourself. ○

C walk or ride a bicycle. ○

D use public transport. ○

2 At home, you

A always have the central heating or air conditioning on in the whole house. ○

B only heat or cool the rooms you are using. ○

C only use air conditioning on unusually hot days. ○

D put on an extra pullover before you turn up the heating. ○

3 When you go shopping, you

A usually buy things which are produced locally. ○

B often ask yourself if you really need something before you buy it. ○

C buy the cheapest things and don't worry about how and where they were made. ○

D buy what you like when you like. ○

4 The main reason for having a job is

A to save money for the future. ○

B to do something useful in society. ○

C to make use of your education and training. ○

D to earn money and buy things you want. ○

5 You get most of your food from

A your own garden. ○

B a local producer. ○

C a supermarket. ○

D a fast food restaurant. ○

6 You choose your food because it is

A produced by people who take care of the environment. ○

B good for your health. ○

C cheap and tasty. ○

D quick and convenient. ○

7 You normally eat because

A you are hungry. ○

B you want to reward yourself. ○

C it's a mealtime. ○

D you feel bored. ○

8 You choose leisure activities

A that require a lot of special equipment and clothes. ○

B you can do at or near your home. ○

C that do not require any effort. ○

D to keep fit. ○

9 For you, the people who really matter

A are your family. ○

B live near you. ○

C are you and your best friend. ○

D can be any human beings. ○

10 You feel that the future of the earth

A is the responsibility of governments. ○

B is the responsibility of us all. ○

C is not something one individual can help to change. ○

D is not something to worry about. ○

Key to questionnaire

1 A0 B1 C4 D3   2 A0 B3 C3 D4   3 A3 B3 C1 D0   4 A3 B4 C4 D1   5 A4 B3 C1 D0
6 A4 B3 C2 D1   7 A4 B2 C3 D0   8 A1 B4 C4 D4   9 A3 B3 C1 D4   10 A2 B4 C1 D0

Key to phonetic symbols

Vowels

Sound	Example
/ɑː/	cart
/æ/	cat
/aɪ/	like
/aʊ/	now
/e/	tell
/eɪ/	say
/eə/	there
/ɪ/	big
/iː/	steep
/ɪə/	here
/ɒ/	pop
/əʊ/	phone
/ɔː/	four
/ɔɪ/	boy
/ʊ/	took
/uː/	pool
/ʊə/	tour
/ɜː/	third
/ʌ/	fun
/ə/	again

Consonants

Sound	Example
/b/	be
/d/	do
/f/	find
/g/	good
/h/	have
/j/	you
/k/	cat
/l/	like
/m/	me
/n/	no
/p/	put
/r/	run
/s/	say
/t/	tell
/v/	very
/w/	well
/z/	zoo
/ʃ/	shoe
/ʒ/	television
/ŋ/	sing
/tʃ/	cheap
/θ/	thin
/ð/	this
/dʒ/	joke

Irregular verb list

THE LEARNING CENTRE
HAMMERSMITH AND WEST
LONDON COLLEGE
GLIDDON ROAD
LONDON W14 9BL

Verb	Past simple	Past participle	Verb	Past simple	Past participle
be	was were	been	lend	lent	lent
beat	beat	beaten	let	let	let
become	became	become	lie	lay	lain
begin	began	begun	light	lit	lit
bend	bent	bent	lose	lost	lost
bite	bit	bitten	make	made	made
bleed	bled	bled	mean	meant	meant
blow	blew	blown	meet	met	met
break	broke	broken	pay	paid	paid
bring	brought	brought	put	put	put
build	built	built	read	read	read
burn	burnt/burned	burnt/burned	ride	rode	ridden
buy	bought	bought	ring	rang	rung
catch	caught	caught	rise	rose	risen
choose	chose	chosen	run	ran	run
come	came	come	say	said	said
cost	cost	cost	see	saw	seen
cut	cut	cut	sell	sold	sold
dig	dug	dug	send	sent	sent
do	did	done	set	set	set
draw	drew	drawn	shake	shook	shaken
dream	dreamt/dreamed	dreamt/dreamed	shine	shone	shone
drink	drank	drunk	shoot	shot	shot
drive	drove	driven	show	showed	shown
eat	ate	eaten	shut	shut	shut
fall	fell	fallen	sing	sang	sung
feed	fed	fed	sink	sank	sunk
feel	felt	felt	sit	sat	sat
fight	fought	fought	sleep	slept	slept
find	found	found	slide	slid	slid
fly	flew	flown	smell	smelt/smelled	smelt/smelled
forget	forgot	forgotten	speak	spoke	spoken
forgive	forgave	forgiven	spell	spelt/spelled	spelt/spelled
freeze	froze	frozen	spend	spent	spent
get	got	got	spill	spilt	spilt
give	gave	given	spoil	spoilt	spoilt
go	went	been/gone	stand	stood	stood
grow	grew	grown	steal	stole	stolen
hang	hung	hung	stick	stuck	stuck
have	had	had	sweep	swept	swept
hear	heard	heard	swell	swelled	swollen
hide	hid	hidden	swim	swam	swum
hit	hit	hit	take	took	taken
hold	held	held	teach	taught	taught
hurt	hurt	hurt	tear	tore	torn
keep	kept	kept	tell	told	told
kneel	knelt	knelt	think	thought	thought
know	knew	known	throw	threw	thrown
lay	laid	laid	understand	understood	understood
lead	led	led	wake	woke	woken
learn	learnt/learned	learnt/learned	wear	wore	worn
leave	left	left	win	won	won
			write	wrote	written